INDIGENOUS METHODOLOGIES:
CHARACTERISTICS, CONVERSATIONS, AND CONTEXTS

What are Indigenous research methodologies, and how do they differ from mainstream Western approaches? Indigenous methodologies flow from tribal knowledge, and while they are allied with several Western qualitative approaches, there are key distinctions. In this work, Margaret Kovach examines the theoretical and epistemological basis of Indigenous methodologies and offers practical guidance to those conducting research in Indigenous communities.

Kovach's study focuses on topics such as ways of knowing, decolonizing theory, story as method, self-location, Indigenous research methods, cultural protocol, meaning-making, and ethical responsibility. In exploring these concepts, the book integrates the stories and perspectives of six Indigenous researchers, and also draws on the author's direct experience. An original and important contribution to the evolving discourse on Indigenous research approaches, the volume will be invaluable to students, faculty, and community-based researchers of all backgrounds.

MARGARET KOVACH is an assistant professor in the College of Education at the University of Saskatchewan.

MARGARET KOVACH

Indigenous Methodologies

Characteristics, Conversations, and Contexts

UNIVERSITY OF TORONTO PRESS
Toronto Buffalo London

© University of Toronto Press 2009
Toronto Buffalo London
www.utppublishing.com
Printed in Canada

Reprinted in paperback 2010

ISBN 978-1-4426-4042-9 (cloth)   ISBN 978-1-4426-1211-2 (paper)

♾ Printed on acid-free, 100% post-consumer recycled paper with
vegetable-based inks

Library and Archives Canada Cataloguing in Publication

Kovach, Margaret, 1964–
Indigenous methodologies : characteristics, conversations and contexts /
Margaret Kovach.

Includes bibliographical references and index.
ISBN 978-1-4426-4042-9 (bound).–ISBN 978-1-4426-1211-2 (pbk.)

1. Native peoples – Research – Canada – Methodology.   2. Indigenous
peoples – Research – Methodology.   3. Research – Methodology.   I. Title.

E76.7.K68 2009   305.897'071072   C2009-903766-1

This book has been published with the help of a grant from the Canadian
Federation for the Humanities and Social Sciences, through the Aid to
Scholarly Publications Programme, using funds provided by the Social
Sciences and Humanities Research Council of Canada.

University of Toronto Press acknowledges the financial assistance to
its publishing program of the Canada Council for the Arts and the
Ontario Arts Council.

University of Toronto Press acknowledges the financial support of the
Government of Canada through the Canada Book Fund for its
publishing activities.

This book is dedicated to the memory of my sister Pat and Trudy

Contents

Acknowledgments   ix

Prologue   3

Introduction   9

1 Indigenous and Qualitative Inquiry: A Round Dance?   23

2 Creating Indigenous Research Frameworks   39

3 Epistemology and Research: Centring Tribal Knowledge   55

4 Applying a Decolonizing Lens within Indigenous
Research Frameworks   75

5 Story as Indigenous Methodology   94

6 Situating Self, Culture, and Purpose in Indigenous Inquiry   109

7 Indigenous Research Methods and Interpretation   121

8 Doing Indigenous Research in a Good Way – Ethics
and Reciprocity   141

9 Situating Indigenous Research within the Academy   156

Conclusion   174

Epilogue   179

References   185

Index   193

Acknowledgments

There are many to acknowledge. I give thanks to all who have given me support and encouragement while I embarked upon this work. To the six individuals who shared their research stories with me, Kathy Absolon, Jeannine Carriere, Laara Fitznor, Michael Hart, Graham Smith, and Cam Willett, I give thanks. I would like to acknowledge Budd Hall, Leslie Brown, Leroy Little Bear, and Barbara Whittington, the mentors who guided me through my doctoral work that formed the basis of this book.

To both my mothers, you are both a continuing source of love and inspiration and I thank you. To both my fathers, though you are in the spirit world I felt your presence. To my siblings, nieces, nephews, aunties, and uncles in both my families, you have given me a belonging in this world, and it is only through belonging that I could embark on this work. I would like to acknowledge my immediate family – Monty and Rachel – for your support and love. I also want to acknowledge all the good friends, too many to name, who have shared this journey and have been a source of inspiration.

I would like to acknowledge and thank everyone at the University of Toronto Press. Thank you to Ernie Scoles, who provided the cover art for this book.

Finally, I would like to acknowledge the financial support of the University of Saskatchewan's Publication Fund for assistance in the preparation of this manuscript.

INDIGENOUS METHODOLOGIES:
CHARACTERISTICS, CONVERSATIONS, AND CONTEXTS

Prologue

This prologue was written not long ago, but not today either. It was written when I was absorbed in the intensity of a research journey that led to a doctoral degree and then this book. Looking back, I see a vision of myself standing in the eye of a tornado, in a protected but fearsome stillness that could snap at any moment. Coming to know about Indigenous methodologies felt like that. I am in a different space now, having survived the swirling winds, but to tell you this story I need to go back in time, back to memory.

Tânisi. Maggie, *nitisiyihkâson,* Kovach, *nitaspiyikasôn.* Hello, I am Maggie, I am Nêhiýaw and Saulteaux, my lineage stems from the traditional territories of the Plains Cree and Saulteaux peoples of the Great Plains. My relations are of the Pasqua and Okanese First Nations in southern Saskatchewan. I was raised within an adopted family on a small, rural Saskatchewan farm. I honour both these influences. This tells you a bit about me, but there is more that I need to share. I am introducing myself purposefully in this prologue for it is relational work. In community, I would share this through talk, I would give enough information about my lineage and those who raised me for people to 'ssess me out.' People would nod; I would know if they understand. It is different in writing.

Graham Smith, a Maori scholar, introduced me to the concept of using a prologue within Indigenous research. A prologue is a function of narrative writing that signifies a prelude. It encompasses essential information for the reader to make sense of the story to follow. While not every written narrative needs a prologue, it can be a useful device. Within Indigenous writing, a prologue structures space for introductions while serving a bridging function for non-Indigenous readers. It is a precursory signal to the careful reader that woven throughout the varied forms of our writing – analytical, reflective, expository – there will be story, for our story is who we are.

I understand my responsibility, so why, then, am I having such difficulty? All that it asks is that I share enough about myself to prepare the reader for this work. I go to write and get tangled in several years' worth of reflections, unable to make choices about what to put on paper. Both a lot and not much is different since I started this venture, and I do not know what exactly to say about it. Persistently, I flip through journal notes and search my memory in an attempt to remember stories and conversations, trying to craft a prelude for my journey into Indigenous methodologies. It is a story of coming to know, with narrative appearing in bits and pieces throughout the text. It is no use trying to separate them. The story will reveal itself. Yet, the story started somewhere, so why the struggle pinpointing its beginning?

As I reflect upon this, I have a memory flash of my partner, Monty, and me driving down Victoria Avenue East in Regina just before Thanksgiving weekend. We are heading to my mother's house. Leaving Regina we drive past the A and W, then the bingo hall, and I see a big Safeway sign in the distance. As we get closer we can read the block letter words: 'Utility Turkey on Sale here.' Who knows why, but it strikes a chord. We get to my mother's place and I ask her, 'What exactly is a *utility* turkey?' As best as I can remember, she says, 'A utility turkey is not a perfect bird, but you can roast it.' It occurs to me that this is pretty much the direction I am seeking with this opening, to share just enough to predicate possible conjectures. It is not a seminal memoir, it is a 'utility prologue.'

So what do I know about who I am? I was born to my birth mother in a rural Saskatchewan hospital. I was registered to Pasqua First Nations at birth. Pasqua is a Saulteaux First Nation and my ancestors were signatories to Treaty Four in the Qu'Appelle Valley. On my mother's side, my bloodline is Plains Cree and Saulteaux. On my father's side, it is Plains Cree. I was adopted at the age of three months. My adoptive parents were of Eastern European, of Hungarian descent, and both spoke the language. I was raised knowing that culture counts. I have maintained relationships with both my families, with my birth family for over twenty years.

Sitting at my desk late at night in Regina, I write in my journal, 'If I have any romantic notions about my life it is that I was born under a prairie sky with a Seger tune playing in the distance.' I know this is romanticism because I was born indoors and Seger did not record until after my birth. Yet, my beginnings allow for a self-constructed story. I imagine that is what happens when you are an adoptee, you fill in blanks. Although a certain mystery follows adoptees, my life has not been that exotic. I was a Native kid who grew up round and about a small rural Saskatchewan town. I was loved but conflicted, questioning where I belonged, trying to stay at distances yet needing connection. I could go on – there are many possibilities for proceeding with the prologue, but I do not want to write a life narrative. This work is about research nested within universities, so I will focus there.

I started university early, and as is the experience for many young Indigenous students of my circumstance and generation, education became a portal for self-discovery. I remember starting my first year at the University of Regina. I meandered around, majoring in psychology but drawn to sociology, then registering in the Bachelor of Social Work program at the young age of twenty-two. My education has taken me back and forth between social work and education, both offering opportunities to explore my First Nations identity. Exploring identity was not easy because of the process of reclaiming unleashed anger that I thought I had worked through. It has also evoked a lot of sadness, though I knew that was always there.

In my mind, identity and education always intersect. I cannot help but think of the first poem that I read by an American Indian poet Chrystos. Much later, an Indigenous professor asked us to explore our narratives and write these musings on found paper. I handed in mine on the back of Chrystos' poem, *I Am Not Your Princess*. If our soul can hold print markings, you would find these words somewhere on mine: 'Don't assume I know every other Native Activist / in the world personally / That I even know names of all the tribes / or can pronounce names I've never heard'; (1988: 66). This poem sticks because my own attempts to conform to an outsider's view of the 'Indigenous Standard' (i.e., 'all Natives are this, all Natives are that') have failed miserably. While I have admittedly been pulled into this unpalatable proposition of my own volition, I become resentful if others expect this of me. I respond to the poem because it does not pull any punches, and I can appreciate that edge. I get angry about the racism that Indigenous people experience. I am writing this here because it drives my work.

My critical perspective on the world was solidified through academia, but it did not begin there. My upbringing was such that I never knew a time when I did not know about Tommy Douglas. I can still hear my dad saying that Tommy Douglas was a good man because he was not a big shot and he fought for the little guy. Running around the kitchen, while the adults (mom, dad, aunties, uncles, neighbours) sat at the kitchen table talking politics, was my first critical social theory classroom. Since then, I have sat in many other classrooms, racking up a few degrees, voraciously taking in the words of brilliant critical theorists (Habermas, Freire). But after distilling the message, the fundamentals are the same: big shot, little guy.

As a social worker, I have worked with First Nations organizations, serving on-reserve communities in counselling and social development, but mostly within adult education. I have taught for several years as a university instructor in First Nations social work and education, but at heart I am a curriculum developer. Curriculum makes space like nothing else I know in education. It can be a mighty tool of social justice for the marginalized. When I went back to university to complete my Ph.D., my initial choice for a research topic was an inquiry into Indigenous curriculum and instruction. I switched topics after being unable to understand why research textbooks did not offer Indigenous frameworks as a methodological option for examining a problem. I could not leave it alone; it was a curiosity that I could not abandon. I switched topics and proceeded to inquire into the intersection between Indigenous knowledges and research.

At some point – I am not sure when – I had this uneasy feeling that my sense of self would intersect with my research. Although I tried to keep my inquiry cerebral, I could feel coyote medicine in the air. I was living on Coast Salish territory, in Victoria, British Columbia. Below is a reflective note from my journal that signifies my burgeoning sense that seeking insight into Indigenous forms of inquiry would cause me to revisit my identity, to retrieve my story from the archive of my being.

> On an early Wednesday morning, I go to the library with Keith Basso's book, *Wisdom Sits in Places*, in hand. I have not looked at the book since my flight to Saskatchewan in September ... Flying over the prairies near Regina, on a crisp autumn day, I can see the golden fields quilted together and feel that customary sense of familiarity with this place. On an intuitive level, I understand Apache Elder Charles Henry's point that, in the grand scheme, the meaning which places have in our lives transcends our own momentary existence. I think of the name-place stories of Pasqua,

my First Nation community – mostly that I do not know them. Yet even with this deficit of the cultural stories, I maintain a powerful connection to this part of the country that has shaped who I am ...

I get home from Saskatchewan and put the Basso book in my 'in pile' for a few weeks. The notion of name-places keeps simmering in my mind and I consider how the sky, water, and earth, among other things, contextualize our life. On a rainy Wednesday afternoon, I decide it is time to return to the book, and I head up to the University of Victoria library. To me, it is intriguing the way the Western Apache stories intermingle knowing with communicating. Basso's analysis of the association between language and ethnography in understanding a culture makes sense, though I question if other variables need consideration. And I wonder how this translates to contemporary urban Indigenous life of Foucault readers, Starbucks, and SUVs versus oral storytelling, black tea, and pickup trucks.

There I was, an expatriate Cree/Saulteaux on Coast Salish territory, a 'small town girl' living in the city, a prairie woman living on an island. A daughter, a sister, a partner, an affiliate (the name that my stepdaughter and I have for each other), an auntie, a friend, a cat owner, a student, a teacher, a curriculum developer, a researcher, a seeker – all of these form my identity. Yet, I had not paused long enough to consider the full implications of my ancestry. I knew that the research would ask this of me. I knew that this inquiry would take me home to find my story anew. The Great Plains of southern Saskatchewan was the lurking variable in my research.

This book emerged from this particular research journey, the questions that I have asked, and the meaning that I have made from abundant and powerful knowledge shared with me. Had this occurred at another time in my life, the interpretations might have been different. We know what we know from where we stand. We need to be honest about that. I situate myself not as a knowledge-keeper – this has not been my path – rather my role is facilitator. I have a responsibility to help create entry points for Indigenous knowledges to come through.

True to form, during this writing I periodically bemoaned to my partner that my voice was not Indigenous enough (whatever that means) for this task. He kept saying, 'Keep going, Maggie, what you're doing is important.' And so I have persisted. This writing comes from the heart, it comes from who I am and all that I am – nothing more, or less for that matter. It comes from my own need and longing to engage with my Nêhiýaw and Saulteaux ancestry, and to say to my academic world that my culture counts. It is written from my voice, in my style, and it reflects who I am. The Elders say that if it comes from the heart and is done in a good way, our work will count. My hope is that this work will count for Indigenous people in a way that is useful – that's all.

Goal

Introduction

A while back, I was presenting before a diverse group of Indigenous and non-Indigenous people in a college setting. Many in attendance were students and faculty. I was sharing the findings from my research into the nature of Indigenous methodologies. A significant part of the presentation was devoted to the methodology of the study, a tribal-based approach with Cree knowledge as the guiding epistemology. Respecting protocol, before starting the presentation I acknowledged the territory and introduced myself. I shared aspects of my background with the audience – tribal and community affiliations, personal background, professional experience – to offer enough identity markers to situate me. I then introduced my research. After unpacking terms like *methodology* and *epistemology* and why I chose to use them when referring to Indigenous research, I spent considerable time focusing on the tribal methodology used for my study. I outlined why I chose this emergent approach based on ancient knowledges, and why I felt that it was the only approach that could respond to my specific research question. I then spoke about the characteristics of the methodology, shared the research question of the study, and offered an overview of the research group and what the participants in it said.

Throughout the presentation, I observed the usual audience responses – some took notes, others sat forward with thoughtful expressions, and still others possessed those unnerving blank stares. After I finished, I thanked those present and asked for questions. I had presented extensively on this research and the comments that followed were similar to those made in other venues. None of the audience members contested the central finding of the study – that there was a distinctive Indigenous approach to research – rather, people were eager to talk about how it could be applied. The tribal methodology used in my research was a natural entry point for that discussion. People in the audience wondered how a tribal-based approach could work for an urban Aboriginal population. Did the methodological approach of my study work only for Cree researchers? Did this approach allow for the participation of non-Indigenous peoples? This book seeks to respond to these questions, but that is not why I share this story nor is it why this talk has stayed with me.

As I was packing up and gathering my effects to accompany my host for dinner and to debrief, a young Indigenous student cautiously came up to me. She said that she enjoyed the presentation, but she was wondering about something. She said that she was of Indigenous ancestry but had grown up in the city and did not have any connections with community. She said that she was drawn to using an Indigenous methodology but did not think that she could go this route because she did not have the necessary cultural connections. We talked about her aspirations and hesitations, and as she was speaking my stomach was churning, for she was not seeking guidance on a relatively straightforward question about Indigenous methodologies. Rather, her query was more complex. It got to the heart of why Indigenous approaches mattered in the first place. I had to choose my words carefully, for standing before me was the future. This young Indigenous student was questioning whether she could embrace her Aboriginal culture. It did not seem that her reasons were stemming from a lack of desire, but more about belonging. I did not ask for specific reasons, but I suspected that some of them were ours collectively born of a colonial history that shadows our being. I listened, shared some of my experience, the ins and outs, ups and downs. I said that our culture, family, kin, kith, clan, and community wait for us. We have the right to know who we are, and that this right involves responsibilities – but there are people to help us out, that we are not alone. I offered her the best guidance I could should she choose Indigenous methodologies – start where you are, it will take you where you need to go. I do not know what choice this student made and will likely never know. I wish I could have been less obscure, but it was not my place to direct another's path. I share this story because I want to acknowledge this Indigenous student and how our talk has kept me going through many a hesitant day of this work. Since this time, I have heard variations of this narrative, not all but many from young Indigenous people who share a story that holds an undertone of a deep desire to come back to one's own culture. Many non-Indigenous young people are attracted to Indigenous approaches as well because, I believe, it has to do with a generation seeking ways to understand the world without harming it.

Leaving this memory, I come back to the present. As I write I feel the *kókoms* and the *mósoms*, the uncles and the aunties sitting with me, and they ask, 'Why are you writing this book?' This young Aboriginal woman comes to mind, but there are other reasons, and I cannot proceed without tending to the question, Why a book on Indigenous methodologies? I know that the motivations underlying this effort are layered. An initial reason for public distribution of this work is inter-twined with the methodological choice for my research study. A premise found in a Nêhiýaw epistemology is about giving back to community, and as researchers we can do this by sharing our work so that it can assist others. Having experiences as both an Indigenous graduate researcher and university research instructor, I knew that a contribution on Indigenous research frameworks would be useful to both Indigenous and non-Indigenous researchers seeking to honour Indigenous knowledge systems. I attempted to share my research through presentations and e-mailing digital copies of my findings to those who requested them. However, such efforts cannot reach the same audience as a publication. The choice of writing a book, as opposed to a series of separately published journal articles, was to ensure that this offering could, and would, be taken up as a holistic unit. These reasons help to explain why a *book* on Indigenous method-ologies. This response was less taxing than the pointed question of why a book on *Indigenous methodologies*. I believe that the ancestors were curious about the latter question, and I share some of my thoughts here.

The catalyst for this book was my doctoral research. My doctoral dissertation is an exploration of ways in which Indigenous academic researchers have incorporated culture into their research methodology. The findings of this research are the basis of this book. Part of the doc-toral project expects that one's doctoral research will be published as new scholarship in some form, be it in scholarly journals or as a book. In completing my doctoral studies, I could no longer evade publica-tion decisions on my research. This represented a new tension, of an ongoing conflict, reappearing throughout my Ph.D. work. On the one hand, this research is deeply associated with Western systems for it is through a doctoral program that I was able to explore Indigenous methodologies. Simultaneously, I struggled with the appropriateness of bringing an oral-based knowledge system into an academic world that has only recently become open to it. Conducting and defending this research, and the knowledges that it holds, ensures a level of exposure within academia. Publication of the research, however, would heighten its vulnerability.

Indigenous contributors to this book cite the risks of bringing cultural knowledges into Western research spaces, and I, too, found myself anxious about the misinterpretations, appropriations, and dismissals that often accompany Indigenous ways of knowing within the academy. The transformative potential for academia in welcoming diverse knowledges is significant, but at what cost to Indigenous peoples? I knew that I was not the first to have such apprehensions, and knowing this heightened my responsibility to be clear on the reasons why I chose to persist.

Cultural longevity depends on the ability to sustain cultural knowledges. At the heart of a cultural renaissance, Indigenous or otherwise, is a restoration and respectful *use* of that culture's knowledge systems. Colonial history has disrupted the ability of Indigenous peoples to uphold knowledges by cultural methodologies. While colonialism has interrupted this organic transmission, many Indigenous peoples recognize that for their cultural knowledge to thrive it must live in many sites, including Western education and research. Contemporary universities are centres where knowledge is created, maintained, and upheld. Research powers this force. By entering these knowledge centres, Indigenous peoples are well positioned to carry out research that upholds cultural knowledges. Indigenous research frameworks are conceptual tools that can assist.

As the academic landscape shifts with an increasing Indigenous presence, there is a desire among a growing community of non-Indigenous academics to move beyond the binaries found within Indigenous–settler relations to construct new, mutual forms of dialogue, research, theory, and action. As long as the academy mirrors a homogeneous reflection of bodies, minds, and methods, our move in this direction is stalled. The infusion of Indigenous knowledge systems and research frameworks informed by the distinctiveness of cultural epistemologies transforms homogeneity. It not only provides another environment where Indigenous knowledges can live, but changes the nature of the academy itself. Indigenous methodologies disrupt methodological homogeneity in research.

To counteract the heinous reputation of Western research in Indigenous communities, one response has been to apply Western methodologies (such as community-based approaches) that are in alliance with the ethical and community dynamics of research with Indigenous peoples. However, there is a need for methodologies that are inherently and wholly Indigenous. The past several years have been marked by a growth in literature on tribal-based methodologies (Wilson, 2001; Weber-Pillwax, 1999), which is built upon the first wave of Indigenous scholarship (Little Bear, Hampton, Deloria) and argues the epistemological basis for this form of inquiry. Linda Tuhiwai Smith's (1999) book, *Decolonizing Methodologies*, has provoked analysis of how methodologies per se impact Indigenous peoples, and we are now at a point where it is not only Indigenous knowledges themselves that require attention, but the processes by which Indigenous knowledges are generated. Thus, Indigenous methodologies are the next step.

There is a need for research that employs a range of methodological options determined by the needs of the particular Indigenous community. However, Indigenous methodologies are not a widely available choice because they are not widely recognized. This is problematic and results in a form of 'methodological discrimination' (Ryen, 2000: 220), which can only be countered by increasing awareness of Indigenous inquiry. On the methodological buffet table, Indigenous methodologies ought to be a choice.

This work has relevance to policy and practice outside academia. Policy and programming grow out of research, and while the influence of research and its methodologies is not always visible in the policy cycle, research is where it starts. Research creates policy and policy generates programs. There has been a crisis in Indigenous educational and child welfare policy (among other sites) in this country. Why? Because the research that influences policy and shapes practices that impact Indigenous communities emerges from Western, not Indigenous, knowledges or forms of inquiry. The proposition is that methodology itself necessarily influences outcomes. Indigenous research frameworks have the potential to improve relevance in policy and practice within Indigenous contexts.

Finally, this book acknowledges the significance of relationships with others in the research community, starting where there are natural alliances, such as qualitative research. The most effective allies are those who are able to respect Indigenous research frameworks on their own terms. This involves a responsibility to know what that means. As Indigenous researchers, our responsibility is to assist others to know our worldview in a respectful and responsible fashion.

This book, then, offers a commentary on differing aspects of Indigenous methodologies. It is both analytical and conceptual, but it is also applied. This work offers conceptual possibilities for research that rests upon tribal perspectives. It is both emergent and exploratory while simultaneously specific, for the fluidity of tribal worldviews creates distinctive philosophies and practices. This book comprises my own narrative, and among secondary research it showcases insights by Indigenous scholar-researchers in Canada and internationally. The intent is to present a variety of Indigenous voices speaking to Indigenous inquiry.

In researching this book, I had conversations with six Indigenous scholars who delved into aspects of Indigenous research methodology while completing their doctoral degrees within Western universities. Their stories, interwoven with my own reflections, explore how Indigenous researchers have integrated Indigenous cultural knowledges into their research frameworks and the challenges of doing so within academia. Cultural knowledges in this statement include the broad spectrum of beliefs about knowledge stemming from an individual's own cultural group; this could include knowledge from the sacred and ceremonial. With their permission, these individuals' research stories are melded into the text here in a format that honours oral conversation. All participant quotes appearing in this book are taken from the primary research for my doctoral dissertation; all of the interviews took place in the spring and summer of 2006. In both the primary research report (my dissertation) and this book, all participants chose to have their names stand with the insights that they shared. The act of sharing through personal narrative, teaching story, and general conversation is a method by which each generation is accountable to the next in transmitting knowledge. As contemporary Indigenous thinker Fyre Jean Graveline asserts, we learn in relationship to others, knowing is a process of 'self-in-relation' (1998: 52). The conversations with the Indigenous scholars are engaging, insightful, and highly instructive about the ins and outs of Indigenous research. They are all Indigenous post-secondary academics, and from an educative perspective their research stories bring powerful insights into Indigenous methodologies. Below are the six Indigenous scholars interviewed for this work, introduced in the order that they appear in this book. A more extensive introduction appears before each of their stories in the respective chapters.

Michael Hart is of Nêhiýaw ancestry from the Fisher River Cree Nation in Manitoba. He completed his doctorate through the School of Social Work at the University of Manitoba. Graham Smith is a Maori educator who holds a doctoral degree in education through the University of Auckland and is recognized as a distinguished professor of education. Jeannine Carriere is a Métis woman and her ancestors flow from the Red River Métis of Manitoba. She received her Ph.D. from the Department of Human Ecology and Family Studies at the University of Alberta. Cam Willett is of Nêhiýaw ancestry from Little Pine First Nation in Saskatchewan. He completed his doctoral work through the Department of Adult Education, Community Development and Counselling Psychology, at the Ontario Institute for Studies in Education, University of Toronto. Laara Fitznor is of Nêhiýaw ancestry from northern Manitoba. She received her doctorate in education from the Department of Adult Education, Community Development and Counselling at the Ontario Institute for Studies in Education, University of Toronto. Kathy Absolon is Anishnabe from Flying Post First Nation. She was raised in Parry Sound and is first-degree *Midewiwin* of the Three Fires Society. Her doctoral degree is from the Department of Adult Education, Community Development and Counselling Psychology, at the Ontario Institute for Studies in Education, University of Toronto. I would like to thank these individuals who took time to share their teachings. Their time was valuable as all are busy faculty members at various institutions, several in tenure-track positions. The conversations are of significant scholastic value, holding within them the richness of oral culture. Theirs is a knowledge source that I simply could not access through written publication given the orality of our traditions. This needs to be recognized.

As defined by the Indigenous scholarly research community, this book offers insight into specific indicators of Indigenous inquiry for those who will either use it or be in a position to assess its use. This book takes the form of three layers or dimensions: (a) situating self; (b) introduction, context (Chapters 1, 2, 9), and conclusion; and (c) the qualities of Indigenous inquiry (Chapters 3 to 8). The most outward dimensions (i.e., situating myself) are marked by a Prologue and Epilogue that contain a personal narrative of my research journey while I was conducting my doctoral work (the basis of this book). Sharing from my story is a conscious way to illustrate 'self-in-relation' (Graveline, 2000: 361). I wish to show the holistic, personal journey, not solely its cognitive component, and how it resonated with all parts of my being. The Prologue and Epilogue give formal uninterrupted space for narrative, and while this form of sharing integrates itself throughout the text, it is intentional that the work begins and ends with story.

The book is blanketed by the Introduction, Chapters 1, 2, and 9, and the Conclusion. These chapters provide the context for the discussions, and reference the landscape within which Indigenous methodologies are situated. The Introduction assists the reader in approaching this work, and identifies its purpose, intention, organization, and audience. Focusing on the broader research context, Chapter 1 positions Indigenous methodologies within the qualitative research landscape. It affirms tribal-based research as a distinctive methodological approach, a methodology establishing its positioning alongside the dominant Western qualitative paradigm. The chapter argues for the presence of tribal-based research and explicates its position. Substantive consideration is given to Indigenous research frameworks as a relational approach within research theory and method, a characteristic that finds alignment with a range of Western qualitative methodologies. The purpose of Chapter 1 is to place Indigenous methodology as a legitimate approach among other valid forms of inquiry.

Chapter 2 comments on the necessity of conceptual frameworks for research generally, and their specific use in upholding Indigenous research. Towards this end, the chapter offers an example of an Indigenous epistemological framework based upon *Nêhiýaw Kiskêýihtamowin*, or Cree (Plains Cree) knowledge used within my doctoral research. This chapter could never give full insight into the nuances, intricacies, and complexities of Plains Cree knowledge (nor does it try to do so). Rather, it provides the reader with enough information about how Indigenous epistemology (i.e., Plains Cree), as a tribal positioning, fits within an Indigenous research framework. Chapter 2 is prefatory to the discussion that follows on the characteristics of Indigenous methodologies.

As this book situates Indigenous methodologies within the larger context of qualitative research, it also situates them within the landscape of Western academia, where, arguably, much of this conversation will take place. Chapter 9 opens with a statement concerning why academia must be examined relative to Indigenous research frameworks. When the rubber hits the road the practice of Indigenous methodologies will be felt in Western knowledge centres. A book such as this would be incomplete without a contextual piece. The tensions and possibilities that forge the creation of a principled ideological space and the opportunities for supportive non-Indigenous involvement are examined in this chapter.

I hesitantly call the final chapter a conclusion for it is more accurately a pause in an ongoing, stimulating discourse on the nature, qualities, practices, and politics of Indigenous methodologies.

Chapters 3 to 8 make up the heart of this book. These six chapters explore qualities that when holistically integrated are indicative of Indigenous research frameworks. The intention is not to be deductive, declaratory, or exhaustive. Rather, the aim is to offer a portal so as to study characteristics that the Indigenous research community has cited as being specific to Indigenous inquiry. Each chapter is written in essay format, each highlighting a particular quality. There will, inevitably, be consistent themes that traverse all chapters given the integrated nature of the topic. I recommend that this book be read as a whole, for each quality is interrelated with the others. It is not one singular aspect of Indigenous inquiry that makes it unique, but the combination of each as they work in concert to form a distinctive whole. While their insights are threaded throughout the entirety of this work, each chapter incorporates a condensed conversation with a specific Indigenous scholar-researcher. For example, Chapter 3 focuses on Indigenous epistemologies and integrates a talk with Michael Hart. Chapter 4 integrates a conversation with Graham Smith, and so forth. The conversations are blanketed between an introduction and a reflective commentary. This is an attempt to provide a range of voices and honour the place of story in Indigenous knowing and researching.

Chapter 3 starts with Indigenous epistemologies as they apply to research choices and design. It is presented in a layered form, beginning with a general discussion of the topic. It then focuses on Plains Cree knowledge. Themes include the connection between Indigenous ways of knowing and place, that the homeland that Indigenous people never left is pivotal in distinguishing Indigenous methodologies. It raises the complexities of integrating holistic knowledge into the research conversation, yet for Indigenous methodologies to flourish this must be upheld. Chapter 3 is also the first of six core chapters to integrate narrative from the six Indigenous researchers. Michael Hart shares his thoughts on Indigenous languages, connection to place, traditional knowledge systems, and living according to the underlying values as they relate to Indigenous research. Grounding his reflections in Nêhiýaw epistemology, his insights show how tribal knowing, as applied to a research method, makes for a distinctively Indigenous approach.

While Chapter 3 sets out the epistemological context, Chapter 4 argues for the integration of a decolonizing theoretical lens that positions Indigenous inquiry as resistance research. Graham Smith effectively argues that attempting to move forward with Indigenous research frameworks without acknowledging the colonial residue inherent in Western educative and research processes will not bring the substantive change required. The means by which knowledge is garnered, valued, and legitimized from a traditional Western perspective contrasts with tribal ways, and exemplifies how the different worlds chafe in the presence of each other. He argues that Indigenous methodologies should be a choice and that, for both political and practical reasons, they are currently not an option.

To further delve into Indigenous methodologies, Chapter 5 invites us to consider the deep connections between knowing, story, and research. The focus of this chapter is not only story, but story as an Indigenous research method. Story is not a culturally neutral form of expression, but is taken up in different ways by different cultures. In an effort to traverse cultural paradigms, the chapter discusses the similarities between story within Indigenous methodologies and reflexivity within existing qualitative approaches. This discussion will be of interest to those who wish to use, or seek to understand the use of, story within Indigenous research. The chapter concludes, appropriately enough, with a story. Jeannine Carriere shares her research story, one imbued with a holistic sensibility that moves beyond thought alone. She explains why it is important to capture in the research the self as it comes to know, and identifies methods for researchers to go about this aspect of research.

Self-location, cultural grounding, and purpose are the essence of Chapter 6. The chapter explores an Indigenous perspective on purpose and self-location as consistent characteristics of Indigenous research. Throughout the chapter, the role of self-location within resistance research, shared by other forms of anti-oppressive research methodologies, reveals itself. Within the chapter, Indigenous researchers share methods for capturing location, grounding, and purpose, such as portfolios and journals, as part of their research methodology. To complete Chapter 6, Cam Willett situates himself in his work, and shares his thoughts on purpose, memory, and motivations within his research.

Chapter 7 is a commentary on the choices made in research, the rationales, and the application of Indigenous methodologies. It focuses on the research 'details' that often cause consternation when traversing cultural paradigms, including differentiating methods in focus group research circles and conversation in open-structured interviews, to name only two. This chapter also integrates considerations for making meaning within Indigenous research, including working with and presenting 'data.' To augment themes arising from the chapter, Laara Fitznor offers a hands-on accounting of the ins and outs that confront researchers engaged in Indigenous research, and the on-the-spot decisions that need to be made to stay congruent with cultural epistemologies.

The final chapter of the central core, Chapter 8, is devoted to conducting research in a good way. The Cree term *miýo-wîcêhtowin* means good relations; *miýo-wîcêhtowin* is the heartbeat of ethical responsibilities within Indigenous research practice. This chapter places ethics as methodology, and positions reciprocity as an ethical starting place. Indigenous research ethics are examined from the perspective of governance, methods, and community relevance. The unavoidable tensions of conducting ethical research according to collectivist traditions in individualist spaces come into the analysis. To augment the points made in the chapter, Kathy Absolon shares her perspective of what it means to conduct ethical research from an Anishnabe point of view.

Who Will Find This Book of Interest?

Several different audiences will find interest in this book. Because Indigenous research frameworks are enjoying growing interest by the research community, the challenge is to make it accessible to a range of audiences. This book was written with many people in mind, certainly members of the academy, both Indigenous and non-Indigenous. They will find this book of general interest given the attention to research methodologies within scholarship. This group includes researchers, faculty, graduate students, adjudicators for research grants, ethics board members, university administrators seeking to recruit more Indigenous students, and those generally interested in emerging methodologies (particularly qualitative). It is intended for both the novice graduate student and the seasoned scholar. It will have relevance for those active in applied research outside academia who have conducted (or seek to conduct) research within Indigenous contexts. It is also offered to the Indigenous community, whose members have a huge stake in ensuring that research is conducted in a respectful way that honours and upholds tribal paradigms.

Yet, throughout I have been guided by a singular question: Will this work assist Indigenous graduate students in their research methodology? While this book is intended to be of interest to a broad audience, it was written especially with Indigenous graduate students in mind, those who have bounded into a research methodologies class and felt the confusion of knowing that something does not fit, but not knowing what that is. As greater numbers of Indigenous students are entering graduate studies, there is a need to meet this group's methodological needs. My wish is that Indigenous graduate students and other interested folk can see this book as a contribution in upholding Indigenous research design, and that it will encourage continued conversation and action among Indigenous researchers and their non-Indigenous allies in the emergent field of Indigenous methodologies.

A Note about Terminology

Throughout this text, I use the word *Indigenous* to refer to Indigenous peoples and culture. However, I periodically use the term *Aboriginal* when referring to a specific Canadian context, such as in reference to Aboriginal rights. Correspondingly, this applies to the word *Indian* (when referring to the Canadian status Indian population) as defined in the Indian Act. In referencing *Indigenous knowledges*, I use this term in the plural. However, I also rely upon the terms *Indigenous epistemologies, tribal knowledge*, and *tribal epistemology* in specific instances. *Tribal knowledge* refers to a specific tribal way of knowing (e.g., Nêhiýaw); the term *Indigenous knowledges*, however, acknowledges both the shared commonalities and the diversity of many tribal ways of knowing.

Arguably, *Indigenous methodology*, like *Indigenous theory*, is a contested term. Referring to the use of the term *theory*, Cree scholar Neal McLeod acknowledges a positioning that thinking beyond the colonial box is 'a theoretical activity,' while others hold the perspective that theory is 'an inherently Western idea and cannot be rendered within Indigenous philosophies' (2007: 98). This same argument applies to the term *methodology*. For the sake of clarity, and to be congruent with the growing literature within Indigenous research approaches (Wilson, 2001; Steinhauer, 2002; Kovach, 2005), I have chosen to use the term *Indigenous methodologies*, in the plural, to describe the theory and method of conducting research that flows from an Indigenous epistemology. Within this book I use interchangeably *Indigenous methodolo-*

gies, *Indigenous research frameworks*, and *Indigenous inquiry*. All these terms describe research methodologies that encompass tribal or Indigenous epistemologies.

Within research, *epistemology* means a system of knowledge that references within it the social relations of knowledge production. It is different from ontology, in that ontology is concerned with the nature of being and reality. In referencing Indigenous (or tribal) ways of knowing and how they apply to research methodology within a research vernacular, I consistently use the term *epistemology*. The term *epistemology* has been most frequently used as a broker word during knowledge discussions that cross the Indigenous-Western divide. Cree thinker Willie Ermine used this term in his seminal piece, 'Aboriginal Epistemology' (1999). The term *epistemology* most closely approximates the 'self-in-relation' (Graveline, 2000: 361) aspect inherent to Indigenous knowledges. The layers of difficulty in bridging cultural paradigms within research most often begin at the level of individual word choice.

Throughout this text, the term *Western* is used as a descriptive term for a particular ontological, epistemological, sociological, and ideological way of thinking and being as differentiated from Eastern thought, an Indigenous worldview, and so forth. It is understood that Western thought is not monolithic or static, that it holds within it rich diversity and contributions; however, this book is not devoted to examining the intricacies of a Western worldview. Still it is a book on Indigenous methodologies and by necessity must examine Western colonialism and its influence on Indigenous knowledge. The purpose is not to propagate unhelpful binaries, but to point out that Indigenous approaches to seeking knowledge are not of a Western worldview, a matter that colonialism (and its supporters) has long worked to confuse.

I conclude this Introduction with a note about the writing style used. This is a research story. It is situated in a time, place, and context. The journey began in a landscape of ocean air and cedar trees, and travelled to a place where strong winds push sage brush across the dry plain. Although the narrative style is present, the writing often shape-shifts to other forms. Like sweet grass, it has three braids, comprising three writing styles: expository, analytical, and narrative. As a method for incorporating narrative, I periodically rely upon the first-person voice. It has the additional benefit of keeping me grounded. Plains Cree scholar Winona Stevenson writes, 'Seldom do you hear a Cree

Elder profess "I know." What is heard is "I believe" or "I believe it to be true"' (2000: 19). Using the first person honours the experiential while engaging the abstract and theoretical. I have made this choice because given all my understandings of Nêhiýaw and Saulteaux culture that have guided me through this journey, the one that keeps coming back is, 'Keep it whole, girl.' This is my way of trying to do that.

1 Indigenous and Qualitative Inquiry: A Round Dance?

Strangely, there has been very little attention paid to Indian methodologies for gathering data, and, consequently, the movement is primarily an ad hoc, personal preference way of gathering new ideas and attempting to weld them to existing bodies of knowledge.

Vine Deloria, Jr (1999)

In writing this section on qualitative research, I seek out a glossary on qualitative terminology to locate the defining characteristics of this approach, and compare them against my own. As I reach for this book, I see Keith Basso's *Wisdom Sits in Places* (1996) nearby in the mishmash of books lining my shelf. I return to the glossary, flip to 'Q' and see 'Qualitative Inquiry.' It reads: 'Qualitative is a not-so-descriptive adjective attached to the varieties of social inquiry that have their intellectual roots in hermeneutics, phenomenological sociology, and the *Verstehen* tradition' (Schwandt, 2007: 247). *Verstehen* (German, meaning 'to understand') is a term associated with the interpretative tradition, emerging in the nineteenth century to contest positivist thought. In the late 1800s, German philosopher Wilhem Dilthey differentiated scientific inquiry into two classifications. One form, *Naturwissenschaft* – 'natural science,' from *Natur* (nature) and *Wissenschaft* (science, knowledge, intelligence) – deals with the abstraction of knowledge, while the second, *Erklärung* ('explanation, interpretation, definition, etc.'), concerns understanding of everydaylife from one's empathetic interpretation (Neuman, 1997). Reflecting upon this, my eyes wander again to Basso's book. I think of Apache Elder Uncle Charlie, whom I have met only through Basso's work, and wonder what he would have to say about that. Would there be a common understanding about knowledge-seeking systems?

In traversing cultural knowledge paradigms, the first level of complexity arises with language. In considering Indigenous philosopher Anne Waters' analysis of the 'dualist binary ontology' of the English language compared with the 'nonbinary complementary dualist construct' (2004: 97, 98) that serves the thought and language of many Indigenous cultures, I am left contemplating how difficult it must have been for Indigenous people and the first visitors to understand one another given each group's distinctive language and culture. With colonization, Indigenous people were forced to forfeit their languages, and so a majority of Indigenous people in Canada now have English as their first language. Having a common language, however, has not served to increase cultural understandings. Rather, it has put Indigenous culture at risk. This suggests that a common language is not the panacea for a common understanding. Instead, understanding is a layered endeavour.

Given the complexities instilled within this word, *understand,* at what point can we say that we do indeed understand something? I begin to ponder my own immediate process of understanding in relation to others. I think of the students who come into my research class. The word *epistemology* sends us off into different directions, creating a dialectical force field. Tensions arise from the need to attach meaning to lofty and effervescent words like *truth* and *knowledge*. It seems that the interpretative nature of understanding fastens itself to the most intimate aspects of our experience, connecting us enough to find both foe and brethren. The space between these two places is deeply political, where representation, method, and meaning vie to be heard, to be understood. It is here, in this interpretative meaning-making, that qualitative research methodologies exist.

Qualitative research offers space for Indigenous ways of researching, yet any understanding of Indigenous methodologies alongside Western-constructed research processes (qualitative or otherwise) triggers recollection of the miserable history of Western research and Indigenous communities. The oft-quoted statement by Linda Tuhiwai Smith says it all: 'the word itself, "research," is probably one of the dirtiest words in the indigenous world's vocabulary' (1999: 1). In response, Indigenous scholars have been unified in their call for methodological approaches to research that respect Indigenous cultural knowings. From this starting place, it is not whether we need to consider Indigenous inquiry, but what approaches to it would look like and how (or if) they might fit into the qualitative landscape. Indigenous researchers are finding ways to apply their own tribal epistemologies into their research work. Yet, why are Indigenous methodologies missing from the buffet table of qualitative methodologies available to researchers (e.g., community-based research, feminist methodologies, grounded theory)? Is there is no desire within Western academia to acknowledge Indigenous methodologies? Or are we simply lost in translation? Can the backdrop of qualitative research be a bridge for traversing worldviews?

This chapter offers a context for locating Indigenous methodologies (and their corresponding conceptual frameworks) within research practice, specifically alongside qualitative research. It positions Indigenous methodologies as distinct from other forms of qualitative inquiry and calls forth several questions. Why attempt to locate Indigenous methodologies within qualitative inquiry? What do they have in common within the *Verstehen* tradition? Before contemplating these questions and posing the argument that Indigenous methodologies are a viable research framework that embodies qualitative characteristics (though not exclusively), it is necessary to provide a preparatory discussion for exploring this positioning. This involves clarifying three philosophical assumptions that underlie claims about methodologies in general and about Indigenous inquiry specifically.

To start, this work is premised on a belief that nested within any methodology is both a knowledge belief system (encompassing ontology and epistemology) and the actual methods. The two work in tandem. Second, Indigenous methodologies can be situated within the qualitative landscape because they encompass characteristics congruent with other relational qualitative approaches (e.g., feminist methodologies, participatory action research) that in the research design value both process and content. This matters because it provides common ground for Indigenous and non-Indigenous researchers to understand each other. Finally, and most significantly, tribal epistemologies are the centre of Indigenous methodologies, and it is this epistemological framework that makes them distinct from Western qualitative approaches.

The Backdrop of Qualitative Research

Given the interpretative nature of qualitative research, it is not surprising that there are different understandings of what exactly qualitative inquiry means in and of itself. Strauss and Corbin are grounded theory methodologists who define qualitative research as 'any type of research that produces findings not arrived at by statistical procedures or other means of quantification' (1998: 11). They argue that qualitative research, as a label, is confusing because different people can interpret it differently. Nevertheless, they formulate a working definition of qualitative research as a 'nonmathematical process of interpretation' for purposes of spotting patterns within the data and from which a theory can emerge (ibid.). Denzin and Lincoln add to this understanding of qualitative research by saying: 'Qualitative researchers stress the socially constructed nature of reality, the intimate relationship between the researcher and what is studied, and the situational constraints that shape inquiry' (2003: 13). To build upon the interactive nature of qualitative research, Rossman and Rallis (2003) accentuate the reflexivity of qualitative research. It is an approach, they argue, that demands that researchers be continually aware of their own biases as a means of consistently locating themselves in the research.

Because qualitative research is interpretive, the stories of both the researcher and the research participants are reflected in the meanings being made. It is likely at this point that qualitative research diverges most clearly from traditional positivist quantitative approaches. Each guided by their own philosophy, one is a seeker of a singular static truth from an objective distance, while the other searches for contextualized realities and acknowledges many truths. These approaches differ significantly, but both stem from a paradigm defined and nuanced by Western thought.

In his seminal book, *The Structure of Scientific Revolutions*, Thomas Kuhn defines paradigms as 'some accepted examples of actual scientific practice – examples which include law theory, application, and instrumentation together – that provide models from which spring particular coherent traditions of scientific research' (1996 [1962]: 10). Whether it is quantitative or qualitative research, Kuhn's description of paradigms encompasses both theory and method. He is, however, contextualizing paradigms within Western thought, which influences this definition. Mertens uses the terminology of paradigms to provide us with a rubric for differentiating between research approaches, and describes how and where qualitative and quantitative methods fit within each schema. This rubric identifies positivism/postpostivism, constructivism, transformative, and pragmatic as each being a distinctive paradigm (2005: 9). Each paradigm is characterized by its own ontology, epistemology, and methodology, all of which, nonetheless, fall within the larger paradigm of Western thought. Paradigms within a paradigm, Mertens' rubric helps to clarify the diverse conceptual frameworks that encompass each distinctive research approach and how it differs from other approaches. Given the range and possibilities evident in the qualitative research tradition, contextualized knowledge (such as an Indigenous one) can find an ally with these paradigms.

The current field of qualitative research is an inclusive place. For example, the use of a self-reflective narrative research process, in conjunction with a philosophy that honours multiple truths, is congruent with a research approach that seeks *nisitohtamowin* (a Cree word for understanding) or 'self-in-relation' (Graveline, 1998: 57). Within qualitative inquiries, there are allies for Indigenous researchers. Participatory action research, a methodology found within the transformative paradigm, has utilized qualitative approaches, offering a research theory, method, and action for giving back to a community through research as praxis (McTaggart, 1997; Stringer, 1999). Phenomenology and narrative inquiry have been useful methodologies for Indigenous researchers who wish to make meaning from story. Denzin and Lincoln suggest that there are 'seven moments of qualitative research' (2003: 19), and that we are entering the seventh moment, where inclusivity of voices in research practice is possible. I am instinctively drawn to the idea of a seventh moment, for I think of seven generations, seven fires with all the hope implied in those terms. Yet my critical side will not be quieted without its say, and my inner critic says that there needs to be due attention to moments one to six, starting with what Denzin and Lincoln refer to as the 'traditional period' (ibid.).

In the traditional period of the twentieth century, qualitative research was largely influenced by positivism. Most prominently, ethnographical research design was employed as qualitative 'objective' studies of the 'other.' Ethnographies of the 'other' in the Americas usually meant depictions of 'exotic' Indigenous cultures (Ladson-Billings, 2003). These early qualitative studies were responsible for extractive research approaches that left those they studied disenfranchised from the knowledge they shared. In early educational ethnographies concerned with the plight of the marginalized 'other,' Native American children were a primary research sample (Yon, 2003). Educational ethnographies became a powerful tool to assist in the enculturation of Indigenous peoples through education. The ethnographers themselves cited as problematic the short-term 'smash and grab' ethnographies that gathered qualitative data from quick in-and-out interview sessions (Martin and Frost, 1996: 606). Still, qualitative research as ethnography, with the powerful imagery of words unavailable to quantitative approaches that depended upon numerical symbolism, allowed researchers entry into the world of 'other.' Gaining access to this world, researchers of this period interpreted their observations from their own cultural stance, resulting in a skewed perception of what they were trying to understand. Perhaps these early researchers did not see this as an imposition, for they certainly did not and/or could not admit to it under the prevailing paradigm of scientific research.

I am not convinced that this is part of the research method's distant past. While critical theory and postmodern analysis have created space within Western science for representation, voice, and a multiplicity of truths, the essentialism of Western thought pervading research has not been fully challenged in the academy. In her recent work on cultural epistemologies, Ladson-Billings points out that Western epistemological privilege pervades the academy and that the 'epistemological challenge that is being mounted by some scholars of color is not solely about racism, however, it is also about the nature of truth and reality' (2003: 402). While anti-racist efforts that attempt to decolonize human relationships within sites of research (e.g., the academy) move forward, albeit slowly, there has been little systemic shift in the ideology of knowledge production.

From an Indigenous perspective, the reproduction of colonial relationships persists inside institutional centres. It manifests itself in a variety of ways, most noticeably through Western-based policies and practices that govern research, and less explicitly through the cultural capital necessary to survive there. The result has been, and continues to be, that Indigenous communities are being examined by non-Indigenous academics who pursue Western research on Western terms. While we may currently be in a more inclusive moment of qualitative research, Indigenous communities are still being 'researched,' albeit with more political finesse. Indigenous researchers have acknowledged the colonial history of Indigenous oppression and the political nature of Indigenous research. Ojibway scholar Roxanne Struthers succinctly summarizes the history of non-Indigenous research in Indigenous communities by saying it was not 'managed in a germane manner' (2001: 127). Within a Maori context, Bishop states that research benefits often went to the researcher, 'not the people being researched' (1997: 36). In providing a context, these scholars remind us that regardless of whether research emerges from a positivist, constructivist, or transformative paradigm, it is still 'researching' Indigenous people, and it is still deeply political.

From a qualitative methodological perspective, I sense that there are two overriding political challenges as we enter into the seventh moment of qualitative research. The first involves finding (and using) a research approach that is not extractive and is accountable to Indigenous community standards on research so as to honour the tribal worldview. The second challenge is dealing with the undeniable. There is a fundamental epistemological difference between Western and Indigenous thought, and this difference causes philosophical, ideological, and methodological conflicts for Indigenous researchers. From the perspective of those who wish to employ a methodological approach guided by their own cultural epistemology, but cannot because it is personally and/or structurally shut out (intentionally or not), it feels as though the space is uninviting. This applies to quantitative research, qualitative research, and the post-secondary research environment in general. This sense of exclusion has a direct impact on Indigenous scholars and students within academia.

Eber Hampton describes the violence directed at graduate students who hold alternative worldviews concerning knowledge. He explains, 'I like the analogy of Cinderella's slipper because we are not Cinderallas; the slipper doesn't fit' (1995: 8). In line with Ladson-Billings, I have come to believe that a significant site of struggle for Indigenous researchers will be at the level of epistemology because Indigenous epistemologies challenge the very core of knowledge production and purpose. While this is not a matter of one worldview over another, how we make room to privilege both, while also bridging the epistemic differences, is not going to be easy. Indigenous methodologies prompt Western traditions to engage in reflexive self-study, to consider a research paradigm outside the Western tradition that offers a systematic approach to understanding the world. It calls for the non-Indigenous scholar to adjourn disbelief and, in the pause, consider alternative possibilities. Given these challenges, how do we situate Indigenous inquiries within qualitative research? Or do we even try?

An Insider/Outsider Relationship

Indigenous methodologies can be considered both a qualitative approach and not. While much of this book focuses on Indigenous methodologies themselves, this section offers a consideration of the relationship between Indigenous methodologies and qualitative research. There is a growing critical mass of literature by Indigenous scholars who attest to the interpretative nature of Indigenous knowledges (Little Bear, 2000; Henderson, 2000; Deloria, 2002; Cajete, 1999). From this perspective, Indigenous epistemologies fit nicely within the narrative aspect of a constructivist paradigm. Indigenous researchers often hear Heidegger's phenomenology calling. From another angle, introducing Indigenous knowledges into any form of academic discourse (research or otherwise) must ethically include the influence of the colonial relationships, thereby introducing a decolonizing perspective to a critical paradigm. Those active in Indigenous community research will look to a form of participatory action research methodology. From this juncture, one could argue that Indigenous inquiry fits within a transformative paradigm. Seemingly, Indigenous methodologies may simply be a subcategory of a Western paradigm that utilizes qualitative research approaches.

This can be helpful in assisting Western researchers in relating to each other on the topic area, and given the limitations of the language of interpretative concepts such as ontology and epistemology, a place to start is a place to start. Yet, I believe that there are at least two fundamental difficulties in presuming that qualitative research, a Western tradition, can fully bring Indigenous methodologies under its wing. The first centres on form or, more specifically, the language that holds meaning in epistemological discourse. Indigenous knowledges have a fluidity and motion that is manifested in the distinctive structure of tribal languages. They resist the culturally imbued constructs of the English language, and from this perspective alone Western research and Indigenous inquiry can walk together only so far. This is a significant difficulty for all those, Indigenous and non-Indigenous, who do not speak a tribal language yet are inquiring into the nature of tribal knowledges.

The other matter relates to knowledge itself. Indigenous methodologies are guided by tribal epistemologies, and tribal knowledge is not Western knowledge. Knowledge is neither acultural nor apolitical. In speaking to Indigenous researchers, the Indigenous scholar Shawn Wilson tells us that it is time to release our dependency on Western

Figure 1.1 Locating Indigenous methodologies in qualitative research

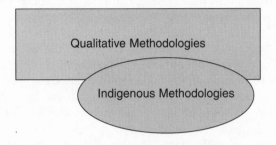

research traditions: 'These are dominant western system research paradigms. Now as Indigenous researchers we need to move beyond these, beyond merely assuming an Indigenous perspective on these non-Indigenous paradigms' (2001: 176). At present, there is a desire to give voice to Indigenous epistemologies within qualitative research, yet those who attempt to fit tribal epistemology into Western cultural conceptual rubrics are destined to feel the squirm. From my perspective, Indigenous methodologies and qualitative research at best form an insider/outsider relationship (see Figure 1.1). Although most qualitative researchers intuitively understand the dynamics of this relationship, it is here that we encounter the messiness of the work. The tension of the insider/outsider dynamic will persist until Indigenous research frameworks have methodological space within academic research dialogue, policy, and practice.

While discourse on the complexities of researching across knowledge paradigms will persist, mention must be made of the 'insider' space that qualitative research and Indigenous methodologies share. This matters because assisting Indigenous researchers (specifically graduate students) requires the involvement of the non-Indigenous academic research community. This is an educative process with a greater likelihood of success if Indigenous researchers and their non-Indigenous allies begin with some general understandings. It is correct to assume that Indigenous academics will be put in a position of educating their non-Indigenous contemporaries. If we do not take on this responsibility, Indigenous post-secondary students wishing to employ an Indigenous research framework will continue to be misunderstood and discouraged. While Indigenous methodology provokes substantive political and ideological shifts within Western research contexts, I believe that an antidote for a certain level of inertia can be found in knowledge translation. Without exposure to Indigenous inquiry, non-Indigenous academics may not know how to recognize an Indigenous methodological approach that flows from tribal epistemologies. This requires intellectual acumen and skill given that the task demands traversing culturally influenced knowledge paradigms. The educative work on behalf of Indigenous and non-Indigenous scholars is critical here, for what cannot be seen is often not acknowledged, and what is not acknowledged is dismissed.

In commenting on the 'insider' space, Indigenous methodologies share two interrelated characteristics with other qualitative approaches (e.g., feminist methodologies and appreciative inquiry): (a) both approaches are relational, and (b) both approaches must show evidence of process and content. Given their holistic nature, Indigenous research frameworks involve evidence of a capital 'P' process within research. What is meant by a qualitative relational methodology in general, and what is meant by Indigenous methodologies as a relational approach in particular? One could argue that if qualitative research is founded upon an interpretive tradition, then it is, by necessity, relational. Rossman and Rallis submit that 'qualitative research is quintessentially interactive' (2003: 35). They go on to suggest that there must be a direct contact between researcher and research participants that includes the complex and varied responses that only an ongoing relationship can achieve. Given that any knowledge that emerges from qualitative inquiry is filtered through the eyes of the researcher, it follows that this new knowledge must be interpretative. A significant contribution of qualitative research, then, has been its ability to gain recognition that the researcher is not a neutral instrument of the research process.

Quantitative research, flowing from a positivist paradigm, assumes that objective neutrality can exist within research so long as lurking variables are controlled. Qualitative research, however, is built upon an interpretative presumption, and assumes that subjectivity within research will be a constant. The supposition of subjectivity and the interpretative nature of qualitative research imply a relational approach to research. *Reflexivity* is the term often utilized within a variety of qualitative research approaches to reference the relational. Reflexivity is the researcher's own self-reflection in the meaning-making process.

Feminist inquiry is a methodological approach that is highly reflexive. It provides a research methodology that allows feminist researchers to share the experience of conducting research and their own subjective experience with their research participants throughout the process. Integral is a gender analysis that contextualizes feminist research (Liamputtong, 2007: 11). Autoethnography, an approach with its foundations in ethnographical research, brings together the study of self (auto) in relation to culture (ethnography). Within this approach, self-reflection moves beyond field notes to having a more integral positioning within the research process and the construction of knowledge itself. As Gergen and Gergen state, 'rather than giving the reader pause to consider the biases, here the juxtaposition of self and subject matter is used to enrich the ethnographical report' (2003: 579). In postmodern research, reflexivity is a central component of the research process. It requires an awareness of the self in creating knowledge (ibid.). In anti-oppressive approaches, self-reflection is described as 'critical reflexivity,' which purposefully gives space for the political examination of location and privilege (Herising, 2005: 136). In line with these research approaches, decolonizing methodologies demand a critical reflexive lens that acknowledges the politics of representation within Indigenous research. It is rare that qualitative research conducted in the past decade does not make mention of the self-reflective component in its methodology, whether referring to it as reflexivity, critical reflexivity, self-reflection, or field notes (Gitlin et al., 2002).

Depending upon the specific methodology, the rationale for giving reflexivity its due can vary. A methodology that flows from a theoretical perspective that highly values 'self-in-relation,' such as autoethnography, will incorporate reflexivity as a necessary method to actualize its approach. For feminist and postmodern researchers, critical reflexivity brings forward the political and representational dimension of research in knowledge construction inherent to their particular theoretical standpoints. From other perspectives, reflexivity is associated with validity as a means of identifying bias within the research. Creswell (2003) situates reflexivity as an indicator of validity within qualitative research. He indicates that there are eight primary strategies to demonstrate validity, one of which is to clarify bias and create a transparency that readers will appreciate. Evidence of self-reflexivity is an acknowledgment by the researcher that her or his subjectivity may influence the research findings. For varied reasons, reflexivity attests to the relational aspect of research that is incorporated within numerous qualitative approaches. From this place, I wish to acknowledge the progressive work by many qualitative researchers for creating the necessary space required by emergent methodologies, such as Indigenous inquiry, that place significant value on the relational, and that allow recognition of the experiential nature of Indigenous research frameworks.

Switching to the specific epistemic roots of Indigenous inquiry, Indigenous scholar Vine Deloria, Jr (1999) explicates the link between a relational worldview and methodology. Many Indigenous worldviews are based upon an animistic philosophy that attests that the human entity is but one clan group within its relational family. Deloria argues that a relational worldview, from a tribal perspective, is one that assumes relationships between all life forms that exist within the natural world. Relationship has a broad inclusive meaning within tribal understanding. Indigenous scholar Gregory Cajete affirms the relational perspective of Indigenous knowledges: they are, he says, about 'honoring the primacy of direct experience, interconnectedness, relationship, holism, quality, and value' (2004: 66).

One methodological tool for such an epistemic positioning is observation. We gather knowledge by observing the relationships within the natural world (Deloria, 1999: 34). Here the words *relationship* and *observing* are equally significant. In making meaning, the relational quality of tribal worldviews suggests a highly interpretative approach. This is recognized among tribal peoples. In referring to her doctoral work, Manu Aluli Meyer states that the epistemology that governs her dissertation 'is an interpretative analysis of my own epistemology, shaped by dream, taped narratives and a lifetime of interactions' (2004: 86). Indigenous forms of inquiry find an ally in the qualitative approaches that assume the relationally constructed aspect of knowledge production. Granted, qualitative approaches are based upon a non-animistic premise, which differs from tribal epistemology, and so deeper questions remain: Relationally constructed via which relationships? What does it mean to privilege human-centric knowledge? Still, the relational significance found in each provides a place for mutual understanding of the other.

An indicator of a relational approach in research can be found within process and content, and the reader must be able to identify both in the methodology. Indicators that this holistic epistemology is present include explicit reference to personal preparations involving motivations, purpose, inward knowing, observation, and the variety of ways that the researcher can relate her own process undertaken in the research. Another way to assess process is to see the inclusion of story and narrative by both researcher and research participant. In an Indigenous context, story is methodologically congruent with tribal knowledges. A product resulting from research using a tribal-centred Indigenous methodology ought to have a strong narrative component as part of its method and presentation of findings.

Researchers wishing to use Indigenous inquiry may use it alongside a Western approach that organizes data differently (e.g., grounded theory, phenomenology), thereby using a mixed-method approach. The data can be coded, emergent themes grouped and bracketed, and so forth, while transparently indicating that it is not an Indigenous epistemological approach to data analysis. This involves presenting research in two ways, but given the newness of Indigenous methodologies to the academy, this may be a strategic concession. The point is that if Indigenous methods (e.g., sharing circles, story, protocol) are being utilized, an Indigenous research framework with a tribal epistemology ought to be recognized, as opposed to assuming that Indigenous methods can be subsumed under a Western way of knowing.

Yet, while tribal epistemologies, and subsequently tribal-centred methodologies, are premised upon a relational perspective of the world, there are other characteristics of this approach that make it distinctive. Thus, Indigenous methodologies can only be categorized as relational to the extent that other relational qualitative methodologies can and are likewise categorized. Feminist methodology, for example, is relational but not generically so. Rather, its relational nature flows from a feminist epistemology that identifies it as distinct from, for example, autoethnography. It follows that Indigenous methodologies are not solely relational, but involve other characteristics that create a distinctive methodological approach. These traits include the tribal epistemology at the heart of this approach and a decolonizing aim, both of which are born of a unique relationship with Indigenous lands.

Furthermore, the relationships within Indigenous research approaches include the respect that must accompany the research process. Within Western research, this discussion is often found within ethical considerations. Relational research is concerned with doing research in a good way. As Wilson affirms, as a researcher 'you are answering to *all your relations* when you are doing research' (2001: 177, emphasis in original). Indigenous scholar Marie Battiste (2007) suggests that one of the most critical aspects of Indigenous research is the ethical responsibility to ensure that Indigenous knowledges and people are not exploited. Research is about collective responsibility: 'we can only go so far before we see a face – our Elder cleaning fish, our sister living on the edge in East Vancouver … – and hear a voice whispering, "Are you helping us?"' (Kovach, 2005: 31).

Indicators and Issues within Indigenous Methodologies

In claiming the distinctiveness of any emergent methodology, the question lingers: Is it *really* different? This is not a surprising query, for it would be easier for the dominant majority if the surface features of the alternate methodology could be understood within the existing paradigms, to continue rather than interrupt a pre-existing, ongoing conversation. In fact, the resistance to epistemological disruptions within academia is so great that it can stymie that which it seeks to create – new knowledge. Within an Indigenous research context, the result has been an attempt to weld Indigenous methods to existing bodies of Western knowledge, resulting in confused efforts and methodological floundering (Deloria, 1999). This can be seen in the increasingly common approach to research within the Indigenous landscape: the non-Indigenous principal researcher (with a significant Western research record) includes a junior Indigenous co-investigator (without a significant Western research record) on the research team. The research design includes Indigenous methods (e.g., research circles) and cultural protocols (e.g., offerings, ceremony), and identifies the research strategy as flowing from a central methodology that has credibility within the Western research community (e.g., community-based approach, grounded theory). The research is institutionally funded, and while there is awareness that this does not really challenge the status quo, it mentors Indigenous researchers to gain the necessary social and cultural capital to reproduce this strategy independently. It is not perfect, but, it is considered better than the 'smash and grab' ethnographers of time past. And the beat goes on, yes, the beat goes on …

On my less cynical days, I believe that this approach is an attempt to recognize the history of Western research within Indigenous communities and make reparations. Yet it is nevertheless problematic. Indigenous methods do not flow from Western philosophy; they flow from tribal epistemologies. If tribal knowledges are not referenced as a legitimate knowledge system guiding the Indigenous methods and protocols within the research process, there is a congruency problem. Furthermore, by not clearly recognizing Indigenous inquiry for what it is – a distinctive methodology – the political and practical quagmire will persist.

There have been attempts to problematize Indigenous methodologies, centring on the use of a specific tribal epistemology within an Indigenous research framework. In my case, I chose to centre Plains Cree knowledge in my methodology (see Chapter 2). Being Cree, I have an understanding of its epistemological premises and subsequent methods and protocols. A common response has been to ask how a researcher can privilege a specific tribal epistemology and still have meaning for other Indigenous cultures beyond that specific tribe. How can a Cree-centred methodology make sense in a Coast Salish context? Why, for example, did I use a Cree knowledge for my methodological approach instead of a pan-Indigenous approach? Primarily, these questions have come from non-tribal people who are well versed in matters of methodology and the like, but are new to Indigenous knowledges. Furthermore, there is a political dimension to this problematicizing that has its roots in colonial history, and often manifests itself in discourses of disbelief, and, within research circles, a desire for universal application.

My initial reply is to clarify why identifying a specific tribal knowledge is important. A part of this response is in itself political. Indigenous peoples have never been appreciative of a pan-Indigenous approach that attempts to homogenize our tribal practices. In a Canadian context, most individuals with a rudimentary knowledge of Indigenous cultures know that the coastal Tshimsian peoples have different practices than the land-based Plains Cree. The unique aspects of our tribal cultures are held in esteem because they emerge from those ancestoral interrelationships found in place. Our tribal affiliations must be acknowledged – it is about identity and respect. This brings me to the second point.

As Indigenous people, we understand each other because we share a worldview that holds common, enduring beliefs about the world. As Indigenous scholar Leroy Little Bear states, 'there is enough similarity among North American Indian philosophies to apply concepts generally' (2000: 79). Thus, when considering Indigenous epistemologies, Indigenous people contextualize to their tribal affiliation. We do this because our knowledges are bound to place. Therefore, if I indicate that, as a researcher, I will be following Plains Cree traditions (because that is my tribal affiliation), other Indigenous people will understand that though the specific custom and protocol may vary, the underlying epistemology for approaching the research is known. In fact, research emerging from a specific tribal-centred approach is often as familiar, if not more so, to Indigenous peoples than methodologies from Western research approaches (even if they are allied).

Other queries centre on whether this approach would work with the urban Indigenous population. My first response is to say that I am an urban Indigenous woman living away from my ancestral territory, and I have been able to apply a tribal-centred approach to research – it is feasible. Second, all urban Indigenous people come from a specific tribal background (or a mix, as in my case), and we need to reclaim that. However, this approach demands that the researcher 'do the work' to honour those tribal knowledges. Right from the beginning, the researcher has to ask: Am I up for the journey?

There are many ways to problematize Indigenous epistemologies; this has been going on since colonial times. There has been a continuous expectation that Indigenous ways must be congruent with Western customs, even though it is understood that the cultures are philosophically diverse. Politically, I understand why this happens, but does it make sense logically? Indigenous researchers and our allies cannot get drawn into the same old, same old. Rather, we need to delve into the possibilities. For the non-Indigenous researcher, the question then becomes: How can a non-Indigenous researcher participate? (This is dealt with more generally in Chapter 9.) These are questions about Indigenous methodologies that require good talk. My first response is that not all research in Indigenous contexts will require an Indigenous methodological approach; it depends upon the inquiry question. However, it should be an option. Second, it may be that the form of scholarly research, with its dependence upon a sole principal investigator model, may need to be revisited. It is possible that non-Indigenous researchers may only participate in Indigenous methodologies where there are structures that allow for equal partnership.

While contrasting opinions about ontological and epistemological differences will remain, and the functional role of methodologies in seeking truth will diverge, this diversity need not be diminished, for it allows relevancy within a range of contexts. However, an enviroment, research or otherwise, that allows for equitable valuing of ideas and relationships in understanding the world, and the living entities within it, is necessary for relational approaches such as Indigenous methodologies to thrive. The context of qualitative research is a fertile garden for such a seed to grow.

Perplexed, I put the Western research methodologies aside momentarily and returned to the teachings. Based upon the work of Indigenous scholars referencing Indigenous forms of inquiry (Atleo, 2004; Bastien, 1999; Bishop, 1997; Cole, 2002; Meyer, 2004) and reflecting upon my culture, I constructed a tribal-centred framework. This involved bridging Plains Cree knowledges and their methods in a manner translatable to Western research. The result was a workable conceptual framework or model. This chapter is a case presentation of this research framework as used in my doctoral research. At times it reads like a methodology chapter, but I have included it here because it offers insight into the application of an Indigenous methodological approach. There remains a dearth of literature in this area, and it serves as a practical example of an Indigenous research framework for those grappling with such tasks. This is, however, only one approach, and there are many ways to illustrate a conceptual framework for Indigenous inquiry. Prior to introducing this framework, I offer a preliminary note about conceptual frameworks in general, highlighting the cautions and possibilities of this aid in clarifying methodological mapping within Indigenous inquiry.

Why Do Conceptual Frameworks Matter within Indigenous Inquiry?

Jiménez Estrada (2005), an Indigenous scholar of Mayan ancestry, uses the Ceiba, or Tree of Life, as a conceptual research framework. This is a representation that both honours Mayan cosmology and gives visual form to the thought behind the research design. When initially considering a conceptual framework for my research, I considered the symbolism of an alder post in a Nêhiýaw ceremonial teepee. The posts (or poles) offer a structural foundation for the hides or branches that enfold them. The ceremonial teepee gives shelter and holds inside it ancient knowledges. These are two examples of many possibilities for conceptual frameworks as a holistic organizational device for Indigenous research. Yet applying the language of conceptual frameworks to Indigenous inquiries can be problematic and thus requires 'unpacking' both the term and its intention.

Maori scholar Graham Smith reminds those of us engaging in a relationship with Western academic institutions that we will be asked from time to time to make 'strategic concessions.' Applying the definitional terminology of conceptual frameworks to Plains Cree ways of

2 Creating Indigenous Research Frameworks

Researchers have the task of applying conceptual frameworks that demonstrate the theoretical and practical underpinnings of their research, and, if successful, these frameworks illustrate 'the thinking' behind 'the doing.' The research on which this book is based was an inquiry into Indigenous scholar-researchers' experiences in integrating cultural knowledges into methodology. In carrying out that research, I was searching for a conceptual methodological framework adequate for the research question. At the time, there was growing scholarship on Indigenous knowledges but a shortage of literature on Indigenous conceptual frameworks (specifically examples) linking tribal knowledges with congruent methodologies for human subject research. As a starting point, I had a choice of Western methodologies that could possibly work. Initially, I chose phenomenology because of its narrative approach and interpretative quality. However, phenomenology did not fully encompass the political dimension of a question requiring a decolonizing perspective, and so I attempted to integrate critical theory. At that point, I was trying to bridge two distinctive Western methodologies flowing from their own knowledge paradigm. It became a puzzle as to how to fit those two differing approaches together. Moreover, I knew that neither could respond to a research question seeking to study Indigenous knowledges as methodology. At the time, I could not articulate why, but I knew that no matter how sympathetic the Western methodology, the question I was considering ruled out a research process based solely on Western thought and tradition. Finding a research framework that could accommodate all three of these considerations became frustrating.

knowing is a strategic concession, for it does not fully capture the relational, holistic flavour of this worldview. The word *conceptual* privi-
leges thought as the sole pathway to knowledge and places feeling,
spirit, and experience as secondary. Furthermore, such frameworks
within research are primarily set out using the written word, and the
abstract quality of written language carries its own complexities in
attempting to represent a worldview based on oral tradition.

Edward Buendía contends that conceptual systems traditionally utilized in Western higher education are culturally and racially loaded
mechanisms that privilege European epistemological thought. Conceptual frameworks put at the centre 'acceptable' epistemological
positions that make sense to the dominant culture. Buendía argues that
the result is 'the imposition of a logic that has created particular types
of coherencies in categorizing and explaining the real' (2003: 51). There
are indeed a range of conceptual frameworks applied to research
methodologies, and the problem is that they inherently centre Western
epistemology, thus manufacturing and reproducing Western epistemology as a normative standard within research. Nonetheless, even
with their inherent bias, Western research frameworks can be adapted
as structural forms that are helpful to the Indigenous researcher for
allowing the entrance of visual, symbolic, and metaphorical represen-
tations of a research design that mitigates the linearity of words alone.
If we see them as aids to elevate tribal epistemology, and if we are
willing to acknowledge their limitations, conceptual frameworks can
be intermediary tools for putting forth a tribal-centred research
methodology.

Conceptual frameworks make visible the way we see the world.
Within research, these frameworks are either transparent (i.e., through
form) or not, yet they are always present. The rationale for explicit representation of one's conceptual framework is that it provides insight
into a researcher's beliefs about knowledge production, in general,
and how those beliefs will impact the research project. The content and
form of the conceptual framework itself assists in illustrating the
researcher's standpoint, thus giving the reader insight into the interpretative lens that influences the research. Karen Potts and Leslie
Brown are anti-oppressive researchers, and they make explicit to the
reader the connection between conceptual frameworks and the interpretation of findings in research: 'We carry our framework, which is
not inherently good or bad, around with us and it is through this
framework that we view the data. Making visible the [conceptual]

luggage is an individual and collective process' (2005: 274). They state that interpreting research findings and presenting those findings inherently involves a power dynamic that can be revealed in order to minimize it, or left hidden to maintain existing power relations.

In conducting research, the explicitness of our choices and the beliefs that influence them sends a purposeful message about who we are as researchers. Potts and Brown (2005) argue that we bring this intentionality to our research from day one. It does not magically appear only when we present our findings, but rather emerges throughout the research via motivations, critical reflection, engagement with others, and overall research choices. Explicit conceptual frameworks allow an opportunity to be honest about our perspective as researchers, and to illustrate how this perspective impacts the methods chosen.

This brings us to the relationship between a conceptual framework and methodology. How do they differ? Conceptual frameworks are also known as theoretical frameworks, epistemological frameworks, or research frameworks, all of which connote a theoretical knowledge system that governs the research. Morse identifies the theoretical framework within qualitative research as that which gives focus to the inquiry rather than solely serves data collection (as cited in Mertens, 2005). While methodology is defined here as encompassing both knowledge system and methods, the purpose of an Indigenous research framework is to illustrate the unification of these aspects. An Indigenous research framework acts as a nest, encompassing the range of qualities influencing the process and content of the research journey.

Too often Indigenous research has been equated with the inclusion of particular methods, such as sharing circles, and commentary on ethical guidelines involving research with Indigenous people and/or communities. While it is an attempt to consider Indigenous ways of knowing within research, methodologically speaking this definition of Indigenous research is problematic. When Indigenous researchers utilize Indigenous methods, there is always a tribal epistemic positioning in operation. However, this tends to be rendered invisible methodologically, and I believe that part of the problem lies within the conceptual framing. The act of searching, be it for knowledge or anything else, is a process in which all cultures have engaged, and it is always informed by that respective culture. When one is hungry, one searches for food in a planned manner, and if all goes well the sustenance is found and one is satisfied. The plan and method for accessing food depends largely upon socialization arising from one's sociocultural group. In research, ideological standpoints and cultural epistemic conditioning determine how this is done. The difficulty is that Indigenous epistemologies are not often explicitly acknowledged where Indigenous methods are at work in research. This has to do largely with epistemological recognition.

From a decolonizing perspective, the use of conceptual frameworks to reveal privileged epistemologies can work towards instigating change or, at the least, mitigate methodological inconsistencies that tend to arise when integrating Indigenous and Western methods. Edward Buendía questions how 'researchers, be they White or researchers of Color, can frame their research narratives to operationalize the epistemological standpoint that allows them to see and write knowledge differently' (2003: 50). From this perspective, a conceptual framework gives researchers a tool to show how their methods are being aligned with a particular way of knowing. Once I understood that I was privileging Plains Cree knowledges, a research framework began to form and give meaning to what I had been doing (or at least attempting to do) but as yet could not name. This was an attempt to honour the tribal knowledge that emerged from a social encounter with my world. In my case, Plains Cree knowledge offered guidance in research choices that reflected values, standards, ethics, and ways of Indigenous peoples generally and Cree specifically, and it demanded that I 'write knowledge differently' than I had been instructed to do within previous Western research training. Once this tribal epistemology was visible, then all research choices were considered against it. My methodology world became, while not easier, certainly clearer.

Still, there are tensions. Because so much of Indigenous ways of knowing is internal, personal, and experiential, creating one standardized, externalized framework for Indigenous research is nearly impossible, and inevitably heartbreaking for Indigenous people. It raises many questions. How are we customizing our Indigenous frameworks to fit within our tribal paradigms while communicating our process to Western academia? And how is the language of frameworks itself ultimately chipping away at our philosophies? Can we carry out tribal-centred research within the academy without this framework language? Although there are limitations in applying research framework language to Indigenous ways of knowing, these frameworks can assist Indigenous researchers by naming and acknowledging three distinct aspects of Indigenous research: (a) the cultural knowledges that guide one's research choices; (b) the methods used in searching; and (c) a way to interpret knowledge so as to give it back in a purposeful, helpful, and relevant manner. The expression of that framework can vary (Estrada, 2005), but the use of a conceptual framework in Indigenous inquiry will still have these consistent aspects.

By explicating one's conceptual framework, whatever form it takes, one allows others entry points in considering the interconnections underlying the approach in question. This becomes particularly important for Indigenous researchers who are faced with carrying out research in a social milieu (i.e., academia) with people who are largely unfamiliar with the depth and intricacies of Indigenous knowledges. Will a framework representing a tribal methodology be recognized and respected in and of itself? The response to that question will depend largely upon the assessor's ideology. However, the clarity of the researcher's conceptual model will be influential. As members of tribal communities, we descend from societies that were/are highly organized in accordance with a collective belief system. It has nothing to do with our ability to plan; we simply did not put it on paper. Within the current research landscape, it may be that we need to write out our plan. Still, at the end of the day it is up to each of us to determine if we will make that concession.

A Nêhiýaw Methodology

Whether it is Indigenous or Western, the way that one goes about doing research holds complexity. The research for this book, based on my doctoral study, was qualitative, involving Indigenous scholars. In seeking their wisdom, I utilized a methodology based upon an Indigenous research framework centred on Plains Cree knowledge. The methodology built upon several key qualities of Plains Cree tradition, but it is also shared by other tribal groups as identified in the literature by Indigenous scholars. These key qualities include: (a) holistic epistemology, (b) story, (c) purpose, (d) the experiential, (e) tribal ethics, (f) tribal ways of gaining knowledge, and (g) an overall consideration of the colonial relationship.

The Indigenous research framework offered is constructed to mirror a standard research design familiar to qualitative researchers. While the form is familiar, centring a tribal epistemology makes the methodology distinctive from other qualitative approaches. In this sense, the design is adapted to accommodate a Nêhiýaw-centred methodology,

Figure 2.1 An Indigenous research (conceptual) framework with Nêhiýaw epistemology

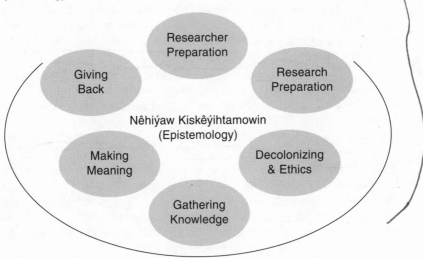

not vice versa. This route was chosen so that this conceptual framework and methodology could be more easily translatable to non-Indigenous researchers. This is a concession made with the hope that the next generation of researchers will not have to worry about such a translation variable. Again, this framework is but one expression of an Indigenous methodological approach.

The epistemic centre of this approach is *Nêhiýaw Kiskêýihtamowin* (Plains Cree knowledges), with research choices made so as to be congruent with this knowledge base. I drafted a pictorial illustration of this framework (see Figure 2.1), but I quite deliberately did not use arrows or directional lines in its construction. Rather than a linear process, this research followed more of an in and out, back and forth, and up and down pathway. I see Nêhiýaw knowledges as a nest that holds within it properties full of possibility for approaching research.

This methodology has several characteristics, as outlined in Figure 2.1. These characteristics include: (a) tribal epistemology, (b) decolonizing and ethical aim, (c) researcher preparations involving cultural protocols, (d) research preparation involving standard research design, (e) making meaning of knowledges gathered, and (f) giving back. The remainder of this chapter is a discussion of this design.

Centring Nêhiýaw Knowledge

As a 'theory of knowledge,' epistemology includes beliefs held about knowledge, where it comes from, and whom it involves. Within research, it addresses questions as to what is considered knowledge – e.g., can subjective knowing count as knowledge? – and what counts as legitimate knowledge (Kirby et al., 2006: 12). Revealing one's epistemological positioning shows the interpretative lens through which researchers will be conducting and making meaning of their research. Identifying one's epistemic positioning makes visible how this positioning guides the research. Nêhiýaw epistemology was the knowledge system guiding my research methodology. (Chapter 3 provides a more specific discussion of the epistemological assumptions underlying Nêhiýaw epistemology.) Within a research document, report, thesis, or dissertation, this would be expanded upon and infused throughout to illustrate how the epistemological assumptions influenced the entirety of the research. These would echo the unique, interpretative narrative of the Indigenous researcher and take a distinctive form. A discussion of a tribal epistemic positioning within research would address specific assumptions about the knowledge system of the tribal group to differentiate it from a pan-Indigenous approach, while still revealing shared assumptions about knowledge among tribal societies. As Leroy Little Bear (2000) has stated, there are many aspects that are shared. An Indigenous research framework has transferability among distinctive tribal contexts.

A consideration of using Nêhiýaw epistemology is a responsibility for protecting this knowledge. It can be difficult for Indigenous researchers to determine how much cultural knowledge to include in a textual format. Fortunately, as a Cree researcher I have had access to documented accounts of Plains Cree culture by Cree Elders in a variety of published forms. As such, these Elders have allowed this knowledge to be shared in the public domain, and so it is appropriate to share. It is for this purpose that Elders and others have agreed to have their words put into text. Furthermore, by observing and talking with Elders, family members, and other Plains Cree individuals with knowledge of the culture, I have gained an understanding of the ways and how they intersect with my life narrative. As a learner of Nêhiýaw epistemology, I have incorporated my understandings into my research and writing, and have done so with great respect and caution.

As stated earlier, an Indigenous research framework that utilizes a methodology based on Nêhiýaw epistemology is a relational methodology, so while I speak of knowledges (e.g., values, language), it should be assumed that they are nested, created, and re-created within the context of relationships with other living beings. While these relational aspects of Plains Cree culture are represented here in the linear constraints of written text, the elements are fluid and they interact with each other in a weblike formation. Each value represents a strand in a web that is integrated and interdependent with the other strands. This is an important point, for I understand Plains Cree culture as being a non-fragmented, holistic approach to the world. Segregating values from ceremony or segregating either from place or language is done at one's own peril.

Decolonizing Aims and Tribal Ethics

Theory is differentiated from epistemology in that the former concerns the knowledge that we privilege. For example, the use of theory in this Indigenous research framework is a critical positioning that only works in conjunction with the tribal epistemological positioning being upheld. Graham Smith defines the following characteristics of Indigenous theory, stating that it is:

- Located within a culturally contextual site
- Born of organic process involving community
- The product of a theorist who has an understanding of the cultural epistemic foundations of an Indigenous worldview
- Focused on change
- Although not universal, portable to other sites
- Flexible
- Engaged with other theoretical positionings (i.e., it is not an isolationist theory)
- Critical
- Workable for a variety of sites of struggle
- User-friendly – people can understand what the theorist is talking about. (Smith 2005: 10)

In conceptualizing a tribal methodology, I have identified a theoretical positioning as having its basis in critical theory with a decolonizing aim in that there is a commitment to praxis and social justice for

Indigenous people. As long as decolonization is a purpose of Indigenous education and research, critical theory will be an allied Western conceptual tool for creating change.

Indigenous methodologies are inclusive of a number of approaches to research. The approach that I have employed in my research puts the tribal worldview of Nêhiýaw epistemology at its centre. However, a decolonizing theoretical perspective is integral to an Indigenous approach to research. Because of the decolonizing terminology, there is an assumption that its focus is on decolonizing relationships between Indigenous peoples and settler societies, thus centring a critical or postcolonial perspective. While this framework decentres the 'settler dilemma,' the problematic nature of this relationship is recognized. Thus the Indigenous epistemological framework incorporates a decolonizing aim. A decolonizing theoretical perspective aligns well with the collectivism of ancestral Nêhiýaw knowledges.

Indigenous research, flowing from tribal paradigms, shows general agreement on the following broad ethical considerations: (a) that the research methodology be in line with Indigenous values; (b) that there is some form of community accountability; (c) that the research gives back to and benefits the community in some manner; and (d) that the researcher is an ally and will not do harm. (These considerations are discussed more fully in Chapter 8.) In considering a Nêhiýaw epistemology, a critical ethical point is that one must be prudent and respectful about what one shares. This requires reflection on both the research topic and one's personal motivations. As mentioned earlier, the research needs to be done within the value *miýo-wîcêhtowin*, meaning 'having or possessing good relations' (Cardinal and Hildebrant, 2000: 14). I was sensitive to protecting Nêhiýaw knowledges, and chose to present Cree cultural knowledges from pre-existing published sources of teachings by Cree Elders. I was also discerning about including aspects of my own personal journey, particularly as they involve other people, while recognizing that I must share just enough. Another way to keep good relations – *miýo-wîcêhtowin* – within primary research is to ensure that research participants understand and accept how their teachings are represented. To that end, they must be given an opportunity to review their contributions and make changes wherever necessary. Depending upon the ethical review policy and procedures, universities may allow research participants the option of letting their name stand, an option that allows for a form of accountability that is found within oral cultures.

If research within an Indigenous context is not located within a specific geographical community, it may not go to a tribal ethics board. Advisory committees or boards can work in this capacity. Tribal ethics review boards (and advisory committees) are instituted by Indigenous communities and have great ability to be stewards of Indigenous knowledges within a research context. However, there needs to be due consideration as to the policy and practice of these boards. With much at stake, tribal ethics boards need the time and capacity to work through the complexities of what their standards of research ethics will mean for Indigenous peoples, communities, and researchers, as well as how they interface with the non-Indigenous research community. From the Western standpoint, all research carried out within the auspices of Western universities must go through an external ethics review. Some ethics review processes will ask specific questions concerning the Indigenous community, whether approval by the Indigenous community was sought, and justification if that approval was not sought or granted.

Researcher Preparations

The term *researcher preparation* describes the experiential aspect of the research. It is about process. There were aspects of this research approach that required preparation and choices grounded in the inward knowing that arises from personal experience. In this framework, I refer to personal preparations to include *miskâsowin*, a Cree word that means to go to the centre of yourself to find your own belonging (Cardinal and Hildebrandt, 2000: 21). From the oral teachings and writings of Indigenous peoples of different nations, the message seems consistent – all we can know for sure is our own experience. My conceptual framework included a methodological approach that encompassed reflexivity in the research. The inward reflection of the researcher is not a new component of research, but arguably it takes up more space in methodology for those following a tribal paradigm because of the value placed upon this type of knowing.

From a Nêhiýaw epistemology, attention to inward knowing is not optional. From a traditional Cree perspective, seeking out Elders,

attending to holistic epistemologies, and participating in cultural catalyst activities (dream, ceremony, prayer) are all means for accessing
inward knowledge. According to Plains Cree culture, teachings come
from many places. We need to open ourselves to those teachings and
then give ourselves time to integrate them so that we can be of use to
our community. This requires preparation by the researcher, something that is unique to each individual. It is a process that can never
lend itself to a check-box, universal approach, rather it is personal
work that must be done by the researcher in conjunction with her
world (both inner and outer).

In qualitative research undertaken by critical researchers, particularly with inquiries that seek to explore issues related to marginalized
groups, there are often unambiguous statements by researchers as to
their insider/outsider status. By reflecting on the insider/outsider
status, researchers prepare themselves for the task. The process of self-
location can be useful for situating one's self in relation to the research.
Closely related to the issue of self-location in research is purpose. In
considering purpose, the work of Eber Hampton (among others)
prompts us to be clear about the motivations, both academic and personal, guiding our inquiry. As a means of capturing personal reflections throughout the research journey, I elected to record my thoughts
in a journal during the course of the research. Unlike field notes, which
I understand to be recordings of observations made during field study,
this journal captured reflections on thoughts, relationships, dreams,
anxieties, and aspirations in a holistic manner that related (if at times
only tangentially) to my research. It offered a means for tracing personal analysis and discoveries of the research that were emerging in
narrative. It became a tool for making meaning and showed evidence
of process and content.

These are some ways that personal preparations are evidenced in
the research process. Chapter 6 discusses this quality in more detail, as
it emerged through the literature and in conversation with Indigenous
research participants. The research took me home to Saskatchewan,
where I connected with community and culture. Other Indigenous
scholars speak about personal preparations in other ways, such as the
inclusion of ceremony in guiding their research. However we define it,
this is about doing the work in a good way. If we are attuned to the
ancestors, Indigenous researchers know what this means and that it
matters deeply.

Research Preparations

Preparing for the research is part of the research strategy. My research framework involved talking with other Indigenous researchers about Indigenous research. It was a qualitative study with an exploratory aim. Some of the specifics on gathering the data included selecting participants, the methods for gathering knowledge, interpretation, and *tâpwê* (truth and trust).

In choosing participants, it is suggested within qualitative studies that research participants be chosen for what they can bring to the study as opposed to random sampling. This study sought depth rather than breadth, and so a small sample group of six research participants was chosen. Participants included a strong representation of Cree people (four of the six participants are Cree), individuals who had a strong sense of their culture, experience in a Western academic doctoral program, and a background in education and/or social work because of the interdisciplinary nature of the study.

Having a pre-existing and ongoing relationship with participants is an accepted characteristic of research according to tribal paradigms. In my research, I had met all the participants through collegial networks of Indigenous researchers and university instructors, so I could be described as having a pre-existing and ongoing relationship with the research participants. In this sense, I was both insider and outsider in relation to the research participants. We all carry our own experiences and knowing about our culture, and while we can share some general insights with each other we are also outsiders. In terms of the power dynamics in the researcher and participant relationship, the power of the researcher is in communicating his or her own interpretations of the teachings. To mitigate this power differential, to value the relationship and be congruent with the methodology, participants had final approval of their contributions.

In line with Nêhiýaw epistemology, which honours sharing story as a means for knowing, conversation is a non-structured method of gathering knowledge. While this may seem like another way of saying interview, the term *interview* does not capture the full essence of this approach. For this was very much a combination of reflection, story, and dialogue. Thus, in my research framework participating in the participants' stories – their experiences with culture and methodologies – was a primary method of the research. In presenting the findings, two processes were employed, a condensed conversation and thematic coding. The condensed conversation was an attempt to ensure the presentation of knowledge congruent with a Plains Cree worldview, which allowed for interpretative teachings and for the voice of the person sharing the story to come through.

The data collection process for my research took place during the time when I relocated from Victoria, B.C., to Saskatchewan. The conversations took place over a two-month period in four general localities (Regina, Winnipeg, Vancouver, and Victoria). That I was based in the general vicinity of my traditional territory was critical to this research. I believe that where we are, and the daily influences of our lives, shape how we think and write. If I were located on Vancouver Island, the flavour and feel of this research would have been drastically different. It would have been the writing of an expatriate Cree/Saulteaux from the cafés of Victoria. I would not have been able to put Nêhiýaw epistemology at the core of my methodology in the same manner, for our Indigenous methodologies are bound to place.

In considering research validity, I hear the Elders' voices: Are you doing this in a good way? There is a Cree word, tâpwê, which means to speak the truth. This is about validity or, relationally speaking, credibility. To do this means to tend to the process in a good way, so that no matter the outcome you can sleep at night because you did right by the process. Checks were included in my research framework that fit an Indigenous research paradigm. To show community accountability, there was a consistent effort at debriefing with other Indigenous graduate students and scholars throughout this process, both formally and informally. Efforts were made to keep the language of this research as accessible as possible, so that it is not mystifying but rather useful to a range of individuals who comprise the Indigenous community. By presenting the conversations and talks through a condensed conversation format, this meets the Cree criteria of tâpwê. For example, participants reviewed and approved their transcripts. They were able to make changes and be comfortable with the both the raw transcripts and condensed conversations.

The primary means of presenting the findings of this research is in story form. I was capturing the participants' stories through conversations and chose to relate these conversations in a condensed format yet staying as true to each story, to the voice, as possible. Each condensed conversation is couched between an introduction and reflective com-

mentary written by myself, identifying the teachings that were particularly relevant to me. It is also an attempt to show self in relation to
others. Presenting the data in this way allows readers to interpret the
conversations from their own particular vantage points and take from
the teachings what they need.

I chose to present data in a secondary Western manner through a
thematic grouping or bundling of themes. As Moustakas explains, I
engaged in the process of 'identifying the qualities and themes manifested in the data' (1990: 51). I used a process that first identified
themes into bundles that aligned with my research question. This was
not an Indigenous method, which I acknowledged. I experienced
some uneasiness in the coding process at times because it felt like I
was extracting the findings from the context of people's stories. In
externalizing the data, I was cautioned about the limitations of
Indigenous research in a textual universe. I am reminded of Vine
Deloria's account of Ruth Beebe Hill, a non-Sioux researcher who
'deliberately interpreted Sioux customs as an extreme form of indi-
vidualism ... She utterly gutted all substance in the kinship tradition
and reduced the Sioux religion to bizarre mysticism' (1991: 458). As I
think about the data analysis and interpretation of Western research
processes, I am reminded to pay close attention to the principles of the
Indigenous research paradigm and the decolonizing aim of this
research. I tried to be as respectful as possible, particularly in the
matter of coding, and hope that the ancestors will not disown me for
this one.

In the past several years, I have watched while Indigenous research
frameworks have become an increasingly present part of the research
vernacular, and to me this is *miýo* (a good thing). I think that we create
space by not letting the subject fade into the sunset. I am reminded of
a quote by Blackfoot scholar Betty Bastien: 'To continue practicing
research outside of one's culture, and attempting to develop research
questions from experiences based on the western paradigm, continues
to create dependency among tribal peoples' (1999:62). I am equally
reminded of Susan Boyd, a critical researcher, who points out that
'knowledge is power' and the choosing of a methodology is a political
act (2005: 1).

This chapter shares an example of an Indigenous research framework based upon tribal epistemology. It reflects much that is familiar
to Western qualitative research and highlights that which is distinc-

tively its own. The next six chapters are an in-depth look at character-istics familiar to the Nêhiýaw research framework – they are tribal epistemology, decolonizing theory, story as method, self and cultural location, purpose, Indigenous methods, interpretation, and ethics as methodology. The starting place for conceptualizing Indigenous research frameworks is the knowledges.

3 Epistemology and Research: Centring Tribal Knowledge

Indigenous scholar Manu Aluli Meyer describes her relationship with epistemology like this: 'Every little thing. I mean, I can see a dead frog on the road, and it relates to epistemology' (2001: 192). It took me a while, but I understand her point of view now. Every decision, every move I have made during my tribal-centred research journey has asked me to consider how it fits with my beliefs about knowledge, the world, and Plains Cree ways of knowing. So much is about epistemology, but knowing this does not make the path clearer.

The deeper that I submerge myself into tribal knowledge systems, the more I resist Western ways of knowing as a given for *all* academic research, even though I know that this demands a long swim against a strong current. I can appreciate Western research methods of coding, bundling, categorizing, and naming according to a set of values and principles to make meaning. My concern is not about organizing knowledge, for Cree society is quite adept at this, but rather it is the worldview, the epistemological underpinning of this organization with which I grapple. For me, epistemology is simultaneously elusive and ubiquitous, woven tightly with a personal identity that shifts over a life span, and though it is holistic it is most often expressed through a cognitive lens. Epistemology and research methodology are a tightly bound, complex partnership. And as Meyer (2004) states, the epistemological presence in life and research permeates. It is frogs everywhere.

As noted earlier in this book, the word *epistemology* is used, as opposed to *ontology* or *cosmology*, because *epistemology* captures the 'self-in-relation' (Graveline, 1998) quality of Indigenous knowledge systems. This chapter is devoted to epistemology, emphasizing the centrality of tribal epistemologies to Indigenous research frameworks. It is this epistemological foundation that differentiates Indigenous research from Western methodologies. Beginning here provides foundational work for the proceeding chapters on story, purpose, Indigenous methods, and so forth, because they are of Indigenous epistemology. It is pertinent to note that Indigenous knowledges can never be standardized, for they are in relation to place and person. How they integrate into Indigenous research frameworks is largely researcher dependent. At the same time, Indigenous methodologies are founded upon Indigenous epistemology, and they will (or ought to) be evident in such frameworks, revealing shared qualities that can be identified as belonging to an Indigenous paradigm.

In moving from a broad discussion of Indigenous epistemologies, this chapter then focuses on Plains Cree knowledge. The reason for focusing on a specific tribal epistemology is to emphasize how the protocols and customs of a particular tribal group assist in making research decisions. It is also an attempt to ward off a pan-Indigenous approach. The chapter concludes with a conversation with Indigenous researcher Michael Hart, who shares his thoughts on the intersection between Cree knowledges and research.

Indigenous Knowledges and Research

When considering tribal epistemologies, there are many entry points, one of which is commentary on its holistic quality. Descriptive words associated with Indigenous epistemologies include interactional and interrelational, broad-based, whole, inclusive, animate, cyclical, fluid, and spiritual. Tribal knowledge is pragmatic and ceremonial, physical and metaphysical. Indigenous cultures have sophisticated and complex cultural practices to access that which comes from both the ordinary and the extraordinary. It is difficult to define, deconstruct, or compartmentalize the different aspects of knowing ('science,' spirit, inward knowing) within an Indigenous context – reductionist tools seem to not work here. As Battiste and Henderson indicate, 'universal definitions of Indigenous knowledge' do not work well either because the knowledge, particularly the knowledge that originates from the extraordinary, is deeply personal and particular (2000: 36).

Subjects not methods

The following discussion of Indigenous epistemology emphasizes its non-fragmented, holistic nature, focusing on the metaphysical and pragmatic, on language and place, and on values and relationships. Within Indigenous discourse, these are aspects of Indigenous epistemologies that consistently emerge. They are all bound by the relational. Relationship is not identified as a specific theme because it is wholly integrated with everything else. Indigenous epistemologies live within a relational web, and all aspects of them must be understood from that vantage point. This is but a snapshot. Many books and articles have been written on Indigenous science, providing deep insight into Indigenous epistemologies. The purpose here is not to mirror such depth, but rather to make visible the breadth of holistic epistemologies as they relate to Indigenous research frameworks.

Ermine (1999) suggests that Indigenous knowledges are born of relational knowing, from both inner and outer space. The outer space is the physical world and inner space is where metaphysical knowing resides. Indigenous scholar Marlene Brandt-Castellano identifies Indigenous knowledges as coming from a multitude of sources, including 'traditional teachings, empirical observations, and revelations,' and she goes on to suggest that revelations comprise various sources, including 'dreams, visions, cellular memory, and intuition' (quoted in E. Steinhauer, 2002: 74). Because of the interconnection between all entities, seeking this information ought not to be extractive but reciprocal, to ensure an ecological and cosmological balance. Much insight comes to an individual inwardly and intuitively. There are myriad examples within Indigenous stories and writing that speak of reliance on this source.

Scholarship on Indigenous science, in one manner or another, references the relationship with metaphysics through creation myths, philosophies on space and time, and an energy source that Indigenous people describe as the sacred (Cajete, 1999; Cardinal and Hildebrandt, 2000; Little Bear, 2000). This suggests that energy reveals itself as knowings stored deep within a collective unconscious and surfaces through dreams, prayer, ceremonial ritual, and happenings (Cardinal, 2001; Ermine, 1999). Suspension of judgment is required for the knowing to surface in its own time (Deloria and Wildcat, 2001).

I can identify this knowledge source in my own life. Early in my research, I had a powerful dream that was particularly relevant. I

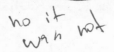

no it was not

knew, culturally, not to dismiss the knowledge coming to me in this form, for within Plains Cree knowledges dreams matter. In conversation with Graham Smith about the intersection between holistic philosophy and research, he said, 'I just see that as part of Indigenous knowledge, frameworks. You need a way to write them in, obviously, but part of the cultural context. I see dreams as being part of oral culture.' He went on to say that the Maori do not have the same traditional beliefs around dreams, but he would not dismiss this as a valid knowledge source. In following tribal paradigms in research, there needs to be space for the choices that will be made in accordance with those paradigms. In choosing Indigenous epistemologies, respect must be paid to their holistic, relational nature. Michael Hart spoke about the range of Cree knowledges: 'It's a lot of reflection back on my time with Elders, with traditional teachers, in ceremony that is my biggest influence. I say ceremonies, because to me I don't hunt so I can't rely on that.' Jeannine Carriere shared the advice given by her Cree colleague: 'Hold your tobacco and see what happens.' All the Indigenous researchers showed respect for holistic knowledges. They held as legitimate inward understanding imbued by spirit.

A holistic orientation is integral, but how do Indigenous researchers apply it to their research? First, they make choices about the knowledge that they will privilege. This cannot be stated more clearly than in Kathy Absolon's words: 'I am an Anishnabe; I want to be an Anishnabe thinker.' Being an Anishnabe or a Nêhiyáw thinker means holding dear a broad range of knowledge, and that one's daily life reflects respect for holism. Privileging tribal epistemology in academic research efforts is easier said than done, but Indigenous researchers are making this choice. Acknowledging these choices and challenges, they are encompassing holism within their research frameworks.

Indigenous researchers are grappling with ways to explain how holistic epistemologies inform their research design in ways understood by Western academic minds. In carrying out her research, Roxanne Struthers (2001) honoured spiritual knowledge by offering a traditional gift of tobacco to her participants, as well as a daily offering of tobacco to the Creator. In preparing herself for the research – gaining guidance as to whether she should continue with her research – she relied on dream knowledge that came to her in the form of three Ojibway grandmothers. Guidance from dreams and spirit became a part of her research. Richard Atleo (2004) introduces the Nuu-chah-nulth method of *Oosumich*, which is a spiritual methodology equivalent to that of a vision quest. He argues that Western methodologies and *Oosumich* belong together because they are two proven methods of accessing information.

The holistic nature of Indigenous science often creates a chasm between it and the beliefs held by Western science. Language bridges gaps by acting as a mechanism to express divergent worldviews. Like inward knowing, language is so powerful because it reminds us who we are; it is deeply entwined with personal and cultural identity. Graham Smith expressed concern about those who were 'claiming Indigenous theorizing' but do not have an appreciation for the nuance of tribal culture that is intricately tied with language. Language matters because it holds within it a people's worldview. Language is a primary concern in preserving Indigenous philosophies, and it is something that must be thought through within research epistemologies.

In connecting language, culture, and knowledge, Anne Waters (2004) offers insights into the structure of Indigenous languages and how form gives rise to a way of thinking and being. Waters suggests that dualist constructs such as like/unlike have resulted in a binary language and thought pattern in European cultures. Conversely, in many Indigenous cultures the language constructs suggest a non-binary, complementary philosophy of the world. Western research that serves to extract and externalize knowledges in categorical groupings aligns well with the categorical premises of Western languages. Inevitably, the question of whether language and method shape thought or thought shapes language and method surfaces. Is it the chicken or the egg? Whatever the causal forces, what can be ascertained is that they live in a profound relationship with each other.

Given the role of language in shaping thought and culture, conflict between Indigenous and Western research approaches (and its involvement in knowledge construction) rests deeply within language and the matter of dualist thought patterns. In tribal epistemologies and Indigenous research frameworks, one must first assert the interrelationship between Indigenous language structure and worldview, and then the manner in which colonialism has interfered with this dynamic. Given this history and interruption, it is no wonder that Indigenous thought tends to dance around the sharp edges of the language binaries that define Western methodologies.

Moving on from linguistic structure and thought, there is also the matter of language, epistemology, and knowledge exchange within Indigenous inquiry. Given the philosophical basis of a complementary, non-binary Indigenous thought pattern, it makes sense that narrative encased in the form of oral history would be the natural means to transmit knowledges (Struthers, 2001). Within the structure of story, there is a place for the fluidity of metaphor, symbolism, and interpretative communications (both verbal and non-verbal) for a philosophy and language that is less definitive and categorical. My sense is that skilled orators, then and now, were able to imbue energy through word choice, and allow listeners to walk inside the story to find their own teachings. The interpretation and the teachings taken become the listener's task. With the listener's involvement, the insight gained from the story is a highly particular and relevant form of knowledge exchange.

An equally important point about language (or vernacular) and knowledge exchange is the ability to make concrete the abstract theoretical findings of research. The skill of making research methodology relevant and interesting to community rests largely with language. The ability to craft our own research stories, in our own voice, has the best chance of engaging others. One strategy is to integrate into our research findings the stories that paint the context of our research. As I write this, I am in Saskatchewan. Being here helps to infuse my thinking and writing with a Great Plains landscape. That a magpie, a thunderstorm, a teepee set against the rolling hills of the Qu'Appelle Valley can make an appearance in my writing seems most possible if I am here. The visitation of anecdotes, metaphors, and stories about place make cerebral, academic language accessible, and reflect holistic epistemologies.

No wonder one of the first approaches to erasing a culture is to attack its language because language holds such insight into the social organization of a people. Without language to affirm knowledge daily, it is easy to lose cultural memory. Milan Kundera, the well-known Czech novelist and philosopher on cultural evolution, has written: 'The first step in liquidating a people ... is to erase its memory ... Before long a nation will begin to forget what it is and what it was. The world around it will forget even faster' (quoted in Dyck, 1986: 132). There is a need for ongoing conversation, such as on the effects of non-fluency on Indigenous epistemologies and research. Many Indigenous people do not know their own language and they are attempting to relearn. However, it will take a lot of immersion to retrain our minds. How to think and be in a non-binary way is a challenge when we live in a binary world. Because language is central to the construction of knowledge, how are we, as Indigenous researchers, approaching the issue of philosophy and language in our research – beyond identifying its importance? These are ongoing considerations for tribal epistemologies.

Language is a central component of Indigenous epistemologies and must be considered within Indigenous research frameworks (Bishop, 1997; Struthers, 2001; Weaver, 2001; Waters, 2004). Still, linguistic structures associated with tribal languages and the deep interconnection between thought and language cannot be extrapolated from other attributes. Indigenous epistemologies, even within the cerebral-orientated conversation of language structures and their influence on thought, cannot be relegated solely to the cognitive realm. Indigenous epistemologies assume a holistic approach that finds expression within the personal manifestations of culture.

Blackfoot scholar Narcisse Blood once spoke about places as being alive, that they are imbued with spirit and are our teachers. Daniel Wildcat considers how place informs: 'You see and hear things by being in a forest, on a river, or at an ocean coastline; you gain real experiential knowledge that you cannot see by looking at the beings that live in those environments under a microscope or in a laboratory experiment' (in Deloria and Wildcat, 2001: 36). As tribal people, there is an understanding of how to proceed based upon a long history of interrelationship with a particular territory. Place is what differentiates us from other tribal peoples, and what differentiates us from settler societies (including both privileged and marginalized groups). Place gives us identity. A Saskatchewan Cree poet and scholar, Neal McLeod, writes about place and how it allows us to transverse time, giving us an immediate connection to the ancestors and reminding us who we are: 'to the circle of old men speaking / echo of generations / gave form to the moment of my birth' (2005: 23).

Place links present with past and our personal self with kinship groups. What we know flows through us from the 'echo of generations,' and our knowledges cannot be universalized because they arise from our experience with our places. This is why name-place stories matter: they are repositories of science, they tell of relationships, they reveal history, and they hold our identity.

In southern Saskatchewan, there is a well-known name-place legend of how the Qu'Appelle Valley received its name. The most familiar version tells of a love story between a Cree man and woman who were soon to wed. Away from home on a hunting trip, he paddles home to her, for they are to marry the next day. As he is nearing her home, he hears a voice calling out his name. He responds *Kâ-têpwêt* (who calls?) in Cree, then *Qu'appelle?* in French, but there is no reply, so he travels on. He arrives at her home and finds her family grieving. They tell him that she has left for the spirit world, but add, 'Twice did she call for thee last night.' Pauline Johnson, a Mohawk poet, wrote *The Legend of Fort Qu'Appelle*, based on a story handed down from the old people of this region. Although there are different versions, this legend, with its tinge of frontier romanticism, is 'likely misinterpreted from a story told by the Indians' (Lerat and Ungar, 2005: 17). Even so, its haunting sadness casts a line back through time to the ancestors. There is an alternate version of how Qu'Appelle got its name. According to this story, 'two groups of people arrived on opposite sides of the Qu'Appelle and since they could not get across to visit, they shouted news across the water, and that is how the river got its name' (ibid.). Either way, these stories situate us in place, they localize history and maintain an oral tradition of passing on knowledge.

Place names make theoretical notions concrete; they offer us tacit meaning. Stories, like name-place legends, give comfort and grounding, and offer the warmth of belonging. It is from here that we can reach out to the world. Stories connected to place are both about collectivist tribal orientation, and they are located within our personal knowing and conceptual framework of the world. Michael Hart reminds us that there is a web of interconnection that forms our way of knowing. He acknowledges the epistemological interrelationship between people, place, language, and animals, and how they influence our coming to know. He acknowledges many gifts from many places and that 'place is key but it is only one component.' From a holistic epistemology, one relationship is not more significant than another. Rather, it is a balance of all. Relational balance is holistic epistemology.

Indigenous epistemologies are action-oriented. They are about living life every day according to certain values. Reflecting on an Indigenous mindset, Leroy Little Bear characterizes the ideal Native American personality as one who is kind, who puts the group first, who is friendly, who 'is steeped in spiritual and ritual knowledge,' who is easygoing and has a good sense of humour (quoted in Alfred, 2005: 10). Inherent within this perspective is knowledge and action in relationship with the world. This reflects a holistic, value-based knowledge system that consistently returns to the responsibilities of maintaining good relations.

Miýo, Cree for good, is an integral quality and a manifestation of holistic, relational epistemology. *Miýo* is about sharing and generosity, respecting the earth and all its inhabitants, working hard, and caring for other people. These qualities are about *miýo-wîcêhtowin* (good relations), which is the heartbeat of the Plains Cree culture. Irene Calliou, a Métis Elder, remembers her Cree grandmother speaking of how these values were part of daily practices: 'My grandmother used to dig up medicinal roots; and once she dug them up, she placed tobacco there [in the hole]. I did not know then why she put tobacco in' (quoted in Ahenakew and Wolfart, 1998: 157). Calliou tells us of showing respect for the earth, of reciprocity, and of the importance of observation and attentiveness in learning as knowledge is transmitted through kinship relationships. The importance of land is tied with the value of collective responsibility and stewardship. A prevailing teaching is that an Indigenous research framework must not solely be an intellectual construct, for it cannot be understood in the absence of its practical manifestations, which involve living life in a way that reflects goodness, that reflects *miýo*.

Indigenous researchers are incorporating tribal epistemologies into their research. What seems equally evident is that these researchers are taking action in at least two ways: (a) they acknowledge the breadth of tribal epistemologies, their relational and holistic qualities, and their necessity; and (b) they *use* tribal epistemologies in preparation for and conducting their research, in documenting the sources and methods of their knowing, and in acknowledging their influence on their research.

Nêhiýaw Epistemology

The following is a small offering on Nehiýaw (Plains Cree) knowledge. The purpose of integrating Nêhiýaw epistemology as part of a chapter on Indigenous epistemologies is to illustrate how a specific tribal epistemology is both aligned with and differentiated from a broader discussion of Indigenous epistemology. Although the themes are similar – place and language, to name two – they are manifested (and presented) through Plains Cree custom and practice. Within an Indigenous research framework, researchers would present their interpretation of the tribal epistemology guiding their research, and they would each do so in her or his own way.

I start this section with a historic practice emerging from place. It exemplifies a Plains Cree conceptual framework on theory and methodology. It is the buffalo hunt. The buffalo – *paskâwo-mostosw* – were the mainstay of the Plains Cree economy. 'In 1870, there were hundreds of thousands of buffalo in the Saskatchewan country; by 1881, there were only a few head, widely scattered' (Mandelbaum, 1979: 51). The slaughter of the buffalo due to the encroachment of European settlement led to the starvation and destruction of the traditional Cree economy. In its prime, when the buffalo were plentiful, the hunt was a central part of Plains Cree life. There were two ways of procuring buffalo, the hunt and the chase. In the autumn and early winter, tribes used a buffalo chute or pound, but in the spring and summer, as the herds moved southward, they used the chase. In reading stories about the hunt, it is apparent how place, values, and ceremony are integral to this act. *Peyasiw-awasis* (Chief Thunderchild) shares a story of the hunt:

In the days when the buffalo were many, there were Old Men who had the gift of 'making pounds.' Poundmaker's father was such a one, and he gave the name to his son. Another was *Eyi-pâ-chi-nas*, and when it was known that he was 'sitting at pound' – that he was seeking the supernatural power to bring the buffalo – hunters would gather.

One winter there were ten teepees, just for these hunters. Working all together, they cut trees to make a circular pound about seventy yards across ... The gate was fourteen feet wide, and out from it they laid two long lines of tufted willows that spread farther and farther apart, to channel the buffalo into the pound. In the centre they set a great lobbed tree.

When everything was ready, other Old Men joined *Eyi-pâ-chi-nas* and sang the buffalo song. Far on the plain, a herd of buffalo was sighted, and two young men rode out to watch. They were to blow their whistles as soon as the buffalo started to move in the early morning ... The buffalo came on between the lines of the wall and through the gate ... Then the hunters closed in, and stopped the gateway with poles and buffalo robes.

We would cut up the meat till late at night, and haul it with dogs to the encampment ... Other bands came to join us and to feast. (Quoted in E. Ahenakew, 1995: 36)

Underlying the hunt was a way, a methodology, that Plains Cree people used to undertake a sacred act that kept the tribe and its people alive. The hunt involved preparation for the hunt, a method, protocol, ceremony, and respectfulness for going about the procurement of these animals and sharing the bounty. In many ways, the story of the buffalo hunt is a research teaching story, an allegory for a Plains Cree conceptual framework for research – preparation for the research, preparation of the researcher, recognition of protocol (cultural and ethical), respectfulness, and sharing the knowledge (reciprocity). The buffalo hunt provides an epistemological teaching, a reference point for how to do things in a good way, born of place and context specific to Plains tribes. Driving through the Qu'Appelle Valley today, it is easy to imagine the hunt in this place, and I can ground my research framework in the place markers of my ancestors.

Like place, language locates Cree culture. There are six different dialects of the Cree language: (a) East Cree (Montagnais and Naskapi); (b) Attikamek Cree (R dialect), which is also spoken in Quebec; (c) Moose Cree (or L dialect), found in Ontario; (d) Swampy Cree (N dialect), found in Ontario and Manitoba; (e) Woods Cree (or TH dialect), spoken in Manitoba and in north central Saskatchewan; and (f) the Plains Cree (Y dialect) found in south and central Saskatchewan and throughout central Alberta. There are additional Cree languages and communities found in British Columbia, Northwest Territories, and Montana (Wolvengrey, 2001a). I am of the Plains Cree Y dialect or *nêhiýawêwin*.

In taking a Plains Cree language course, I was intrigued to learn how the language constructs fit with my understandings of a Plains Cree worldview. It reinforced for me why language is so important when considering a Nêhiýaw epistemology. The linguistic paradigms that we studied included the imperative, delayed imperative, the indicative, and the subjunctive. The subjunctive paradigm is the conjugation of the AIV in the 'ing' mode. If I were writing, 'I am sleeping' in Cree, it would look like this: *ê-nipayân*. 'I am getting up' would be *ê-waniskâyân* (adding the *ê-* to the beginning of the word and *yân* to the end makes singular the first-person subjunctive) (F. Ahenakew, 1987).

I am told that fluent Cree speakers most often speak in the subjunctive, or 'ing,' mode. The subjunctive is the opposite of declarative and suggests a worldview that honours the present, what we know now. It also suggests a worldview that focuses as much, if not more, attention on process than on product or outcome. Cree Elder Joseph E. Couture explains this concept: 'Everybody has a song to sing which is no song at all; it is a process of singing, and when you sing you are where you are' (quoted in Friesen, 1998: 28).

When Cree and Saulteaux Elders talk about the world as being alive, as of spirit, it makes sense because this is reinforced on a daily basis in the language. Animals, tobacco, trees, rocks are animate, and hence they merit respect. Learning about the structure of Cree language gives me a sense of the way that fluent Cree speakers would have related with their world. Although one may not become a fluent Cree speaker, having an understanding of how language influences Cree knowledge is a key aspect of a research framework based on Plains Cree epistemology.

Ancient knowledge is still alive in Cree communities. The most sacred form comes through dreams, fasts, sweats, vision quests, and during sacred ceremonies. Historically, there were different sacred gatherings among Plains Cree people, many of which still occur today. One of the most sacred is the Rain Dance, which is held at a specific time each year, and individuals who participate (stall dancers) do so for solemn and personal reasons. 'Traditionally, Cree and Saulteaux votaries often made vows in time of great stress such as when a family member was very ill or when an individual confronted immediate danger' (R. Brown, 1996: 44). The lodge is constructed in a specific manner, and there is specific protocol around the dance, dress, and ritual practice of the rain dance. The Saulteaux and Cree of the Qu'Appelle Valley share similar rituals in carrying out the Rain Dance. R. Brown documents Tommy Anequad's explanation of the Rain Dance, which points to the complexity of ritual and method within this ceremony: 'The drums, the whistles, the chanting, the sweet-grass incense, fasting, the Thunderbird's nest, the ritual and ceremony are used to create the proper atmosphere ... to help the person under vow who participates ... to attain cosmic consciousness' (1996: 150).

From teachings conveyed through oral tradition, these practices are said to be timeless, and while there have been some changes the internal integrity of the Rain Dance has remained. Through ritual and ceremony, individuals give of themselves for another, and in this sacrifice the dancers are able to make a connection with the spirit powers to receive spirit blessings for loved ones on whose behalf they dance. During the ceremony, a dancer may receive a vision or dream that offers guidance or assistance. As Brown (1996) recounts, if someone is unsure about a vision, he or she can offer tobacco to the Rain Dance sponsor or a known sweat-lodge leader who assists in interpreting the meaning of the vision. Not only are ceremonies sources of knowing, they also sanction acts of great importance to the people.

The pipe, the drum, the songs, and prayer are integral parts of Plains Cree ceremony, and ways in which to honour the Creator and seek blessing. Once an act is carried out with the sanction of the pipe, it is considered sacred. In Saskatchewan, according to Elders, the treaties are a sacred accord that was sanctioned by the Cree people through one of the most sacred of ceremonies, the pipe ceremony. According to Plains Cree Elder George Rider of Carry the Kettle First Nation, Treaty Four tells us that 'the pipe is holy and it's a way of life for Indian people ... The treaty was made with a pipe and that is sacred, that is never to be broken ... never to be put away' (quoted in Cardinal and Hildebrandt, 2000: 28). Sacred knowledge is not *really* accepted in Western research, other than in a peripheral, anthropological, exotic kind of way. This can create a difficulty for the Indigenous researcher, for if one chooses to embrace Plains Cree knowledges one must honour all that they are.

Plains Cree ways of knowing cannot be an objectified philosophy for this knowing is a process of being. This epistemology emphasizes the importance of respect, reciprocity, relation, protocol, holistic knowing, relevancy, story, interpretative meaning, and the experiential nested in place and kinship systems – all of which ought to be in a research process that encompasses this way of knowing. My ancestors were highly strategic peoples in both the practical aspects of life as well as within ceremonies and rituals contextualized in place and manifested in ways of knowing. Plains Cree knowledges are bound with and exist within a relational universe, and research choices flowing from this positioning must be congruent with these foundational, holistic beliefs.

The proposition of integrating spiritual knowings and processes, like ceremonies, dreams, or synchronicities, which act as portals for gaining knowledge, makes mainstream academia uncomfortable, especially when brought into the discussion of research. This is because of the outward knowing versus inward knowing dichotomy. It also has much to do with Western science's uneasy relationship with the metaphysical. Yet, all ways of knowing are needed, and the Cree ancestors knew this. They knew about inward knowing and valued it highly. In fact, this inward knowing was a central, integral component to how they approached the buffalo hunt and their most deeply sacred ceremonies. They were able to share teachings through stories about their experiences, passed on using the oral tradition, and it was respected as legitimate. Why would research be different?

As I write, my mind goes back to early memories. I grew up on a farm, and when I was young I played by the slough, in the trees around our house, and sometimes on the unbroken prairie between our house and my Auntie's place not too far way. I remember running around on the prickly grass, picking dandelions, and collecting odd-shaped rocks. I knew from a neighbour that arrowheads used to be commonly found on the prairie. I must have been five or six, old enough to understand that arrowheads were from Indian people, and that I, too, was of Indian ancestry. This was an early memory of my Cree identity, connecting those arrowheads with the land and circling it back to me. This is about *miskâsowin* – about about finding belonging – and it became part of my research story. The gift of holistic epistemologies, of Nêhiýaw, is that though they do not demand, but rather provide an opportunity for *miskâsowin*. In doing so, in finding belonging, research becomes more than gathering and presenting data.

A Conversation with Michael Hart

To complete this chapter, Cree scholar Michael Hart shares his reflections on Cree knowledge. Michael Hart is Nêhiýaw (Cree) from the Fisher River Cree Nation in Manitoba. He lives in Winnipeg and currently holds a faculty appointment at the University of Manitoba. He has doctoral degree in Social Work. I have been familiar with Michael's work for several years. As a post-secondary instructor and curriculum developer, I have used Michael's book, *Seeking Mino-Pimatisiwin: An Aboriginal Approach to Helping* (2002), which has been useful in illustrating an Indigenous cultural approach to contemporary social work practice.

I am scheduled to meet Michael at his home in Winnipeg in the afternoon, so I hit the Trans-Canada Highway heading east from Regina in the early hours of the morning. By the time I get to Michael's place, I am a little tired, frazzled, and nervous, but I immediately feel comfortable. He offers me coffee and food. We sit at his kitchen table and start to talk about what is becoming a very familiar topic to me – Indigenous research methodologies.

MAGGIE: What do you think are some of the challenges that we are having in trying to explain our methodologies to academia?
MICHAEL: I would step back even further. I would go back to looking at – again it's a Western concept – worldviews. The challenge with bringing out worldviews is language, overall. There are concepts that we have in Cree that don't have English translations. Right off the bat we are going to lose some of the meanings, and we are also going to change some of the meanings. At the same time, we need to do that because we don't have the choice at this point. I have been trying to learn Cree for a long time, but I have a long, long way to go.

  I was just remembering something ... about protocol. The way I've been dealing with things – let's say I will come to a ceremony, come to understand protocols, but it's not the ceremony that gets transferred, it's the underlying meanings. What I am doing now is looking at the different things that I have been through with Elders, with traditional teachers, and try to understand the underlying teaching, what values are being demonstrated. What am I supposed to do and how am I supposed to act? I will try to transfer those pieces into the new context, which to me reflects what we have to do in life. What we have to do right now in terms of decolonizing – I wish there was [another] term because decolonization focuses on colonization. My intent is to focus on our own ways. What ends up coming to me again is that it goes back to language and place.

  I am Indigenous, I speak English, and that's where I come from. I am trying to understand that perspective because it reflects my reality. My mother was fluent in Cree. I have listened to her growing up, speaking Cree, but when she spoke to us she spoke English. My Mom said that we didn't want to learn, so there is always that piece. It doesn't mean that I am not Cree, but I have a different understanding than a Cree speaker. The journey for the fluent Cree speaker or the Saulteaux speaker isn't the same journey that you or I would take. The journey you and I would take wouldn't necessarily be the same, but they are all part of being Cree. If we deny that, then we have to deny ourselves, and my understanding about our peoples is that we don't do that. We are inclusive, we bring people in. They may come from a different place, have a different journey, but they are still part of us and they are still brought in. It's only when it's to the detriment of the group.

For me and how I value language, it can be hurtful not to speak the language in terms of the peoples. If it gets to the point if there is not enough [Cree] speaking, then we [have] lost that aspect for the future, not just within us, but as peoples. I know it needs to be retained.

MAGGIE: How do Indigenous researchers approach the cultural aspects of Indigenous knowledges when making methodological choices? [*We talk about dream knowledge.*]

MICHAEL: In spending time with these Elders, they [may help you] come to understand a dream, but it's knowledge when you put those dreams, or that dream, into the physical reality. I am trying to explain this without speaking of a particular dream ... Let's say I dream about a smoke lodge, a dream about a particular aspect of a smoke lodge, the way you have to go to the smoke lodge. The dream in and of itself has informed me, but the knowledge process is just more than me having that dream. It is more than me taking that dream and talking with an Elder about it. It includes that process of doing whatever I have to do for that dream to become reality. The methodology isn't just the dream, it isn't just you sitting back and coming to understand the dream, but what you do with that dream, how you put it into reality. So for me, when I think about how I approach research, the issue of research method-ology – I never thought of it as an issue but that's an interesting point in and of itself – that's how I understand methodology. When I talked about there being no single methodology, this is another example. I see people focusing just on the one, maybe on the dream. I had this dream and therefore I came to know, which I won't dispute, but I think there is more to it.

There's a longer process that needs to be involved in bringing the dream to life. It's already alive, but bringing that dream into this world. So that whole piece, how you came back, how you ended up home. To me, that is speaking about the methodology. It would be like doing interviews and saying the interviews are the methodology. There is more, there is a whole bunch of other pieces that are tied to that.

The dreaming would almost be part of the method. Methodology is bigger than that. So how do I approach it? Through a lot of reflection back on my time with Elders, with traditional teachers, in ceremony – those are my biggest influence. I do readings on other areas and talk with other people about their experiences, but I approach it more from there [Elders, ceremonies] because I want to try understand it the best I can in a way that reflects how we do things. I say ceremonies because to me I don't hunt, so I can't rely on that process. A key piece for us that reflects our culture is the ceremonies. To me, they have probably been influenced the least [by other cultures] as opposed to other things.

As an Indigenous researcher, how do you understand an Indigenous approach to research? Well, like I said, it depends upon which approach you take and which understanding you have. I think it takes a lot of self-reflection, not just self, but self in relation to the Elders, the ceremonies, your academic life. I mean, when we go out fasting we are opening ourselves and inviting the spirits to be with us. We are reflecting on ourselves as well, so, to me, both of those aspects would be present in Cree ways of approaching research.

Postscript: A Written Correspondence from Michael Hart after the Interview

What follows is an e-mail that Michael sent me after the interview, and I feel that its inclusion, with his permission, is an important continuation of our conversation:

> I know there is much more to conducting Indigenous research, or more specifically Cree research since I am writing as a Cree man who has and is learning from Cree Elders across Alberta, Saskatchewan and Manitoba. We have several tools to help us enter a place, a sacred, beyond physical place (I am realizing place does not capture what I want to say, since place is too often limited to physicality or the more post-modern/post-structural conceptualization of location) and these tools are aspects of our

means to access knowledge. I guess even before we get to that we need to consider 'what is knowledge?' For me, knowledge is that which helps people move forward in their lives. It may help one person, or it may help many. I guess that is one of the differences I see in my understanding of Indigenous knowledge and Amer-European knowledge, particularly Amer-European knowledge based in positivistic empiricism: That knowledge can be applicable to one person. However, it [knowledge] is beyond one person in that it is between that person and the sacred world. Anyway, back to my commentary.

It seems to me that tools are significant. These tools include our pipes, our songs, our rattles, and our sacred items that we care about, including plant and animal medicines. These items are catalysts in our processes. While by themselves, they may mean very little. But, these items have arisen through at least one of several processes. These processes include dreams of the items before they arrive, the interpretation of the dreams of these items, the acceptance of these items as catalysts, and the passing of these items from one person to another. As I was reading your proposal and thinking on Indigenous ways of coming to know and what is it that we know, I was listening to some stickgame songs. While these songs are not on the level (which suggests a whole other discussion since level implies a very significant consideration) as sundance, smoke lodge, chicken dance, or sweat songs, they did remind me that part of our processes, hence methodologies, including a reliance on such catalysts (I do not know what words to use to express my meaning other than catalysts). They are physical manifestations of sacred experiences. So when I have prepared for my research for my Ph.D., my methodology includes the use of these items, particularly a pipe and songs. I have also partaken in other activities to seek guidance, specifically ceremonies. Finally, I will continue to rely on these sacred items for support as I complete my degree. Hence, our methodologies are bigger than we can easily explain. I think your task is an honourable, but large one as it is bigger than we can imagine. I should speak for myself: Bigger than I can imagine.

As a listener, I interpreted and took teachings from what Michael Hart said. He reaffirmed that there is a distinctive Indigenous methodology based upon tribal worldviews. In doing so, he stressed the significance of Indigenous methodologies. Although Indigenous people share many methods, one's own distinctive culture provides a

[handwritten marginalia, left margin: "stupid even if false"]

[handwritten marginalia, left margin: "2 ares?"]

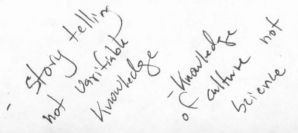

[handwritten notes, bottom margin: "story telling not verifiable Knowledge" — "Knowledge of culture not science"]

unique underpinning to a particular methodological approach. Michael proposed that epistemology is found in language. He talked about the relationship between language, place, and people.

As he spoke, I thought about my desire to learn the Cree language and the resistance that I felt while living on Vancouver Island. It was not that I had any philosophical problems with the notion of learning Cree on Coast Salish territory. Instead, I just could not get into it – I am not sure why, but maybe this helps to explain. When I returned to Saskatchewn and began *Nêhiýawêwin* instruction, one of the first phrases my classmates and I learned was to introduce ourselves. It goes like this: Tânisi, Maggie, *nitisiyihkâson*, Kovach, *nitaspiyikasôn*, Pasqua *iskonikanik nipê-ohcin*. The *iskonikanik*, identifying the community of belonging, loosely translated means *little piece of land that the white settlers didn't want*. This one word has so much connection to Plains Indigenous people, the relationships with white settlers, treaty lands, farmland, and buffalos – it is a single word loaded with the historical context of my homeland. My conversation with Michael helped me understand why learning this word, from a Cree instructor amid other students who were Cree, Saulteaux, and non-Indigenous Saskatchewanians, fit. His thoughts on the connection between specific place, language, and relationships as the basis of tribal knowing resonated with me. Each nation has its *iskonikanik* that tell a big story in a little word, and I believe that is what Michael was saying.

In our conversation (though not in the excerpt presented here), Michael urged care in sharing knowledges coming from the sacred, especially in settings such as universities, where their legitimacy as knowledge sources may not be recognized. This is an important caution, and it left me questioning how much to share without sharing too much – this is an ethical consideration of Indigenous research with which I still grapple. Ceremonies, protocols, and ways of Cree people cannot be separated from their underlying values. Rather, they are there to affirm values. This is integral to a holistic tribal epistemology. Being kind, being inclusive, being community-minded in combination with ceremonies, protocols, and ways is the power of Cree culture. In relating this, Indigenous researchers have great guardianship and responsibility for the research flowing from a tribal epistemology.

Indigenous epistemologies and research frameworks are undoubtedly imbued with complexity. However, given the challenges, growing numbers of Indigenous researchers are finding ways to integrate valuable tribal epistemologies within their research frameworks. This is causing a stir in the larger research community. Yet, progress is dependent upon decolonizing colonial spaces.

4 Applying a Decolonizing Lens within Indigenous Research Frameworks

All problems must be solved within the context of the culture – otherwise
you are just creating another form of assimilation.
– Maurice Squires (in Bruyere, 1999)

'What knowledge do you privilege?'(Boyd, 2005: 1). This question
seeks to unmask the personal choice of epistemology. It is also about
the politics of knowledge. A variety of critiques have dealt with this
query by analysing the political nature of knowledge construction in
marginalized communities (Fanon, 1963; Memmi, 1965; Henderson,
2000). From an Indigenous research perspective, Linda Tuhiwai Smith
(1999) applies a specific decolonizing analysis that reveals the degree
to which Indigenous knowledges have been marginalized within
Western research processes. Much has been written, and while few
within the non-Indigenous community would openly contest the historical existence of colonialism, praxis has been minimal, with a small
community of allies at the forefront of action. Within the academic
environment, part of the difficulty lies with a theoretical positioning
that, in its very name, obscures historical analysis. For example, critical theorists argue that *postpositivism*, *postmodern*, and *postcolonial* uni-
versalize marginalization and work to diffuse sites of contestation.
Tuhiwai Smith critiques the 'post' in *postcolonial* and suggests that
'naming the world as "post-colonial" is, from indigenous perspectives,
to name colonialism as finished business' (1999: 99). In focusing on the
'post' perspective, it frees one from historical analysis. Within a Canadian Aboriginal context, this is problematic because the non-Indige-

nous majority are adept at forgetting this country's colonial history, thus maintaining its reproduction.

While the colonial visage of our ancestors' time has shifted, the relationship continues. On an international level, this is felt through globalization and consumerism, which feed an economic system that preys on Mother Earth striving to sustain the human species even as we abuse her. Colonial interruptions of Indigenous culture continue, and there is no way to address tribal epistemologies and Indigenous research frameworks without considering these relations. It is a dilemma that is distinctively Indigenous and sets us apart from other marginalized groups. It has become part of our collective experience and a burden that our pre-contact ancestors did not have to shoulder. The relationship with the settler society impacts our world daily, in the supermarket, in neighbourhoods, and in educational institutions. In post-secondary education, Indigenous students experience the burn of colonial research on a consistent basis most evident in the suppression of Indigenous knowledges. Postcolonial? There is nothing post about it. It has simply shape-shifted to fit the contemporary context.

This chapter must necessarily recognize the historic Indigenous–settler relationship and by doing so reveal the relational dynamics between Indigenous and Western science that permeates Indigenous research discourse today. In view of the contemporary challenges of representation and voice, there must also be commentary on why a decolonizing lens matters within Indigenous methodologies as a theoretical positioning, a form of praxis, and how decolonization becomes personally embodied within the lives of Indigenous researchers. In underscoring the significance of continued anti-colonial efforts, to complete the chapter, Maori scholar Graham Smith offers insight into the relationship between Indigenous research frameworks and decolonizing praxis.

Going Forward Means Looking Back

Recognizing the colonial influence in knowledge paradigms and revealing how Indigenous ways of knowing have been marginalized in research requires a brief historical detour. When the first European ships came to the Americas, followed soon thereafter by the boats carrying settlers, they were packing aspects of their material culture that caused serious harm to Indigenous communities and cultures. They were also bringing an attitude about the world (and who owned it) that was in sharp contrast with Indigenous peoples' worldviews. While colonization came to affect every aspect of Indigenous life, Western science in particular has worked to first subjugate and then discredit Indigenous knowledge systems and the people themselves.

In the colonization of Indigenous people, science was used to support an ideological and racist justification for subjecting Indigenous cultures and ways of knowing. Darwin's evolutionary theory displaced a creationist approach and proposed that life evolved slowly and incrementally, with the superior forms of life prevailing and the inferior dying out. As Vine Deloria Jr points out, this theory fit extremely well for the elite in Europe who were engaged in the exploitive endeavours of colonialism and industrialism: 'Survival of the fittest, the popularization of a Darwinian concept, became a means for justifying social piracy' (2002: 17). The racism inherent in this evolutionary paradigm contributed to the genocidal policy towards Indigenous peoples in the Americas. Furthermore, science was responsible for increasingly effective weaponry, which in conjunction with a colonialist agenda was used as a means to attempt to force Indigenous cultures to capitulate.

On a philosophical level, the new European scientific paradigm had long-lasting impacts on Indigenous peoples. This science fundamentally contradicted the philosophical perspectives of Indigenous ways of knowing (or science). Pam Colorado (1988) identifies some characteristics of the Western scientific paradigm that were in conflict with Indigenous knowing: (a) the universe is empty space where atoms and particles live autonomously and independently of each other; (b) the universe is static, and atoms and particles do not shift or change; (c) God, through Newtonian physics, no longer has a role in the cause and effect of the universe; (d) prophecy or greater purpose does not exist, life is simply a cause and effect mechanistic dynamic; and (e) all energy patterns can be measured and accounted for by human intellect, hence humans are all-knowing. Because Indigenous people did not separate reason and spirit, and because they did not espouse an evolutionist theoretical perspective, their beliefs have been viewed as superstitions (Deloria, 2002). Further Indigenous knowledges could not be understood from a reductionist analysis because they could not be fragmented, externalized, and objectified. Without an appreciation for Indigenous ways of knowing, Indigenous people were excluded from knowledge construction as defined by Western thought.

Traditional Western science, based on a rationalist, secular paradigm, discounts the possibility that knowledge arises from happenings that cannot be explained through reductionist means (Atleo, 2004; Deloria and Wildcat, 2001). Arguably, Western science can be broadly or narrowly defined. A broad definition of science is that it is an attempt to understand the workings of the universe from a variety of sources. This definition fits well with the multiplicity of sources comprising Indigenous ways of knowing. However, a more conventional definition of science relegates it to that which flows from a scientific method of inquiry. Within this European-oriented philosophy of knowledge and science, research practices, firmly rooted in the principles of Descartes' and Bacon's scientific method, were established as legitimate routes for the creation of knowledge. Positivist approaches, with their propositions of neutrality and their service to a political and economic agenda of capital (more currently globalization), philosophically conflict with Indigenous social values. Furthermore, critical scholars, Indigenous or otherwise, point towards the primacy of 'objectivism' within positivism, which narrows what knowledge can entail. Seemingly, it is the emphasis on external evidence, testing and universal laws of generalizability that contradict a more integrated, holistic, contextualized Indigenous approach to knowledge. Granted, the landscape of qualitative research is changing, but it has only been a recent shift.

The epistemological conflict alludes to the differing paradigmatic characteristics of Western and Indigenous science, and suggests that they approach knowing from different entry points. From a critical perspective, analysing how Western science approaches knowledge offers insight into the inherent tensions that exist between Western and Indigenous research. There have been at least two types of ideological responses to the conundrum of Indigenous epistemologies within Western knowledge centres. Initially, the reaction was to view traditional Indigenous systems of beliefs as having no relevance whatsoever as knowledge sources. However, as E. Steinhauer (2002) suggests, the increasingly common response is to equate Indigenous knowledges with a cultural exoticism and thus relegate them to the periphery of the 'real' work of knowledge construction. Both responses lead to the marginalization of Indigenous knowledges. The Indigenous exotic response can have disastrous implications because it can lead to a totemic understanding (and exploitation) of the more visible aspects of Indigenous culture without due consideration of the knowledges upon which these traditions are based. Additionally, it is a form of fragmenting Indigenous culture and extracting aspects that serve a mainstream purpose. It can also lead to a dismissal or disbelief by Western academia that Indigenous knowledges have relevancy within the construction of knowledge. (There is a small community of non-Indigenous scholar-researchers in the academy who wish to support Indigenous research frameworks. However, at present, there is a dearth in the literature on Indigenous inquiry, which slows decolonizing efforts.)

In critically analysing the primacy of Western thought in research, a product of mainstream academic institutions, one quickly sees the politics of knowledge and inquiry – i.e., both the epistemologies (our understanding about the world) and ideologies (what should count as knowledge and who gets to make that choice) – used to maintain Western privilege. Bridget Somekh and Cathy Lewin propose that to understand modernity, postmodernity, and the evolution of current academic disciplines one must 'look squarely at race' and how it has served capitalism and 'how it served as an ontological and organizing foundation in shaping how one thinks about and does research' (2005: 76). Conventional scholars have become formidable gatekeepers of this system by objectifying knowledge into criterion-defined models, paradigms, and 'truth.' Yet, within this academic research discourse, we are fortunate if we are able to engage in discussions of knowledge – what qualifies as knowledge, what is its source, and how does new knowledge emerge? As an Indigenous researcher, it has been liberating to unveil the political nature of how knowledge is constructed. Unravelling the influence of white privilege has revealed how alternative ways of knowing have become marginalized and how it is that Indigenous inquiry has been left off the 'buffet table' of methodological options. Much of what dominant society perceives as legitimate knowledge is generated by a rather small, homogeneous group of people in formal institutions of higher learning. As Budd Hall (1998) indicates, universities have claimed a monopoly on what does and does not count as knowledge. To assert Indigenous research frameworks, there is a need to critically interrogate this monopolistic knowledge enterprise. Applying a decolonizing lens prompts this action, thus becoming a quality of Indigenous research methodology.

Decolonizing Perspective within Indigenous Research Frameworks

For this discussion, it is useful to begin by clarifying how a decolonizing theoretical lens fits conceptually within Indigenous research frameworks and their utility for method choices. In focusing on the 'how' and 'why' of a decolonizing lens within Indigenous inquiry, it is then possible to reflect upon the decolonizing embodiment experienced by Indigenous researchers holding dual accountabilities to divergent communities. Before advancing into this discussion it is helpful to reassert the various ways that a decolonizing theory fits within an Indigenous research design.

Graham Smith (1997) observes that a decolonizing approach, built upon critical theory, is particularly effective in analysing power differences between groups; that it provides hope for transformation; that there is a role for both structural change and personal agency in resistance; and that Habermas' notion of finding victories in small struggles resists a purist tendency towards an all-or-nothing approach to social transformation. For these reasons, it makes sense to incorporate a decolonizing lens within Indigenous research frameworks. This lens can be positioned at least three different ways.

One approach, best called a *tribal methodology,* puts tribal epistemologies at the centre as the guiding force for research choices. Tribal methodology calls for a minimal integration of decolonizing theory into methodology through the documenting of the historical experience of colonial relations. The sole focus is on tribal knowledges. This approach works best in institutions where there is a critical mass of Indigenous academics and where resistance to holistic epistemologies is not as great.

Another approach utilizes a decolonizing theory as its centring epistemology, thus becoming easily associated with transformative research. It is possible to situate decolonizing methodologies as falling under the umbrella of an Indigenous research framework, but given its critical theoretical basis, it is more aligned with Western critical research methodologies. In this framework, there would be an indication and acknowledgment of a transformative theoretical base.

A third possibility is the inclusion of a decolonizing lens within a tribal-centred methodology that goes beyond identifying the colonial impact and seeks change. However, tribal-centred methodology does not centre the colonial relationship. An example of this is the Indige-

nous research framework presented in Chapter 2. It situates a decolonizing lens as an integral component within the methodological
design, but not as its epistemic basis. From a knowledge paradigm
perspective, this conceptualization clearly identifies an epistemological positioning distinct from Western ways of knowing, but weaves a
decolonizing analysis throughout.

No matter how it is positioned, a decolonizing agenda must be
incorporated within contemporary explorations of Indigenous inquiry
because of the persisting colonial influence on Indigenous representation and voice in research. Furthermore, a decolonizing agenda is a
forceful unifier that continues to shape our distinctive experience as an
Indigenous collective.

'How do researchers write their interpretation without "othering"
their research participants, exploiting them, or leaving them voiceless
in the telling of their own stories?' (Liamputtong, 2007: 165). In her
book, *Researching the Vulnerable*, Pranee Liamputtong poses this question. Any response is intricately related to issues of representation in
research. It will originate from a researcher's own beliefs about accurately representing the voice of a research participant and how this
manifests itself in all aspects of research, including the choices made
about gathering and interpreting story.

Representation and voice have particular relevance within qualitative research, whether this form of inquiry asks participants to share
personal experience of an event, occurrence, or phenomenon. Choices
made about representation in research and how participant 'voice' is
presented reveal to the critical reader the researcher's assumptions
about knowledge. This is entangled with the researcher's assumptions about power. There is a continuum of perspectives among qualitative researchers. It ranges from those who believe that knowledge
is highly contextualized and participants should have a holistic participation in research to those who believe that knowledge can be
decontextualized, leaving the researcher to control the research.
Beliefs about the purpose of knowledge and research are integrated
into this continuum – is the purpose of knowledge and research solely
to serve the researcher's interest or must they serve society in a beneficial manner? Of course, this begs the further question, beneficial by
whose definition?

A decolonizing lens, in conjunction with tribal knowledge, identifies
the centrality of voice and representation in research. From a social
justice standpoint, Indigenous methodologies require methods that

give back to community members in a way that is useful to them. Giving back involves knowing what 'useful' means, and so having a relationship with the community, so that the community can identify what is relevant, is key. This can be identified as both participation and representation in research.

Indigenous research frameworks shift the power of the researcher in controlling the research process and outcome. Methodologically, this means gathering knowledge that allows for voice and representational involvement in interpreting findings. A powerful method for achieving this desire is the use of story, life history, oral history, unstructured interviews, and other processes that allow participants to share their experiences on their terms. The specifics of these methods are discussed in subsequent chapters, but the point here is that decolonizing theory and methods that work in tandem with tribal epistemologies shape-shift the traditional social relations of research. Such methods act to give power back to the participant and the participant's community. Selecting research by inductive (as opposed to deductive) methods is congruent with Indigenous epistemologies and decolonizing methodologies.

Representation and voice in research put the researcher knee-deep in the muddy waters of the objectivity/subjectivity discourse. Too much story, with its inherent subjectivity, can find itself out of favour with those who ascribe to empirical quantification or qualitative generalization. Too much story can be subjected to the label 'experimental research' and risk being discredited by conventional academics. Those involved in Indigenous research experience this dynamic in several ways. Their research methodology may be highly congruent with an Indigenous worldview, but not understood by Western knowledge keepers and thus not recognized or diminished. A more common difficulty is that in an effort to serve both Indigenous and Western audiences, without clearly identifying epistemologies the methodology becomes ad hoc (Deloria, 1999: 33) and difficult for either audience to assess. While the resolution to this dilemma requires more than a decolonizing lens, incorporating such an analysis brings awareness of this contradiction, thus readying it for transformation. The function of a decolonial objective is to provide Indigenous researchers with a context-specific analytical tool for making visible contradictions and bringing Indigenous approaches out from the margins.

The Political Is Personal

In moving from participant experiences to those of the Indigenous researcher, a decolonizing perspective reveals the experiences and complexities of conducting research in colonial sites. The significance of integrating an anti-colonial approach within research is clear; however, it takes its toll. The decolonizing embodiment is a holistically layered process where theoretical positioning intersects profoundly with the personal conflicts of navigating two distinctive worlds.

In considering the social relations of research, a decolonizing analysis helps to sort out the tensions. In traversing academia and community, Cree scholar Cam Willett reflects, 'It's these two worlds that we are living in. The one world you are honoured with the eagle feather and the other world you are honoured with the doctoral degree.' Arising from these two differing worldviews are differing expectations of research. Numerous examples exist of the stress associated with this location. Certainly, there is the shared angst between fellow minority sectors that are advocating an alternative view in the classroom, meetings, and hallways. Within research, working with a cautious eye to the culturally imbued force that is research methodology, trying to adapt critical ethnography, grounded theory, or narrative inquiry to tribal epistemologies is a persistent intellectual challenge that is exhausting and potentially futile. However, I would like to focus on a particular issue germane to the decolonizing embodiment. It is a useful case example of the social relations of scholarship that cause frustration for Indigenous researchers. It is the publication of research.

A relatively uniform network exists of scholars who assess and teach graduate research work, adjudicate research funding proposals, and are sought for peer review of research publications. It is an established system that, consciously and not, works to mentor conformity to a time-honoured system, thereby establishing a collegial process that can absorb alternative points of view without major wounding. The act of compiling and organizing research findings for publication in and of itself presents a tension for Indigenous researchers who do not wish to compromise or diminish the power of oral culture in knowing. Yet, to remain viable in academia, our research must be written, assessed, and published. By and large, individuals assessing our work will not be Indigenous scholars or even necessarily Indigenous-friendly scholars, unless a journal is Indigenous-specific. The incorporation of narrative, story, and self-location found within Indigenous writing is perceived as indulgent rather than being recognized as a methodological necessity flowing from a tribal epistemology.

Certainly, there are pockets of support, but the flexibility of form necessary to present a holistic epistemology contests established norms of academic research writing. It is an uneasy fit because the peer-reviewed formula for scholarly publications focuses on a discussion of findings extracted from context. Thus it is not surprising when a submission is questioned or rejected. This would be less problematic if there were abundant Indigenous-specific journals or sites for publication that garnered academic respect equivalent to that given conventional scholarly publications, for Indigenous scholarship could then be assessed and valued on its own terms. The difficulty is that it is measured against a contrasting worldview that holds a monopoly on knowledge and keeps divergent forms of inquiry marginalized.

Yet, as Indigenous scholars rise through the ranks and manage to sustain their Indigenous identities, they are asking for a validation of Indigenous scholarship, which is reflective of tribal knowledges that move beyond a critique of colonialism. I have been asked to provide peer reviews of research articles for publication in scholarly journals. In assessing Indigenous scholarship, I look for distinctive qualities such as engagement with tribal knowledges, colonial implications, purpose, integration of narrative component, and considered discussion of what has been learned through the research. While by Indigenous scholarship I mean scholarship that is based on a tribal epistemology, it is recognized that Indigenous academics will carry out research not flowing from Indigenous research frameworks; there needs to be that choice. I assess the ability to offer knowledge presented in an Indigenous form, for I worry if it resembles mainstream scholarship too closely. Still, I recognize the pressure on Indigenous researchers to present research findings in a manner that does not radically contest established standards lest they risk entering into the publication void. This is a concern that raises the risk of tribal epistemology being morphed into something that it is not, merely to become palatable to mainstream academic evaluation. This exemplifies a site where decolonizing efforts could come in handy.

out up front. In the end, I was using Western and Indigenous theory and method as appropriate.

I want to elucidate this issue of using Western and Maori tools a bit more. The example of Gramsci's 'hegemony' helps me clarify this point here. The critical notion of hegemony is a great tool for understanding how Indigenous peoples become complicit in forming their own oppression and exploitation. It helps us to understand how common sense itself can become co-opted. As such, it is a useful tool to allow this insight. It helps Maori understand the processes of colonization and that's all. I am not going to say Western theory is useless, that it's white man's knowledge and we shouldn't use it and all that stuff. That's a load of bull – we need to use all the very best available theoretical and methodical tools, and where necessary develop new approaches when these tools are inadequate.

Kaupapa Maori is Maori-centred. It is Maori cultural, Maori political, Maori social – a Maori-centric positioning. It reinforces Maori academic work because it takes for granted Maori language, knowledge, and culture as not only being valid, but also being important. It acknowledges that Maori language, knowledge, and cultural interests are at the centre of the project. It also connects with the epistemological foundations and basis in the way we think, act, and live out our culturally preferred values.

The politics is another dimension that is important here because within the Kaupapa Maori framework, we really need to understand the politics of colonization, although I don't like to talk about colonization. This is because such expression (colonization) puts the colonizer at the centre of the discourse and we are positioned to become reactive. I prefer to use the term and talk about *conscientization* rather than colonization because such a term is more positive. It puts a focus on us at the centre rather than the colonizers, and it also centres concerns about our development.

The point here is that we need to learn the critical illiteracies that are required to unpack all of these colonizing processes. Doing a thesis and doing intellectual work is a political process if you are from a minority cultural group because you are often working in an institution that is ruled by the dominant societal groups. There is a need to have a way in which to defend yourself with some critical and political understandings.

MAGGIE: When we bring Indigenous methodologies into the academy,
what is the risk?

GRAHAM: There is risk, and we definitely should be careful around
this. But what I say to my students is that you have to question
why you are bringing it in. There is some Indigenous knowledge
which is already out there. In this sense, it's already public domain
knowledge in our own communities and perhaps even known and
accessible in non-Indigenous contexts. On the other hand, there is
some knowledge which is regarded as being sacred or restricted,
and if bringing such knowledge into the academy is going to cause
angst to others, then it shouldn't be brought in. The reason I say
this is because I can't guarantee that this particular institution, for
example, can look after it, treat it with respect, and preserve it in
the way that you need it to be preserved, taking regard of the community's expectations. It's unfortunate, but I would rather that you
keep such knowledge safe by keeping it outside. There are plenty
of other things to write about, research, and study for a thesis that
do not open up Indigenous knowledge to disrespect, exploitation,
and colonizing.

[As Indigenous researchers,] you have to make some decisions
as well, take some responsibility about guardianship. Why would
you put sacred knowledge at risk within an academic institution?
Indigenous researchers need to act responsibly, as well. Why put at
risk our culture and knowledge for the sake of an individual thesis
or research project? Are you just opening it up and making it vulnerable? I think there is some onus on ourselves here. There is a
need for us to exercise some agency. Then again, critical theory
gets me to think like that, so this is an example of how critical
theory can assist us. The point being that it [critical theory] helps
us make space for ourselves, our culture, our ways of thinking.

Graham uses the metaphor of needing 'more tools on the wall' to
argue that Indigenous researchers must respond adequately and advo-
cate effectively for the needs of their community. Critical theory and a
decolonizing approach have assisted in providing an analysis for
making visible the power dynamics within society, as well as developing the tools to think, write, and be in a way that furthers social justice.
My conversation with Graham reaffirmed that theoretical tools like
critical theory are useful to the Indigenous researcher, but it is not
enough to stop there. There must be Indigenous methodological tools,

as well. It is, as Graham states, not an either/or proposition, but rather advocacy for a more inclusive approach to research within the academy that respects methodologies from the margins.

Recalling this conversation, I must admit to a certain nostalgia. As a young student at the University of Regina I was part of a social activist student group. It was a heady time, and along with the political organizing and demonstrations, I remember having long philosophical conversations about social Marxism as an analysis for understanding the oppression of the poor and working class. At that time, race was not on the radar. Later, when I returned to Carleton University for graduate work, critical theory was more pervasive, offering an analysis on race, class, and gender. Critical theorists have been instrumental in creating space in the academy for decolonizing thought and Indigenous knowledges, and their contributions ought to be noted.

The stress that Graham places on praxis within Indigenous research is central to our methodology. We can call it decolonization, we can call it Indigenous praxis, or we can call it resistance. The point is that Indigenous research needs to benefit Indigenous people in some way, shape, or form – that is the bottom line. The whole notion of 'knowledge for knowledge's sake' does not fit an Indigenous research framework at this point. Maybe someday we will have that luxury, but not right now.

As I write this, Vine Deloria Jr, who has so inspired me on this journey, has left the physical world to be with the ancestors. In honour of Vine's passing, the American Indian Movement of Colorado (2005) has asked us to remember a quote from Deloria's *Custer Died for Your Sins*: 'Ideological leverage is always superior to violence … The problems of Indians have always been ideological rather than social, political or economic … [I]t is vitally important that the Indian people pick the intellectual arena as the one in which to wage war' (1969: 251–2). As I think about my own work and what it means to be an Indigenous researcher, Vine Deloria Jr reminds me that as Indigenous scholars, researchers, thinkers, and writers, we have an obligation to challenge the ideologies that shackle us. The purpose, then, is to push the edge of the ideological certitude of what counts as knowledge and research in the academy.

5 Story as Indigenous Methodology

Stories remind us of who we are and of our belonging. Stories hold within them knowledges while simultaneously signifying relationships. In oral tradition, stories can never be decontextualized from the teller. They are active agents within a relational world, pivotal in gaining insight into a phenomenon. Oral stories are born of connections within the world, and are thus recounted relationally. They tie us with our past and provide a basis for continuity with future generations.

Stories originating from oral traditions resonate and engender personal meaning. 'In Blackfoot the English word 'story' literally translates as involvement in an event. If a Blackfoot asks another Blackfoot to tell a story, he is literally asking the storyteller to tell about his '"involvement" in an event' (Little Bear, 2004: 6). Jo-ann Archibald reflects upon how stories capture our attention and tells us that stories ask us 'to think deeply and to reflect upon our actions and reactions,' a process that Archibald calls 'storywork' (2001: 1). As a form, it is no wonder that narrative is the primary means for passing knowledge within tribal traditions, for it suits the fluidity and interpretative nature of ancestral ways of knowing.

This chapter focuses on the inseparable relationship between story and knowing, and the interrelationship between narrative and research within Indigenous frameworks. In considering story as both method and meaning, it is presented as a culturally nuanced way of knowing. To honour the richness of narrative, Métis scholar Jeannine Carriere explains how story evokes the holistic quality of Indigenous methodologies.

— Academic Knowledge
— practical Knowledge
— Historical his

Within Indigenous epistemologies, there are two general forms of stories. There are stories that hold mythical elements such as creation and teaching stories, and there are personal narratives of place, happenings, and experiences as the *kōkoms* and *mósoms* (Aunties and uncles) experienced them and passed them along to the next generation through oral tradition. Both forms teach of consequences, good and bad, of living life in a certain way. Edward Ahenakew writes of the Elders' responsibility in ensuring a moral code and history of the tribe, and it was through storytelling that they fulfilled this obligation (1995: 37). Stories are vessels for passing along teachings, medicines, and practices that can assist members of the collective. They promote social cohesion by entertaining and fostering good feeling. In times past, as now, stories were not always transferred in lexical form, but through visual symbols, song, and prayer. The pictograph by Chief Paskwa that was recently repatriated to the Pasqua First Nation (*Dibajiimo Masinahikan 'Newspaper,'* 2007) recounts the chief's perspective on the signing of Treaty Four. This pictorial narrative, the only known document of its kind on the treaty relationship, signed in 1874, stands as a historic interpretation of a defining relationship in Canada, from Indigenous eyes. Although the form varies, stories reveal a set of relations comprising strong social purpose.

The interrelationship between story and knowing cannot be traced back to any specific starting time within tribal societies, for they have been tightly bound since time immemorial as a legitimate form of understanding. Cree scholar Neal McLeod writes of the centrality of narrative and memory for Cree culture in his book, *Song to kill a Wîhtikow*, that '*mistahi-maskwa* was an inspirational Cree visionary because he held the imagination and collective memory of our people at a time when a great darkness, a metaphorical *wîhtikow*, fell on the land' (2005: 8). As with many oral cultures, narrative functions as an intergenerational knowledge transfer (Cruikshank, 1998). The stories hold information about familial rights associated with territorial stewardship, and though the prominence of story in maintaining generational responsibilities is ancient, it has only recently been recognized in Western jurisprudence. In the 1997 Delgamuukw decision, the Supreme Court of Canada ruled that oral testimony has the same weight as written evidence in land entitlement cases. Within Western sites, the significance of story within Indigenous culture is less contested. Rather, it is the nature and structure of story that causes difficulties for non-tribal systems due to its divergence from the temporal narrative structure of Western culture. For tribal stories are not meant to be oriented within the linearity of time, but rather they transcend time and fasten themselves to places (McLeod, 2007). No doubt, this narrative structure creates discomfort, born of unfamiliarity, for those new to it. It creates a significant challenge for research, where 'non-bracketed story' as method and meaning is relatively new to the qualitative landscape.

The anthropological focus on the rich oral traditions within tribal societies has tended to relegate story to a historic cultural method that lacks currency within contemporary knowledge centres. The underlying assumption is that oral tradition is of pre-literate tribal groups that no longer has the same application in a literate and technological world. Within research, a particularly lettered activity, a challenge for Indigenous researchers is to find openings to honour this integral quality of Indigenous inquiry. Within qualitative research, Indigenous researchers struggle to maintain oral tradition for a number of reasons. One reason is to be congruent with tribal epistemologies that honour our rich ancestry. Another equally forceful motivation is to ensure that holistic, contextualized meanings arise from research. The holism of tribal knowledges explored in Chapter 3 undergirds this approach. The oral rendition of personal narrative or formal teaching story is a portal for holistic epistemology. It is the most effective method for capturing this form of knowing in research.

Those well-versed in qualitative research methods will confirm that story is not unique to Indigenous knowledge systems. Story is practised within methodologies valuing contextualized knowledge, such as feminism, autoethnography, phenomenology, and narrative inquiry. Terminology like *life history* and *oral history* is familiar to these forms of qualitative inquiry. Life history is associated with a study of the totality of a person's life, while oral history concerns a particular aspect of an individual's experience that pertains to the research topic at hand (Liamputtong, 2007). It is recognized that story as both form and method crosses cultural divides. However, the way that a culture employs story differs. In reference to art (a form of story) and method, Kandinsky makes the point: 'The borrowing of method by one art form to another can only be truly successful when the application of the borrowed method is not superficial but fundamental' (1977: 20). Story, as a method, is used differently from culture to culture, and so its application falters without full appreciation of the underlying epistemological assumptions that motivate its use. Indigenous people versed in their culture know that sharing a story in research situates it within a collective memory. Likewise, Indigenous researchers ought to know of the deep responsibility of requesting an oral history – i.e., an individual recounting of a particular happening. A researcher assumes a responsibility that the story shared will be treated with the respect it deserves in acknowledgment of the relationship from which it emerges.

Concurrently, the use of story as method without an understanding of cultural epistemology, defined broadly, can create problems with understanding the totality of Indigenous narrative. Cultural specificity of Indigenous story is manifest in teaching and personal narratives and can have profound implications for the interpretation of story within research. Gerald Vizenor, a Chippewa literary critic, advises that within any Indigenous story there is a both a trickster and a tragic element at work, serving to show the irony of living in an uncertain world. He argues that tribal storytellers must pay specific attention to how the actors involve themselves in social encounters. Vizenor goes on to argue that often in the interpretations of these stories 'these encounters are clouded by racial misrepresentations that emerge from a long history of "hyperrealities" about Indians' (quoted in Buendía, 2003: 61). The notion that everyone understands story and that it is an effective means for gaining insight and making sense of the world is not contested. What is contested, however, is that story is an apolitical, acultural method that can be applied without consideration of the knowledge system that sustains it. From that perspective, engaging with tribal stories means understanding their form, purpose, and substance from a tribal perspective. To attempt to understand tribal stories from a Western perspective (or any other cultural perspective) is likely to miss the point, possibly causing harm. This has been a significant finding since the dark years of anthropological research on Indigenous culture. Against this backdrop, there are a number of practical aspects accompanying story as knowing within Indigenous research frameworks.

Story and Inquiry

After considering the importance of story, my own and others', in communicating the breadth of tribal knowledges, I grappled with the methodological complexity of attempting congruency between my philosophical standpoint, data-gathering choices, and the meaning-making strategy within my research. While this research was located within the contextual enterprise of Western research production, the research question itself was deeply cultural. I knew from a Nêhiýaw point of view that knowledge and story are inseparable and that inter-pretative knowing is highly valued, that story is purposeful. I knew that listening to people's narratives would be the primary knowledge-seeking method in my research. This left me with several methodolog-ical quandaries. Rather than pedantic responses to specific questions, this chapter considers story as method in light of the relational quality of story, representation in narrative, data-gathering choices amiable to story, and the challenges of writing story from an Indigenous perspec-tive. In consideration of the previous chapter, there must be commen-tary on the utility of how story works as a decolonizing action that gives voice to the misinterpreted and marginalized.

Story and Indigenous inquiry are grounded within a relationship-based approach to research. The centrality of relationship within Indigenous research frameworks, and the responsibility that that evokes, manifest themselves in broad strokes throughout research in the form of protocols and ethical considerations. (From a methodologi-cal perspective, the same undergirding value of respect applies to all choices made within the research design.) This is significant in Indige-nous qualitative methodologies involving story where there is a primary relationship between researcher and research participant. For story to surface, there must be trust. Given the egregious past research practices in Indigenous communities, earning trust is critical and may take time, upsetting the efficiency variable of research timelines. Cree scholar Laara Fitznor spoke about the significance of pre-existing rela-tionships with research participants: 'They know me, I have a good rep-utation and they know that I would be trustworthy.' Such relationships hold a history of shared story with one another. If a pre-existing rela-tionship is not in place, such a process must begin. In asking others to share stories, it is necessary to share our own, starting with self-location (see Chapter 6). For many active in Indigenous research, this comes nat-urally, as a part of community protocol. The researcher's self-location provides an opportunity for the research participant to situate and assess the researcher's motivations for the research, thus beginning the relationship that is elemental to story-based methodology.

Within the research relationship, the research participant must feel that the researcher is willing to listen to the story. By listening intently to one another, story as method elevates the research from an extractive exercise serving the fragmentation of knowledge to a holistic endeavour that situates research firmly within the nest of relationship. This relationship, as Coast Salish researcher Robina Thomas suggests, is not bound solely to research interview sessions. In hearing the stories of residential school survivors, she acknowledges the deeply personal quality of her research methodology. Thomas' storytelling methodology evokes a deep and personal response, and demands that she, as researcher, be available to hear the stories when the tellers are prepared to share. 'On one occasion, a storyteller phoned and asked me to come over that evening and tape record; he was ready to tell more stories' (quoted in Brown and Strega, 2005: 247). This experience represents the holistic journey of both parties. It alerts prospective researchers that such an approach asks for a deep respect associated with the relational quality of this approach. As mentioned in Chapter 1, it can never be a 'smash and grab' approach to seeking knowledge (Martin and Frost, 1996).

The privileging of story in knowledge-seeking systems means honouring 'the talk.' To provide openings for narrative, Indigenous researchers use a variety of methods, such as conversations, interviews, and research/sharing circles. For her research, Laara Fitznor employed 'research circle-talking circles' to give space for story. It was a method where 'I could ask questions and people would share what they had to share.' It provided a forum for people to relate their stories in a holistic fashion that was not fragmented by a structured interview process. Jeannine Carriere comments on how she used a qualitative in-depth interview method to hear the stories of her participants. 'The best methodology that I found was in-depth interviews, because that gave me the space ... to at least guide people in terms of a question guide, but not be very strict in terms of what to say and when to say it. It was a more open approach.' The importance of less-structured research tools is documented in Anne Ryen's research. Ryen was involved in a qualitative research project with the Institute of Management in Tanzania. From her experience, the more structured the interview the less flexibility and power the research participant has in sharing his or her story (2000). Through this less-structured method, the story breathes and the narrator regulates.

Once individuals have agreed to share their story, the researcher's responsibility is to ensure voice and representation. That participants check and approve the transcripts of the stories is essential for meeting the criteria of accurate representation as perceived by research partici-pants. This ought to be standard practice within research generally, but because of the misrepresentation of Indigenous cultures and commu-nities within research, it is essential within Indigenous methodologies. In presenting a story in research findings, researchers will often have to condense it. It is necessary to give participants an opportunity to review this condensed story form and approve its presentation. By ful-filling this responsibility, the researcher ascertains authentic, ethical representation. Story, then, is a means to give voice to the marginalized and assists in creating outcomes from research that are in line with the needs of the community. Reliable representation engenders relevancy and is a necessary aspect of giving back to community.

Along with a choice of method for hearing others' stories, there are implications for a co-creation process that interpretative narrative invites. In co-creating knowledge, story is not only a means for hearing another's narrative, it also invites reflexivity into research. Through reflexive story there is opportunity to express the researcher's inward knowing. Sharing one's own story is an aspect of co-constructing knowledge from an Indigenous perspective. Absolon and Willet (2004) remind us that our experiences, which live in memory, are vital to Indigenous research. They propose that our experience of being Indigenous, our identity factor, becomes integral to interpreting our research. Through a co-creative, interpretive tradition, Indigenous story offers knowledge relevant to one's life in a personal, particular way.

In presenting research, a complexity of Indigenous story-based research is transferring what is intended to be oral to written text. In *kôhkominawak otâcuniwiniwâwa — our grandmothers' lives as told in their own words*, Ahenakew and Wolfart present textually the stories of the *kókoms* speaking in Cree as closely as possible to the oral spoken story. Introducing the stories, they tell the reader, 'The style of these remi-niscences is casual, familiar, and marked by numerous interruptions and exchanges' (1998: 19). It is a challenge to capture textually the non-verbal nuances of these conversations, yet this form contains much knowledge. The ability to capture the reflections of these *kókoms* as they remember their *kókoms* and *mósoms* give an insider's perspective of a Plains Cree way of being, and the role of kinship systems in passing knowledge. In Western culture, narrative has predominantly been textual, implying a set of assumptions and implications. The nar-rative has less immediacy in that the storyteller need not be physically present with a story listener. In written narrative, the story becomes finalized as a written product to be read and considered according to the reader's interpretation. Once written, the relationship between the reader and the storyteller is conceptual, not tangible. In an oral culture, story lives, develops, and is imbued with the energy of the dynamic relationship between teller and listener. The story can only exist within an interdependent relationship of the narrator and audience. Writing story becomes a concession of the Indigenous researcher.

Cree scholar Winona Stevenson recounts the time that she spent reflecting upon the ins and outs of recording oral teachings that she received during her research, and the ache of putting them into written text. As many of her sources were stories shared in the Cree language, she had the challenge of first interpreting Cree into English and then writing meaning. In her research report, the style of writing shifts back and forth, from analytical commentary of discourse surrounding oral histories to a narrative style of her experience with Cree culture – one is abstract knowledge and one is story. These two ways have differing knowledge-sharing assumptions because the analysis in declarative form illustrates how knowledge conflicts with the interpretive teaching method assumed in Indigenous stories. 'All stories are didactic to varying degrees, but they hardly ever have built-in analysis – analysis is the job of the listener' (Stevenson 2000: 233).

This provides insight into the intricate sophistication of Cree oral tradition and worldview. As it pertains to research, the comparative discussion of oral history from an Indigenous, as opposed to a Western historical, point of view is intriguing. Stevenson states that Indigenous oral histories do not share conventional categorical boundaries: 'the package is holistic – they include religious teachings, metaphysical links, cultural insights, history, linguistic structures, literary and aesthetic form, and Indigenous "truths"' (2000: 79). She goes on to discuss the disciplinary objective of Western scholarship when using story as means of collecting data: 'It often is the case in mainstream scholarship, that once a story is shared and recorded, "facts" are extracted and the remaining "superfluous" data set aside.' She further states that 'the bundle is plundered, the voice silenced, bits are extracted to meet empirical academic needs, and the story dies' (ibid.). Thus, there is a need for linking Indigenous epistemologies to story as Indigenous method, otherwise contradictions would abound. This begs the question: Is story of epistemology or is story epistemology? It does not likely matter for the question implies segregating the two. From a tribal perspective, they are inseparable.

In using story methodology, Robina Thomas shares her hesitation about writing stories down. She acknowledges 'times change,' and for Indigenous stories to be heard they need to be written down. The challenge is to serve the integrity of oral stories by adapting them to this new form (2005: 242). Can we ever bring the full nuance of the oral tradition into Western academia? Not likely. Gerald Vizenor points out that a holistic knowing is lost when stories are not delivered orally: 'So much is lost in translation – the communal context of performance, gesture, intonation – even the best translations are scriptural reductions of the rich oral nuance' (quoted in Stevenson, 2000: 19). Sitting in the now of story can never be captured through the research transcription. The knowledges that we gather in the ephemeral moment of oral story, as told by a teller, as we sit in a specific spiritual, physical, and emotional place, are of a different sort. The immediacy of the relational stands outside the research, and at best we can only reflect upon it. To make visible the holistic, relational meaning requires a reflexive narrative by the researcher.

The question undoubtedly arises – how is this different from journalism? With its emphasis on story, is it *really* research? The response, of course, depends upon the respondent and how he or she defines research. Is research a form of knowledge-seeking that is amenable only to quantifiable generalizations? If that is the belief, it shuts out the possibility of Indigenous research frameworks where generalizabilities are inconsistent with the epistemic foundation. If research is about learning, so as to enhance the well-being of the earth's inhabitants, then story is research. It provides insight from observations, experience, interactions, and intuitions that assist in developing a theory about a phenomenon.

Inevitably, the personal nature of a story will bring to light questions about the legitimacy of knowledge. Does relationship imply subjectivity? Does subjectivity contaminate evidence of 'real' knowledge? In Western research, this is about the validity of research. Knowledge then becomes that which can be proven true. From a traditional Cree perspective, truth is bound in a sacred commitment. 'So when the Old People accept tobacco from one seeking knowledge, and when they share the pipe, they are saying that they will tell the truth as they know it. They are bound in the presence of the Creator as witness to speak from the heart, to speak their truth' (Stevenson, 2000: 249). Stevenson goes on to say that when a storyteller uses the term *tapwê* (truth), it means that the storyteller is telling the truth according to how she or he heard it. As Indigenous researchers, we are bound by this cultural imperative.

In my research, the exchange of tobacco signified that what was spoken was truth as each person knew it. There was a further recognition that the person's story would become a part of the social and historical fabric of the people, a historical truth, through their honour. It requires belief in another's integrity, that there is a mutual understanding that speaking untruths will upset the relational balance. If relational balance is not a high cultural value, such methods of 'validity' will fall flat. Relational validity is only questionable (or suspect) if one's worldview does not ascribe to it. From a methodological perspective, researchers who employ story as part of their research framework will need to be aware of the objectivity bias in research so as to support their own claims.

Story as methodology is decolonizing research. Stories of resistance inspire generations about the strength of the culture. Yet, there are political implications of Indigenous research that need to be figured into the equation. We cannot forget that the relationship between Indigenous knowledges and research is carried out within a contemporary colonial project of post-secondary studies. Thus the stories, and the content that they carry, must be shared with this appreciation to protect them from exploitation or appropriation. The use of narrative in inquiry means that the researcher must accept the guardianship of bringing oral story into academia during this particular historical moment.

A Conversation with Jeannine Carriere

It is appropriate to conclude this chapter with story. Through Jeannine Carriere's story, we can remember a past and imagine a future of knowledge shared through narrative.

Jeannine Carriere is a Métis woman whose ancestral lineage flows from the Red River Métis of Manitoba. Jeannine completed her doctoral studies through the University of Alberta, Department of Human Ecology and Family Studies, focusing on the connection between health and First Nations adoptees. Jeannine has an extensive background in supporting Indigenous children in Alberta, and I met her through her advocacy work in First Nations child welfare. I have a connection with Jeannine because of our shared experience as Indigenous adoptees. I had a sense that even without saying too much, she would 'get me' and the motivations for my research.

This conversation took place in mid-August of 2006 when I returned back to Victoria. We met at her office. I was eager to hear about her research story as she had recently completed her dissertation. She shared with me the story of her research journey and how it was about 'getting to home' in more ways than one.

MAGGIE: Jeannine, what was your research topic and program of study?

JEANNINE: I was teaching in Hobbema, coordinating the Hobbema College program of the University of Calgary. Here I was, teaching at a First Nations university that was very impacted by the oil industry, and I was interested in how it impacted the family structures. I went to the Elders and made my offerings. I got encouragement to pursue it, but it just didn't feel that it was my research. It was with that kind of discomfort that I ended up in Saskatoon at the 'Prairie Child Welfare' symposium – the very first one. We sat in a circle on the last day, and I can't even remember how many people there were, but it was the largest circle I ever sat in. We knew at the beginning of the day that it was going to take all day. The reason for concluding with that kind of circle is that Aboriginal people who attended the first two days were getting increasingly frustrated that even though this symposium was organized to discuss Aboriginal child welfare issues, the government was doing all the talking and the universities were doing all the talking. Where were our voices and our process?

With some advocacy during the evening, we arranged to have this circle as the last discussion. In that circle, I ended up one of the last people to speak. Everybody started talking about their own experiences as opposed to the policy and what should be done in practice. It was more like, 'This is my experience with child welfare.' I felt this thing rising in me, because I thought, 'Can I really do this? Can I really talk about what [was] my experience as opposed to my work experience? Can I talk about my family experience of being adopted and reconnecting, and the whole experience around that?' As the circle kept going, it got closer to my turn, and I knew I didn't have a choice. I had to be authentic in what I said, and it had to be about my experience. I got through it without weeping too much, but after I spoke and the circle concluded I couldn't stop crying. Luckily, I had good friends there and my partner came to pick me up, and he's 'What happened to you, you were at a conference, why are you doing all this crying?'

We were driving to Edmonton and I was trying to compose myself, but what kept occurring to me is, 'Why are you searching for all these research topics? You should be doing this research on adoption. This is who you are, this is your story and this is what you should be contributing.' It was this sort of messages coming to me. I got home and called my friend from an agency I worked at right away, and said, 'This is what I think I should do. This is the third time I am changing the topic, and people are going to think I am nuts.' She said, 'You know that I have been wanting to tell you for a long time now, give your head a shake, why aren't you doing your research on adoption? It needs to be done. We need your help in this area, all the other First Nations do as well.' To make a long story short, that's how the topic came to be, and how it came to me. I knew that in my own life I attributed a lot of stuff to the adoption experience, always looking for something and damaging myself in many ways while I was looking.

MAGGIE: [*At this point we were talking about the personal preparations that became a part of our methodologies.*] There is also part of my methodology that is about me going home.

JEANNINE: Mine, in a way, has lots of parallels. There were cultural pieces for me that were happening in Alberta and I had a lot of supports there, ceremonial support and traditional approaches there. But, as with you when it came to writing, I had to go home. I went home to Manitoba. It's funny how the Creator works, because my partner had an opportunity to work in Winnipeg and I was getting a sabbatical from the U[niversity] of C[algary] to write. Away, we went, but you know what, I mean, nothing is a coincidence, right? I was supposed to go there, and not to disrespect my partner, but he became a kind of instrument for me to get there [*laughter*].

There I was in Winnipeg, transcribing tapes and writing. I was in my head, and not connecting in my heart and my soul, not stopping to think, 'Wait a minute, this is where it all happened for you, Jeannine.' Where I grew up in my adopted parents' home is twenty minutes from Winnipeg. Why wasn't I going there? There was part of me that really wanted to go, but I was scared. I was surrounded by my birth family members, my siblings, my nieces and nephews, and that was wonderful, but that was not the whole story. I kept wondering, 'What is keeping me from that? In order for me to write about connectedness, why aren't I connecting?' I kept feeling this physical sense of discomfort, and I wasn't sure where that was coming from. A good friend of mine from Edmonton said, 'You need to go back there, you need to go to the graveyard, you need to visit your adopted parents there, you need to try and get into the house where you grew up.' I didn't think I could do that. She said, 'Pray about it, hold your tobacco and see what happens. And I think your sister needs to go with you.' She was referring to my sister, because she was the one who found me when I was twelve.

The end of my sabbatical was coming and I knew I had to get back to Alberta, and I thought if I am going to do this, I have to do this now. My partner was going away for a weekend, and I thought this is a perfect opportunity, so I invited my sister to come for the weekend and told her what I wanted to do, and asked her come with me. She said, 'Sure.' She said, 'Maybe after we are finished with [place deleted], we can go to [place deleted],' which was where she lived the longest in a foster home, not a pleasant experience for her either. We thought that we could bring some closure to these experiences together. Away we go, we decided to go to [place deleted] with a first stop at the graveyard to visit my adopted parents. I truly wanted to go and thank them for what they tried to give me, because, you know, it really was my stuff, my resistance, more than anything they did really. Sure they could have been a little less racist, a little more of this or little more of that, but all in all they were pretty good folks. They weren't the problem. It was the policies, it was the way things were done.

I am visiting the graveyard and we come to my parents' grave, and by then I am mess. I said to my sister, 'Can you say a prayer because I just can't do it.' So she started to pray and thanked them for giving me what they could. It was a beautiful prayer and I felt so much more at peace. We start walking out of the graveyard, and now I wanted to go to this house where I grew up, but I haven't spoken to anyone in my adopted family for twenty years, and I didn't have the courage to do that. I kept asking myself, 'Where am I going to get courage to do that, how am I going to do that?' My adopted sister is living in my parents' house, and ended up calling us when they passed away. I haven't seen her since my mother's funeral, so how do I go up to this house? I had all kinds of feelings of animosity toward my adopted sibling. I always felt like I was the different one, that I caused so many problems for my parents, that I wasn't as good as them. I didn't want to knock on that door and reopen that can of worms. I mean, what if she closes the door?

We are walking out the graveyard, and I see this woman walking into the graveyard, and she is going to my parents' grave. I say to my sister, 'That is ... my adopted sister.' My sister said, 'What?' I said, 'Yeah, that's her.' She said, 'This is a sign. You need to go and talk to her.' I said, 'I don't think I can.' She said, 'Of course you can.' I said, 'What if I scare her?' She looked at me, then looked at her, and said, 'She looks like she can handle it' [laughter]. I thought, okay, so I started walking toward my sister and I called her name. When she heard, she looked up and went like this [shades her eyes with her hand] because the sun was bright, and when she did that she was the spitting image of my adopted mom. I told her who I was, and she just couldn't believe I was there. I couldn't believe she was there, and we had a bit of a superficial conversation in the graveyard. Then she said, 'Would you like to come back to the house?' That was a gift! I said I would love to and we went.

We didn't go into the house right away. I savoured the yard for a while because there was the tree that I used to climb on when I was a kid to run away. I was always running away to the creek, to the trees, whatever. I thought, 'My tree is still there.' So I had to take pictures of my tree, me and my tree, my sister, me, and my tree. It's a tree, alright! [laughter] Everything was just so special. At first we sat in this sun room that she built onto the garage. She started telling my sister stories about when I was a kid. It made me kind of nervous because I thought she was going to say all bad things, but, no, it was good. It was obvious that they loved me, which is something that I never thought they did. There were humorous stories.

MAGGIE: Did you write that experience?

JEANNINE: I did, right at the end. I think it's important to capture your own process, and I think Western methodology and Indigenous methodology meet in that way. It's very critical, and if you don't, you are really doing a disservice to yourself and to your audience because it's important to present what you found in the

most accurate and impactful way you can. If you don't acknowledge your own self in the research process, then you will always
have a piece missing. I had seen portfolio work with the students
who I had taught and I had also been able to give guidance in
using portfolios through teaching a course itself. I thought, 'What
a wonderful way for me to use this as a research approach to
capture my process.'

After hearing Jeannine's story, I returned to Saskatchewan. I went to
see Buffy St Marie perform, and it was wonderful to see this strong
Plains Cree woman in Regina not far from her traditional territories. In
introducing one of her songs, she said that there is a need for all of us
to find room in our plans for life. It made me think about Indigenous
methodologies, about Jeannine's research story and my own. The
holistic, relational, and at times raw nature of holistic research meant
making room in methodology for life, for the unexpected, for the path
that emerges rather than the one initially planned. Both Jeannine and
I had the experience of returning to our home communities, though
this was not part of the initial plan, for we had both enrolled in universities far from where we grew up. For me, I could chart out many
good and rational reasons for heading home, yet the decision to go
back was an emotional one. It came from my heart, involving both
angst and longing, and had it been otherwise I am not sure I would
have came back.

  How do we explain or articulate this aspect of Indigenous inquiry
that we may not even understand until long after our research has
been stamped 'Finished'? If we have a chance, it is through our stories.
Stories are who we are. They are both method and meaning. Stories
spring forth from a holistic epistemology and are the relational glue in
a socially interdependent knowledge system. In listening to the
research stories of others, it is evident that research stories reveal the
deep purpose of our inquiries.

6 Situating Self, Culture, and Purpose in Indigenous Inquiry

I have returned home from the Federation of Saskatchewan Indian Nations annual powwow. As the Elder gave a prayer and the carriers raised the pipe, I stood watching the grand entry, then the dancers enter the stadium in regalia, viscerally knowing their role in maintaining culture. I thought about my research journey, why I locate as a Nêhíyaw and Saulteaux researcher. Deep down, I wanted my research to help uphold the culture, for it certainly gave occasion to come home, and this in itself made it purposeful. From my current vantage point, I am thankful for this opportunity, yet there were days during the research when my gratitude was tempered. Indigenous inquiry is holistically demanding, and knowing purpose in what can be emotionally challenging work matters when spirits are low.

Experience and research told me that Indigenous inquiry involves specific multi-layered preparations particular to each researcher. Preparatory work means clarifying the inquiry purpose, which invariably gets to motivations. Preparation assumes self-awareness and an ability to situate self within the research. It requires attention to culture in an active, grounded way. There is no formula (nor could there be) for this preparation. Nor do the details of this work need to be explicitly retold, for they are not preparations amenable to academic evaluation. Yet, they are often referenced by Indigenous researchers, and consistently appear in tribal methodologies (P. Steinhauer, 2001; Bastien, 1999; Struthers, 2001). It is these preparations that count should an Elder ask: 'Why did you do *that* research, and why did you do it in *that* way?' Focusing on self-location, purpose, and cultural grounding, this chapter offers insights into the preparatory aspect of Indigenous inquiries. Integrated into this chapter, Indigenous scholar Cam Willett shares his thoughts on purpose within Indigenous research.

Locating Ourselves

Within Indigenous research, self-location means cultural identification, and it manifests itself in various ways. Indigenous researchers will situate themselves as being of an Indigenous group, be it tribal, urban, or otherwise. They will share their experience with culture, and/or they will identify the Indigenous epistemology (or epistemologies) of their research. Often, they will culturally locate in all three ways. To resist pan-Indianism, identifying the specific tribal epistemology (e.g., Plains Cree) is a necessity. For many Indigenous people, this act is intuitive, launched immediately through the protocol of introductions. It shows respect to the ancestors and allows community to locate us. Situating self implies clarifying one's perspective on the world (Meyer, 2004; Hampton, 1995). This is about being congruent with a knowledge system that tells us that we can only interpret the world from the place of our experience.

Self-locating in research is common among many qualitative approaches, though the extent that it is integrated varies. Within feminist methodologies, researchers are encouraged to locate themselves, to share personal aspects of their own experience with research participants. This is a means of building 'reciprocity, rapport and trust between the researcher and researched' (Liamputtong, 2007: 13). Anti-oppressive inquiries integrate self-location to identify and then mitigate power differentials in research. Anti-oppressive researcher Susan Strega proposes that within the 'system of domination and subordination,' where the perspectives of the marginalized are not fully appreciated, those of us who have this experience need to share it, voice it, and give it space (2005: 224). For if we do not, who will? From this perspective, self-locating is a powerful tool for increasing awareness of power differentials in society and for taking action to further social justice.

Postmodern approaches use self-location to illustrate multiple truths. Through autoethnographies and autobiographical narrative inquiries, researchers reveal how the intuitive and experiential work constructs knowledge. In this research, what is 'central in autobiographical narratives is "I," our accounts of the world, which are constructions, made up of language and meanings, and our own histories'

(Kimpson, 2005: 75). This form of reflexivity allows the researcher-self to participate as co-constructor of knowledge in specific and defined ways.

Regarding the social constructivist tradition, such as phenomenology, Max Van Manen makes this comment: 'How can we pursue the questions of what constitutes (phenomenological) knowledge in such a way that our way of addressing this question may become an example of what the question in the questioning seeks to clarify?' (2001: 46). Van Manen's point underscores the epistemic purpose of self-location, revealing the beliefs that shape our lives and what we take as 'truth' and knowledge. It is not only the questions we ask and how we go about asking them, but who we are in the asking. Van Manen goes on to clarify his point by saying that 'the question of knowledge always refers us back to our world, to who we are. … [I]t is what stands iconically behind the words, the speaking and the language' (ibid.). This stands in strong alignment with holistic epistemologies that emphasize self-knowledge, though always in relation to other.

Specifically within Indigenous inquiry, Absolon and Willett (2005) tell us that location is important. They remind us that self-location anchors knowledge within experiences, and these experiences greatly influence interpretations. Sharing stories and finding commonalities assists in making sense of a particular phenomenon, though it is never possible (nor wise) to generalize to another's experience. 'Location ensures that individual realities are not misrepresented as generalizable collectives. Our ancestors gave us membership into nations and traditions; location both remembers and "re-members" us to those things' (2005: 123). Self-locating affirms perspectives about the objectivity/subjectivity conundrum in research. Cree scholar Winona Stevenson tells us that Cree Elders will most often preface statements by stating, 'I believe it to be true' (2000: 19). These words espouse relational validity, qualify knowledge as personal reflection from one's own life experience, and recognize other truths. Tribal epistemologies cannot be disassociated from the subjective. Tribal epistemologies are a way of knowing that does not debate the subjectivity factor in knowledge production – subjectivity is a given. To embrace Indigenous methodologies is to accept subjective knowledge. This is difficult for sectors of the Western research community to accept, and it is where much of the contention about Indigenous research arises.

In addition to epistemological congruency, there are several reasons for the purposeful monitoring and locating of oneself within Indigenous inquiry. Critically reflective self-location gives opportunity to examine our research purpose and motive. It creates a mutuality with those who share their stories with us. Critically reflective self-location is a strategy to keep us aware of the power dynamic flowing back and forth between researcher and participant. It prompts awareness of the extractive tendency of research. And it endorses tending to the personal and cultural in research.

As a reflexivity method of research, situating the self authorizes expression of the relevant narrative from personal experiences, those reminiscences of life rooted in our earliest experience that shape our understanding of the world. Indigenous scholars, in my study, affirmed the necessity of reflexivity in research. Laara Fritznor shares why situating self matters: 'I was raised in northern Manitoba not on the reserve ... I was Cree with Scottish and German ancestry. For me, it's always important to acknowledge those, that part of who I am.' Keeping one's location front and centre is a way that individuals can consciously assert from where their strength comes, and ensure that their integrity will not become compromised by the trials of academic research. Kathy Absolon advises that if you 'went and found out what it was like and if you feel that you can't be yourself, you can't be who you are, then you can leave.' In my research, writing my personal story was necessary. I was raised outside the culture, yet I was researching Indigenous methodologies. I could not proceed with this research without stating that I write from a specific place. Doing this work shows respect to culture, community, the research audience, and to myself. Being truthful does not culturally disenfranchise. Michael Hart points out that the diversity of personal stories does not preclude collective belonging: 'The journey you and I would take wouldn't necessarily be the same, but they are all part of being Cree.' Inclusiveness is a Cree value. Within Cree culture there is myriad of life experiences among Cree peoples, and locating oneself honours the personal among the collective.

The methods of integrating self-location within Indigenous inquiry are many, and their manifestations differ among researchers. Graham Smith situates himself as Maori through a prologue to his research. Through prologue, personal story offers authenticity, and is recognized as integral to knowledge construction. The prologue is where the writing can shape-shift from an 'objective accounting' to holistic narrative, revealing how the self influences research choices and interpretations.

As a method for reflexivity during my research, I kept a reflective journal. This went beyond conventional field notes to a chronicling of my struggles, dreams, fears, hopes, and reflections. This excerpt is from my research journal:

> I am taking Cree, it is my first class today. Walking into the First Nations University there are Indians everywhere with shiny hair flying as both instructors and students race down the hall to class. The instructor is Cree, Plains Cree, he was raised with the language, says he has been teaching here forever. This class is full of young students, not just Indigenous but of a variety of colours and cultural offerings. Though I am comforted as the Instructor reads off the class list – Tootoosis, Cyr – these are names I know. These are the Crees. The Instructor asks who is Cree, we put up our hands. He asks why we do not know our language. He points to me. I say adopted. He nods.

My reflective journal is a mix of research observations, reading analysis, field notes, annotations of family dinners, ceremony, vibrant dreams, road trip reflections, my on and off relationship with French fries, and so forth. It was that process of consistently self-locating that assisted me in saying, 'I believe this to be true.'

Reflexivity was intensive within my journey. This may not be true for all Indigenous researchers. There is flexibility, though it does need to be evident in some manner to show contextualized knowing. It supposes self-knowledge. A Cree *kôkum* shares a memory of her personal history and the the fascination which the fabled attractions of modern life – such as lipstick or mail-order catalogues – held for her' (Ahenakew and Wolfart, 1998: 24). Such insights not only tell others of oneself, they tell self.

Purpose

Not long ago, I attended a workshop led by a non-Indigenous scholar who was presenting research on the socioeconomic conditions of Indigenous people. I felt that the research was fascinating and was curious as to the researcher's motivation. During the time allotted for questions, I asked him about his purpose for doing this research. What compelled him? To my mind, it was a fairly straightforward question about the motivations that provoked his study, yet he seemed a bit unsure of what I was asking. Afterward, I thought perhaps I was not clear about what I meant by purpose or maybe this just was not a common question. I was perplexed because by this time I had spent considerable energy focusing on Indigenous research approaches, and many Indigenous scholars were consistently saying that knowing one's own purpose and motivation for research was fundamental. This seemed consistent with Western research approaches, and yet my question seemed somehow out of place to that workshop leader. However, I knew instinctively that purpose – Indigenous style – and research curiosity were deeply linked.

Research questions anchor and direct research. There is much attention to the formulation of research questions within academic research, for they can be difficult to craft. The research question ought to be specific enough to render focused findings and at the same time allow for discovery. The research question can emerge from a personal curiosity or be tailored to a specific need as identified by the public or private sector. It can be developed solely by an individual researcher, a research team, or in collaboration with a community or a stakeholder (such as a research advisory committee). Regardless of the origin of the research question, it ought to respond to a need. Furthermore, the researcher should be able to show that there is a gap in the knowledge that the proposed research can assist in filling. Often, in research textbooks, the section on developing research questions is situated by the purpose statement.

In academic research design, there is an expectation that the researcher will identify through a purpose statement the reason behind conducting the research. Here the research indicates that the researcher's curiosity and the purpose statement help clarify the research question and plan. Within Indigenous methodologies, crafting a research question remains a necessity, though it may surface more organically. However, the purpose statement is more elasticized, asking for greater commentary on personal motivation.

In his paper entitled 'Memory Comes before Knowledge: Research May Improve if Researchers Remember Their Motives' (1995), Eber Hampton describes the relationship between memory and research. He advises researchers to go back in time to unfold the sacred medicine bundle that holds memories and consider how memory shapes personal truth. This matters because researchers need to know their personal motives for undertaking their research, and they are usually found in story. Indigenous research frameworks ask for clarity of both the academic and personal purpose, and it is the purpose statement within Indigenous research that asks: What is your purpose for this research? How is your motivation found in your story? Why and how does this research give back to community?

In Plains Cree knowledge, value is placed on experiential knowledge. Inherent within this perspective is the value of personal responsibility in maintaining good relationships. One maintains good research relationships by identifying one's purpose and motivations behind the actions. It is about being honest. Among the scholars I interviewed, there was a consistent belief that research should be collectively relevant. In their own research, the personal meaning was bound with community relevancy. Purposeful research was inseparable from the value in giving back, that what we do has to assist. Kathy Absolon expresses a decolonizing purpose of her research found in community relations: 'One of our core missions in decolonizing and in our life is to figure out who are we, and in order to do that you are not going to find that out in a university, in the absence of your peers and your culture.' In picking her research topic, Jeannine Carriere struggled to find a topic. After considering several options, then reconsidering, she found her research purpose (and subsequent question) in exploring the lives of Indigenous adoptees. A friend helped Jeannine focus her inquiry into the experience of Aboriginal adoptees, saying to her, 'That is who you are, that is your story and that is what you should be contributing.' Michael Hart articulates the connection between purpose and contemporary research. He says, 'I am doing this because we can't all live in teepees forever, ... our realities have changed, and they are going to continue to change.' These scholars demonstrate the strong connection between self, community, memory, reciprocity, and research. Deciding upon a research direction after having examined one's purpose makes its utility transparent and the research strong from day one.

Cultural Grounding

What does cultural grounding mean within an Indigenous research framework? For Indigenous research, cultural grounding is best defined within the context of a person's life and relationship with culture. As with non-Indigenous researchers, its significance may depend upon their life context and how they engage with culture. This

commentary defines cultural grounding as the way that culture nourishes the researcher's spirit during the inquiry, and how it nourishes
the research itself. There are levels of cultural involvement within
research. Some customs are shared openly, others privately. This needs
to be respected. Given this caveat, Indigenous research frameworks
reference cultural grounding specifically or generally, and permeate
the research in a manner consistent with the researcher's relationship
with his or her culture.

Blackfoot scholar Betty Bastien (1999) provides an example of cultural grounding in her research. Her study is an inquiry into the infusion of *Niitsitapi* (Blackfoot) ways of knowing into Bachelor of Social
Work curricula for the Niitsitapi community. It was couched within a
pre-existing relationship with community and utilized methodology
congruent with a Blackfoot worldview. She had a '*Kaahasinnon* –
Grandfather for the Sacred Horn Society' (1999: 88) guide her research.
The site of gaining knowledge from the grandmothers and grandfa-
thers was a convocation that integrated cultural protocols, gift offerings, food, ceremony, and prayer. This cultural guidance assisted her
in determining the parameters around sharing Niitsitapi knowledges
in the research. 'The guidance and advice shared by the grandparents
about common knowledge of the *Niitsitapi* I share here is meant to be
shared with the uninitiated' (ibid.: 95). By involving Elders, Bastien
was offering cultural grounding for the research itself.

Researchers incorporate ceremonial practices to show respect and
give protection to the knowledge shared. A Cree protocol is to offer
tobacco to teachers. Showing respect is a consistent value among most
tribal groups; the ritual for doing so is not. Thus, it becomes necessary
to locate a specific tribal ontology. Cultural grounding of the research
may involve ceremony, though the form of ceremony will depend
upon the tribal epistemology. These are significant considerations. (For
a more detailed discussion on protocol see Chapter 7.)

Encompassing culture is part of the notion of researcher-in-relation.
Betty Bastien's personal preparations for research involved visiting
sacred sites and participating in ceremony. Laara Fitznor spoke of the
personal sustenance that she gained from culture. There was a time
during her doctoral research when she was at a loss as to how to
proceed – her computer crashed with all her research on it. 'I smudged
my papers, I smudged my computer and I said, "you know Creator I
need help, help to get me onto the next stage." All of a sudden I had
this burst of energy and I just wrote.' She called upon spirit to see her

through. My own experience led me home. I had received dream knowledge that helped me to understand that my research necessitated a return. In Saskatchewan, I was able to connect culturally in a way unavailable to me in British Columbia. That said, grounding is not solely found in our ancestral territory. It can also be found in the larger Indigenous community. Returning to British Columbia, I participated in a Coast Salish ceremony on the morning of my doctoral defence. I left knowing that the ancestors stood with me.

The choices are many; there is no dogma. For this is about spirit and connecting with the ancestors. The extent to which the researcher chooses to share these efforts may be great or minimal. It does not matter that it is shared with all as there need be no thick descriptions here. What matters is that there is room within Indigenous research to acknowledge the meaningful role of culture within our inquiries.

A Conversation with Cam Willett

Cam Willett reflects upon how personal history informs purpose by sharing the motivations behind his decision to enter into doctoral studies and research.

Cam Willett is Cree from Little Pine First Nation in Saskatchewan. He received his doctoral degree from the Ontario Institute for Studies in Education, University of Toronto, and has been a post-secondary educator for many years. I offered Cam tobacco for his teachings and started by asking Cam some general questions about his background. First I asked Cam why he went back for a doctoral degree. This is his response:

MAGGIE: Cam, what precipitated you going back to get your doctorate?

CAM: Is it about community for me? I guess, but it seems more personal. I was thinking about that as you were talking and remembering. I think about my elementary education and my secondary education, and which were fine until Grade 12. I dropped out of school because of a lot of life pressures. I was working full-time and had an hour-and-a-half bus ride to school and back. One day, these three teachers ambushed me in the hallway – going from one to the next to the next – saying things about me, 'You sleep in my class, you're really lazy.' I stood up and said, 'Well, fine, I quit,' or whatever, and walked down the hallway. The vice-principal was walking down the hallway, and I say to him, 'I quit right now.' He said, 'Well, you should think about it.' And I said, 'No.' I got on the phone and I called my dad. He came and drove an hour to the school, and we sat down with the vice-principal. He said I should think about this and that, but I couldn't be convinced. That was it for me. I went to Saskatoon and started delivering pizza and worked for a while, then went back to school.

I think the reason I am talking about this is because at that time I was thinking to myself, 'Gee, am I really capable of graduating from Grade 12? Can I do this?' I was really questioning my intellectual ability and whatever. I used to think, 'Yeah, I could,' because I remembered my experiences from before where I did pretty well at school. I am a fairly smart guy, I could do it. So, after going through a lot, I didn't really have any choice. I went back to school. I did great and my confidence was restored, and so I went into university. It was just sort of the logical thing. What else was I going to do?

So why did I start my Ph.D. program? Because it's related to all that. I was coming out of my master's program and the opportunity was there. I knew it wouldn't always be there, and I felt I should just do it. At this point, I was starting to wonder what the heck I am doing this for. How will this benefit my community? How does it benefit me, even? I think my major reason for continuing is to finish what I have started. You don't want to just bail. I know I can do this and that's my motivation. As a young person, thinking back about my experience in high school, a lot of that was pure racism. Today, I know that, and at the time I was trying to figure it out. Has it made me happier to know that racism is so powerful in this province, in this country, today? I don't know. I find now that I can't read the newspaper. I just sort of skim through it. My mind deconstructs everything very quickly and it's frustrating. I deconstruct everything, my mind is less – I wouldn't say it's totally decolonized – but it's certainly a lot less colonized than it was. I don't know. What good does that do? I guess there is a benefit in teaching for the students that are there. It's not just me instructing them to teach the same old colonial curriculum. I don't want my students to go off into Black Lake and teach colonial curriculum. That's not what I am teaching them, I want them to be critical.

When I was taking a course in a master's program, I was talking to my professor during a break, and we were talking about how far I would go in my program. Would I become a faculty member or would I get a Ph.D.? Of course, when you are a student you have the privilege of being radical. You can go into a classroom and say, 'I defy school. I think we should tear down all the universities because it's all bullshit.' But then he pointed out to me, 'Well, you know, if you don't get the Ph.D., will people ever listen to you? Will Western-minded people ever value what you have to say?' That's the thing. It's these two worlds that we are living in. The one world you are honoured with the eagle feather and the other world you are honoured with the doctoral degree. Maybe that's one of the big reasons why I wanted to finish the Ph.D. I guess finishing is partly for validation, though it's not really that important to me. But if that's what it takes for people to listen to you, well then ...

You know, we were saying something about feeling alone and that was a pivotal point in my research. The first year you're learning all this Western stuff, reading all these books that don't have anything Aboriginal, and you're the only Aboriginal person in these classes with no Aboriginal faculty. You start to feel really alone. I think when you do any ceremony, you do reach some of these portals, and you do realize that you're not alone. People are always talking about the language disappearing, cultures disappearing. I think that's a load of bull, because if you put your tobacco down and you go to ceremonies, I believe that all transcends time and space. You can't be lost or killed because all you have to do is sweat and ask, and the songs will come back to you. That's the power of them. Our knowledge and legacy can never be erased. We are very strong and that makes me proud. The legacy of our people is this land.

Cam alerted me to several significant qualities of Indigenous research during our conversation. He affirmed Hampton's advice that knowing purpose is wise in any endeavour, and that we find purpose within our personal narrative. When Cam spoke of his high school experience, I was taken back to memories of elementary school and how the residue from it left me questioning my abilities. What were *my* motivations for returning to school? Would I have pursued doctoral studies if I did not feel that I had something left to prove to the educational system? And when does that stop? The conversation got me thinking.

We talked about story, purpose, self, and the relevance of being holistically true to one's worldview. Was it okay to apply a worldview (e.g., feminist, Indigenous) to our research but not practise it in our lives? It was not really a question about the merits of purity or applying an impossible orthodoxy to one's life. Rather, Cam's point was that epistemology ought to be congruent with life choices in general, not just in research. I was reminded of the holism inherent in Indigenous epistemologies and thought of how we teach research methodology classes in Western universities. We assume that people can select methodologies solely in relation to a research curiosity without a reflection on the self. No wonder it can be a 'head trip.'

Cam spoke about the traditional knowledges that value dreams, the ancestors, and the timelessness of ceremonies, and I knew that regardless of whether they were identified in our methodologies, they were guiding our search for knowledge. I left the conversation with Cam, knowing that Indigenous research frameworks require a purpose statement about one's own self-location and worldview, and that this meant honouring the *kôkoms* and *mosôms* by remembering them. Right off the bat, this was no small order. Knowing why we are carrying out research – our motive – has the potential to take us to places that involve both the head and heart. We need to know our own research story to be accountable to self and community.

7 Indigenous Research Methods and Interpretation

In the previous chapters, there has been a reflective analysis that suggests a range of qualities consistent with Indigenous inquiry. Thus far, there have been arguments for the use of Indigenous research frameworks, the significance of incorporating a decolonizing lens within Indigenous inquiry, and insight into how tribal epistemologies undergird tribal-based approaches to research. There has been attention to story as knowing within Indigenous inquiry and the centrality of self-location, as well a cultural and personal grounding within Indigenous research frameworks. The ways in which these qualities are manifested within Indigenous methodologies vary and shape-shift, resulting in an array of research decision points that need to be aligned.

This chapter focuses on the considerations that accompany these research choices, including the knowledge-gathering methods, sampling, and protocols that take on a particular character within Indigenous methodologies. In addition to highlighting the various challenges and possibilities that arise in the practicalities of Indigenous inquiry, the discussion moves to the complexities of analysing data and making meaning within tribal interpretations. While a host of qualities within Indigenous research frameworks, as put forth in previous chapters, are an integral aspect of knowledge production, it is within an applied context of methods and meaning-making, within the details, that the process becomes concrete.

Because research is about the weighty endeavour of creating new knowledge, it can provoke haughtiness from those who have the acquired skills and arouse fear in those new to the field. My anecdotal observations tell me that research courses in both undergraduate and graduate programs are what students dread most. This is unfortunate because, as Eber Hampton (1995) states, research is fundamentally about learning and ought to be looked upon as such. Still, for the Indigenous researcher coyote medicine lurks in the air as we strive to incorporate methods, arrive at meaning, and present research in a manner that is congruent with Indigenous epistemologies and understood by the non-Indigenous community. That I felt coyote nearby as I wrote this 'methods' chapter is not surprising, for there is no one way to perform tribal-centred research, which explains my hesitancy to include a methods chapter that could be taken up as such. The isolation of method, methodology, and epistemology from each other suggests that each component can work independently rather than as an interdependent relational research framework.

In sitting with this discomfort, I paused to consider the variety of ways that methodology is understood. The narrower understandings of methodology focus primarily on research methods (e.g., data collection and coding; see Alford, 1998), while a broader definition of methodology enlarges the discussion to incorporate the theoretical assumptions about choice of methods or procedure (Creswell, 2003). Pillow suggests that if one believes that methodology is solely comprised of method, then one also ignores the depth of knowing that is found within its epistemological foundations (2003: 185). Expectations of methodology are unambiguous when approaching research from within a qualitative research paradigm – that is, one's methodological choice should encompass both theory and methods. While qualitative researchers may cite methods separate from methodology, they accept that epistemology, theory, and methods need to be in alignment and that methods are drawn from the choice of methodology (Kirby et al., 2006: 125). Throughout this text, this perspective has been upheld and an attempt has been made not to isolate (or elevate) any one particular aspect of the research process. That said, there is a need to focus attention on specific knowledge-gathering methods and their implications within Indigenous research frameworks.

Who we are as researchers cannot help but influence our choice of epistemological framework and theoretical lens, and it follows that this will influence the choice of methods. Some find comfort with qualitative methods, some instinctively choose quantitative approaches, and others yet prefer to avoid human subject research altogether. The partiality towards a particular method has bearing in the personal, social, and cultural construct of the researcher's experience. It is not uncommon for student researchers to identify a particular method as the first decision of their research design, often before developing the research question itself. However, as the research question is formulated and honed within a qualitative design, the research framework shifts. In concert, the epistemic positioning of the chosen methodology becomes increasingly paramount. While decisions about the appropriate theoretical lens, methodology, and method are made in a strategic manner to best respond to the inquiry question, there can be no denying that method preference is influential in determining the research journey. I knew that I had a preference to hear stories and gain insight from words. My research curiosity allowed me that opportunity. In making that decision – a clear epistemic position – the number of research methods narrowed and the strategy came into focus. After making this decision, I had to consider the implications for story as a method of gathering knowledge in an Indigenous research framework.

Why story matters within Indigenous inquiry was discussed more fully in Chapter 5. However, story needs further exploration specific to a method discussion. A first matter for consideration in using story as a knowledge-gathering method is ensuring that the research question is open enough for the task. This is a concern for all qualitative researchers conducting narrative exploratory research, and so is not particular to Indigenous methodologies. The second matter concerns choosing a structure – be it interviews or focus groups – to hear the stories. The selection of a method for hearing stories does have specific implications for Indigenous inquiry.

When it comes to Indigenous research methods, there is a continuum of ways to access information. This continuum runs from the most personal, internal knowledges that guide our research to the external knowledge that comes from others. There are a variety of data collection methods that we use to capture this type of research (e.g., storytelling, research circles, conversations, journalling). There are distinctive means of gathering outward knowledges that align with tribal epistemology and are generally less researcher-dependent, where the researcher's needs dominate the research interview. Highly structured interviews are not congruent with accessing knowledges that imbue both the fluidity and regulation of the storyteller's role within oral tradition, or that respond to the relational nature of Indigenous research.

Methods that are congruent with tribal epistemology include approaches such as a conversational method that involves an open-ended structure that is flexible enough to accommodate principles of

native oral traditions, and is thus differentiated from a more traditional interview process. Conversation as method is unlike standard
structured or semi-structured interviews that place external parameters on the research participant's narrative. An open-structured conversational method shows respect for the participant's story and
allows research participants greater control over what they wish to
share with respect to the research question. It is an approach that may
take longer and require more sessions than with highly structured
interviews. Sharing circles, as utilized in Laara Fitznor's research, is an
open-ended method that invites story. Research-sharing circles have
recently surfaced as a method for gathering group knowledge in academic and applied research. For many tribal cultures, the act of sitting
in circle, as a collective means of decision-making, is familiar. This
form of knowledge-gathering is based upon cultural tradition and has
been adapted to contemporary settings as research.

One may wonder how research-sharing circles differ from focus
groups. Laara Fitznor explains that the tribal protocol around the
social encounter within a circle differs from the epistemological
underpinnings of a focus group. She says, 'When you ask about the
quality difference from the focus group, it is that everybody gets a
chance for input. I was prepared to be there for a good one, two, three,
five hours.' While protocols may differ according to tribal group, there
is a general set of guidelines around research-sharing circles. They nor-
mally require the accompaniment of food, and there is a meditative
acknowledgment of all those who are in the circle, including the ancestors that sit with us. An Elder or cultural person often leads the circle.
Like the conversational method, the research-sharing circle is a
method to engender story. It is meant to provide space, time, and an
environment for participants to share their story in a manner that they
can direct.

There are several differences between these methods and more
highly structured research data-gathering approaches. These methods
are more elastic, and this gives research participants an opportunity to
share their story on a specific topic without the periodic disruptions
involved in adhering to a structured approach, as in an interview
format. Research participants accustomed to the oral tradition of
sharing through story will self-regulate their response to ensure that
the question is being respected and answered. They will also provide
the necessary contextual detail. It becomes less about research participants responding to research questions, and more about the partici-

pants sharing their stories in relation to the question. They may do this in a direct or indirect fashion. Even within story-gathering methods, it is wise to alert participants as to what the research is about so that they have an opportunity to consider what they wish to share. When asking participants for their stories, the researcher must be an able listener and be comfortable with the fluidity of story. The onus is upon the researcher to honour this more exploratory approach and try not to interrupt a story through repdirectional prompting. This means that interrupting a story to 'get back to the question' is not recommended. Robina Thomas reflects on the organic flow of story: 'The beauty of storytelling is that it allows storytellers to use their voices and tell their own stories on their own terms' (2005: 242). The power lies with the research participant, the storyteller. This would doubtless frustrate those interested in a 'just the facts' approach. However, for those who value story as knowledge, this method allows for a breadth of knowing to enter into the research conversation that the researcher alone may not have considered.

not Valid Knowledge

Using open-structured methods, the task of researchers is to intuitively respond to the stories, to share as necessary their own understandings, and to be active listeners. Because sharing story triggers memory, the conversation may bring forth a range of human emotions, so the researcher needs to be prepared. Indigenous research frameworks have a decolonizing agenda that involves healing and transformation. When asking Indigenous people for their stories in research, a researcher must be aware that the choice of this method opens a door for healing associated with decolonization. This may manifest itself on a personal level or more generally, but with story there are responsibilities accompanying this approach that the researcher must accept in using such methods.

Research is imbued with a power hierarchy, with the researcher having final control over the research design, data collection, and interpretation. The choice of methods is a solid indicator of the power dynamic at work. The more structured the method, the more control the researcher maintains (Ryen, 2000). Given the extractive, exploitive history of research within Indigenous communities, efforts to mitigate power differentials in all aspects of research are warranted, whether using an Indigenous methodological approach or not. The attention to methods should encompass both pragmatic and political considerations.

Other method decisions within Indigenous inquiry, such as sampling, call forth similar tensions. Sampling is largely dependent upon whether the researcher is interested in generalizations or theory development. Once that is determined, there is a range of strategies for selecting a sample population for research. Probability sampling is equivalent to random sampling of a population group, and it is often used when a goal of the research is to generalize findings. Non-probability sampling is used when the goal is theory development, thus it is often a sampling technique found within qualitative designs. Purposive sampling or criterion sampling suggests that a sample population has been selected for a specific reason, while snowball sampling indicates a small number of individuals who were selected for a study because of particular characteristics (Somekh and Lewin, 2005).

Within Indigenous research frameworks, the relational quality of Indigenous inquiry manifests itself in a special way when it comes to selecting people for research. In conducting her research, Indigenous scholar Cora Weber-Pillwax notes the relationship factor. She says that she connected with people she had known for years, 'not in terms of knowing their personalities, but knowing their connections' (1999: 170). Michael Hart comments that his research participants are those with whom he has some form of pre-existing relationship. Relationship was a central theme that re-emerged and had particular relevance in discussions of methods because people make contact with their community and need to have that relationship in place to offset the mistrust of research within Indigenous communities. Laara Fitznor comments that, in her research, part of the relational aspect of sampling is directly connected to the trustworthiness of the researcher. She says that people choose to be a part of her research because they know her and she has a good reputation in the community. To have an identity as an Indigenous researcher is not necessarily enough (though it helps) to establish trust. There also has to be evidence that the Indigenous researcher is approaching this work respectfully. Because of the relational factor in sampling, it is not simply a matter of the researcher choosing the participants. This process is more reciprocal.

Inward knowledges are equally important within Indigenous inquiry, and so there need to be methods to record these types of knowing so that they become a formal part of the meaning-making aspect of research. On the significance of inward knowledges as method, Kathy Absolon shares this perspective: 'We will hear people say that our methodologies exist in our dreams, in our fast ... by community forums, by sitting in circles and by engaging in ceremony.'

Recognition of inward knowing flows naturally if one is coming from a tribal epistemic positioning. Methods for this form of knowing are varied. As mentioned by Absolon, the methods of engaging with this knowledge can emerge through fasts, ceremonies, and dreams, as well as through walks in nature, or silence. Michael Hart referenced dream knowledges. The method that I used to document this way of knowing was a journal. However, other options exist. For example, Jeannine Carriere used a portfolio, similar to a journal, to write her feelings, intuitions, and reflections on the research process. This was a place for her to reflect upon the holistic knowledge that informed her research. While we need to protect these types of knowledge, Graham Smith maintains that it is clear that there should be no need to justify them. It is likely that this form of knowledge matters to non-Indigenous researchers; however, the crucial difference is that Indigenous researchers count inward ways of knowing as part of knowledge construction and referencing methods, subsequently legitimizing them in academic research.

An aspect of Indigenous inquiry associated with methods is the use of cultural protocol, which is a set of guidelines for interacting with those holders of knowledge whom a researcher seeks out. Cultural protocol varies depending upon the tribal practices. Within research, the tribal epistemology identified in the research framework and advisory committee for the research will determine the protocol used. In my study, several researchers of Cree ancestry referenced as protocol the use of tobacco as a gift that signifies respect and reciprocity. Cree researchers Michael Hart and Laara Fitznor respectfully spoke about approaching Elders and research participants with tobacco. Ethical protocols in research work hand-in-hand with cultural protocols. Ethical protocols in research respond to the political dimension of research within Indigenous contexts and protect against previous extractive approaches to research. (For greater discussion of ethics, see Chapter 8.) Overall, protocol is about respect. From that perspective, it applies to all aspects of the research process, and the researcher needs to be aware of protocol for the particular context and/or tribal epistemology being used. Indigenous advisory committees for research are helpful here.

With story as method, a number of practicalities surface. Indigenous researchers sometimes express discomfort in recording research conversations. However, to keep the stories alive, this approach has its defenders. During the early days of the Federated Saskatchewan

Indian College, there was discussion as to whether cultural knowledges should be recorded. Cree Elder Jim Kâ-Nîpitêhtêw welcomed his teachings, which were on the Treaty Six pipestem, being recorded 'so that our relatives might learn by hearing about it in this way' (cited in Stevenson, 2000: 238). Laara Fitznor explained to her research participants that the use of tape recorders was the best way of ensuring that their voice came through as truly as possible. Another issue involves the use of transcripts. Fitznor explains that she transcribed the research interviews herself as a means of protecting the words of her research participants: 'That's why for me it was good for me to transcribe as opposed to somebody else because they might have excluded it because well that's not part of the participants so they might exclude Elders' words.'. I found transcribing interviews exceedingly beneficial and powerful. It was a way to relive those conversations with people and to hear the stories anew. Jeannine Carriere shares how the process of transcribing evoked a transformative moment in her research: 'There I was, transcribing tapes and writing, in my head, and not connecting in my heart and my soul, wait a minute this is where it all happened for you Jeannine.' These are but a few examples of how various Indigenous research methods are taken up. As Indigenous methodologies grow, discussion of Indigenous methods will flourish.

Indigenous researchers have been constricted by the limitations of Western sites of research. Indigenous researchers have included cultural methods by incorporating them in the research design, but not as formal data-collection methods. For example, Patricia Steinhauer (2001) shares that she facilitated a talking circle to prepare her participants for the research, then conducted interviews to collect the data. Research-sharing circles have only recently appeared as a formal data-collection method. This has less to do with debate on the inherent effectiveness of Indigenous methods, and more to do with the legitimization process within knowledge centres. The manner in which the Western tradition confers legitimacy upon a specific method is through the theoretical and practical investigations emerging from research and its subsequent publication. The method is recognized as valid and as being utilized by more researchers.

Written publication is central in establishing legitimacy; oral culture, of course, does not have a history of following this tradition. Many concede that engaging with Western research involves acknowledging such traditions. We do not, however, have an extensive history within academia. In crafting a research framework consistent with Indigenous epistemology and methods it complicates matters when there is limited literature to reference. Thus, part of our task as Indigenous researchers is to both use Indigenous methods and publish findings.

Gathering knowledge is an intrinsically rewarding aspect of research. Interpreting data and presenting those interpretations is less congenial for many researchers. Thematic groupings conflict with making meaning holistically. Analysis for the learner is the task of the learner, not necessarily the researcher. This is in contrast with much of Western research. If we choose to write our research findings, then we must find form and content that honours them. Form and content must reflect the conceptual, the enigmatic, the tangible, and the schema of our frameworks. The insights rise up from the passion and toil of self-in-relation. If it all comes together, the process cannot be separated from the product because they belong together, they complete each other. Making meaning within Indigenous inquiry demands this much.

Meaning Making within Indigenous Inquiry

As an educator and researcher, I believe that the time has come to break the cycle of dependency, and to begin research from within the tribal paradigms of indigenous cultures. Research must be designed to explore solutions to problems from within the tribal interpretation.

– Bastien, (1999)

Blackfoot scholar Betty Bastien asserts that returning to our tribal core will snap the line of colonialist dependency upon Western empiricism and disenfranchise the colonial project. She calls for Indigenous people to engage in an epistemological reckoning, to open us to the full cosmological ontology and the breadth and sophistication of the conceptual mappings flowing from our tribal knowings. My sense from Bastien and others is that we have to find a way back to core values of what is responsible, respectful, and kind, to that which is ours not someone else's. Waking up to a new fully decolonized day would be wonderful if unlikely. The process is more fluid and modestly incremental with 'strategic concessions' all over the place, but we are making headway. After all, co-dependency is one wicked little web from which to disentangle. Reclaiming tribal interpretations within contemporary sites requires many minds, and so the following offers initial thoughts on interpretation within Indigenous research. To begin, it helps to sort through qualitative meaning-making generally.

Qualitative research methods involve both interpretive and analytical approaches to finding meaning from the insights of an inquiry. Interpretation and analysis are simply two ways of understanding the world. Interpretive meaning-making involves a subjective accounting of social phenomena as a way of giving insight or to clarify an event. It involves an inductive way of knowing. Analysis involves reducing a whole to the sum of its parts in order to explain a phenomenon. Research analysis within the majority of qualitative approaches requires the organizational grouping of data for the purpose of showing patterns that build a theory. Analysis works to decontextualize knowledge through the organizational act of sorting data. The practice involves working with transcripts to arrive at a 'meaning unit,' or what is commonly referred to as coding (Ely et al., 2001: 162). Depending upon the qualitative methodology, there may be more emphasis on contextual interpretation (i.e., autoethnography) or on thematic analysis (i.e., grounded theory).

With respect to presenting findings, theorists such as Harry Wolcott argue that there are three components. 'Wolcott (1994) made distinctions between three aspects of qualitative writing … description, analysis and interpretation' (quoted in Ely et al., 2001: 160). Ely et al. go on to stress that while the three are often viewed as separate within the research process, the researcher engages with all three ways of knowing throughout the entirety of the research process. In focusing on the analytical aspect of research, Kirby et al. suggest that within social science research there is an 'analytical ladder' that moves in a linear manner and includes epistemological issues, theoretical issues, contemporary issues, social issues, and lived experience (2006: 219). They further suggest that inductive qualitative research utilizes this conceptual framework to organize, understand, and record data. In line with this perspective, Potts and Brown (2005) say that making meaning also includes clarity as to whom the research is going to benefit, recognizes the implications, and accepts the responsibilities of the knowledge that one is constructing.

The more conventional analysis of research is a reductive way of knowing, and contrasts with Indigenous epistemologies that are non-fragmentary and holistic (Atleo, 2004). This is where there is a fundamental divergence between Indigenous and analytically based Western research. This is not to say that Indigenous peoples did not rely on a form of analysis, if analysis means observing patterns and behaviours and making sense of those observations. In many Indigenous communities, individuals with the training and experience to inductively analyse patterns were the knowledge-keepers and were highly esteemed. Scholars such as Deloria (1991) and Cajete (1999) have documented this form of knowing within Indigenous knowledge systems. However, the patterns and observations were highly contextualized and particular, and did not assume that this knowledge could or should be generalized to other instances.

J.P. Spardley established a six-level grid of generalities in research. It helps to situate highly contextualized analysis. Level One is equal to universal statements, while Level Six encompasses 'specific incident statements: writing that takes the reader immediately to a particular behaviour or particular events, demonstrating cultural knowledge in action' (quoted in Coffey and Atkinson, 1996: 117). From this perspective, an Indigenous knowledge system would align with a Level Six analysis. While there is emerging scholarship on meaning-making generated from inductive analysis, there is little that informs research writing (Indigenous or not). How to interpret and present self-in-relation analysis has not been explored deeply, leaving it open to new ideas. The presentation of story in research is an increasingly common method of presenting finding. Interpreting meaning from stories that do not fragment or decontextualize the knowledge they hold is more challenging. In response, some Indigenous researchers have incorporated a mixed-method approach that offers both interpretative meaning-making and some form of thematic analysis.

The interpretative aspect of qualitative research is less of a conundrum than thematic analysis because tribal knowledge systems value the interpretative and the subjective. The process of interpreting and making meaning within Indigenous inquiry is equally systematic, though less linear. For Indigenous researchers, there is a propensity to present findings in story form. Thus, the stories are introduced, often condensed. As with most qualitative research, they go through a member check. The stories stand, with the researcher reflecting upon the stories. Working with story as a means of making meaning requires that the research be presented in its contextualized form. In her research, Laara Fitznor integrated thematic coding, but was clear that the individual research stories were presented as much as possible in their own voice. The truths of the stories are held within the life context of the storyteller. While another storyteller may share a similar experience, truth cannot be abstracted from the life.

The use of procedures that organize knowledge to Western terms limits Indigenous cultural inquiries. Until the conventional qualitative approaches of coding data and presenting findings as a standardized activity prevail, the Indigenous researcher will likely have to utilize a mixed method approach for her research to be seen as credible within the larger research community. I used mixed methods to ensure that a story was available for interpretive analysis by others. This allowed for story and self-in-relation interpretations and integrated thematic groupings. An interesting anecdotal note is that the thematic grouping section of my research is often referred to as 'the findings,' as opposed to both the condensed stories *and* the thematic groupings *or* the stories alone. This suggests to me that there is still work to do. The decolonizing response is for Indigenous researchers (and their allies) to build scholarship in this important aspect of research.

The conventional scholarship demand for written findings creates complexities for Indigenous forms of inquiry. Within qualitative research, 'interpretation means drawing meanings from the analyzed data and attempting to see these in some large context' (Ely et al., 2001: 160). The expectation of the majority of qualitative research methodologies is that the findings will be presented in some categorical way, usually in a written report. Writing is a process of defining, thus the power resides in the writer; it is reciprocal, but only to an extent. This contradicts oral culture, where, as Winona Stevenson (2000) suggests, the analysis is the responsibility of readers to take what they need from the teachings. Much has been written on the topic, but it requires still further research and examination.

In considering how meaning is made within an Indigenous research framework, I wish to close with a note on research credibility. As with research methodology, research itself can be defined broadly as a search for knowledge, focusing on new knowledges for purposes of learning (Hampton, 1995). Qualitative research concerns itself with uncovering knowledge through human subject research via observations and inquiry into phenomena. Qualitative research does not claim to arrive at generalizations arising from research and is more associated with theory development. On a more specific level, qualitative research has been conventionally defined as a set of techniques (methodologies) used to respond to a question connecting 'theoretical claims, method and empirical claims (evidence)'

(Schwandt, 2007: 265). Evidence and credibility within research are closely aligned.

The credibility of research findings is generally evaluated according to the trustworthiness of the methodology used for accessing said information. In an effort to ensure credible research, considerable effort and thought have been invested into standardizing research methods and analysis. Each specific methodology has its own 'code,' but that code does not stray too far from the standards of other methodologies. For example, grounded theory has its own set procedures, participatory action research uses its particular methodology, and so forth. While different approaches allow for some flexibility, the methods and theory behind a particular methodology have been agreed upon and affirmed by the scholars who conduct that form of research, even if the standard or code may not always be visible. The degree to which a research framework identifies and then follows the agreed upon procedures for a specific methodology is an influential factor in determining the credibility of the research. Researchers within a given discipline will evaluate the credibility of that research, assessing the extent to which methodological procedures have been followed. It is a system that has both its strengths and drawbacks for all those engaging in Western research.

For Indigenous research frameworks founded on tribal epistemologies, this poses a specific sort of dilemma. Research carried out through Indigenous methodologies, of necessity, requires individuals who are in a position to evaluate both the framework and subsequent findings according to specific procedural guidelines and protocols. Arguably, this responsibility should rest with the Indigenous researchers who hold this knowledge. At present, the Indigenous research community is small, and there is a dearth of writing on meaning-making within Indigenous inquiry. Clearly, more scholarship based on Indigenous research frameworks is needed. This will ensure that Indigenous research practice, method, findings, and meanings will be judged as credible according to tribal epistemologies. Without work in this area, Indigenous inquiry is vulnerable to being misjudged.

To uphold a tribal methodology that is congruent with a tribal compass, we first need to commit to its values and demands. After making this commitment, it becomes a matter of absorbing the vernacular of research language. For Indigenous researchers, there are often three audiences with whom we engage for transferring the knowledge of our research: (a) findings from Indigenous research must makes sense to the general Indigenous community, (b) schema for arriving at our findings must be clearly articulated to the non-Indigenous academy, and (c) both the means for arriving at the findings and the findings themselves must resonate with other Indigenous researchers who are in the best position to evaluate our research. We can choose to disengage from either of these communities, but if we enter into academia we must traverse these different worlds.

A Conversation with Laara Fitznor

What follows is an excerpt from my conversation with scholar Laara Fitznor. In sharing her research story, she highlights the intricacies involved within the pragmatics of Indigenous methodologies.

Laara Fitznor is a Cree woman from northern Manitoba. She completed her doctorate in education through the Department of Adult Education, Community Development and Counselling Psychology at the Ontario Institute for Studies in Education (OISE) at the University of Toronto in 2002. Laara is a faculty member at the University of Manitoba, and has been cutting trail for Indigenous people in education for many years. It was personally meaningful to have an opportunity to speak with a female Cree scholar who has completed her doctoral research and has stayed true to the Nêhiýaw ways and herself.

I had the opportunity to meet with Laara a couple of times prior to this interview. We both presented at a Canadian Studies conference in Scotland and at the *Shawane Dagosiwin* Aboriginal research conference, the latter of which Laara was a key organizer. We met at her office, where she told me her story. I was particularly intrigued by what I understood to be her Cree approach to research sampling and methods of gathering data.

MAGGIE: Laara, what was your research topic? Could you talk a little bit about that?

LAARA: At the time, there was an Aboriginal circle of educators [in Winnipeg] which was called the Aboriginal Teachers Circle. I got involved with the Teachers Circle, and as I sat with [them], I began observing what was unfolding. [They were talking about] issues around advocacy, racism, isolation in the workplace, wanting to incorporate Aboriginal perspectives. [I was] trying to understand them, trying to work in an Aboriginal way with Aboriginal knowings and processes. In observing a number of things, I started to think, 'Geez, maybe I can do something with my research that involves this group, to look at their stories.' In that sense, you look at a methodology. I wasn't wondering what methodology I would use. I would be getting the stories from them with the basic question being, How do Aboriginal teachers or educators see their experience as Aboriginal professionals who work in primarily Eurocentric systems?

They [Aboriginal Teachers Circle] were excited. I was excited about the idea, and everybody wanted to be interviewed. They were telling me that they had stories to tell. I had worked with my thesis advisor. I said I would like to work with the educators circle. Of course, then you are up against all kinds of things that they talk about in research, such as saying that you can't be too close to your subjects. One of the things that he [the supervisor] recommended was a pilot study with the group. Instead of doing that, I had these initial observations, which were in lieu of a pilot study, I developed in my proposal from what I observed. There were five themes, which ended up being themes of the stories. I worked with my committee, saying, 'Now I have got something here, to interview the teachers one-on-one, and to do sharing circles.' Those were methodologies. The sharing circles, the one-on-one interviews, and working with our medicines, such as tobacco. Offering tobacco, much like you did, to the participants, explaining what that is all about, and if people were not comfortable to take it, I wouldn't expect them to take it, that it's just a little gift. The people who were part of the Teachers Circle already knew that smudging was part of opening meetings there. There wasn't anything new that I was doing. It would be unusual for somebody in the circle not to know about these practices.

The sharing circles were a common thing happening in the community and in the schools, so a lot of people knew about sharing circles. I was talking of a research circle/talking circle where I could ask questions and people would share what they had to share. I was actually doing this in terms of methods. Because I knew circles would be known and familiar for the group, as opposed to, 'I am going to come and ask you questions.' Following the circle, I had intended to interview maybe one person from each circle, just to further clarify ...

I was hired to teach at OISE [Ontario Institute for Studies in Education in Toronto], and I knew that I gotta collect my data before I go [leave Winnipeg]. That pushed me to do data collection with the circles, because I had already done the biographical survey. I called the members, as many as possible, particularly the ones that submitted their surveys. They were all willing. I think everybody said yes. I panicked because I wanted to do a simple random sample, selecting only so many of them, but I thought if I am working in a Cree way, this is forfeiting my Cree perspective. So what do I do? I included everybody, which meant that I would have as many circles as people want, because I am getting data from people that you can always merge anyway. I thought, okay, sharing circles are not written up in any research methodology, in a methods book. I saw focus groups, so I wrote a long rationale in the initial part of my research explaining the importance for sharing circles. They both get at maybe the same information, but in focus groups people are just talking and in sharing circles it is quite different. It is more of a ceremonial, sacred space where I am building in the cultural pieces of it, as opening and closing with an acknowledgment or a prayer, and opening with a smudge. I used tobacco offerings.

In two of my five circles, I had an Elder that was involved. I had the Elder do an opening or closing for two of my circles. The premise was to bring an Elder into each of my circles, but I couldn't organize it for three of them. When I couldn't [have an Elder in attendance] I did the opening and the closing. I have done so much work with circles in my own teaching and in my own development through sitting in Elders circles, whether it's in the lodge, sweat lodges, or just sitting around listening to Elders talk and having an opportunity for people to respond and talk about themselves and who they are, their own developments. I have team-taught with Elders, so I have learned a lot from Elders.

When I was doing the circles, when you ask about the quality difference from the focus group, [it] is that everybody gets a chance for input, everybody has that air time, they can take as long as they want. I was prepared to be there for a good one, two, three, five hours. I reminded each of them about that, because a lot of them knew sharing circles. I said, 'Keep in mind that although I am saying this could be around two hours, likely it might be more.' I think they were all about two to three hours. When each person

spoke, sometimes it seemed ten minutes, twenty minutes, sometimes a half an hour. When we went through another round, it
would be the same. The smallest size circle that I had was three,
which was interesting because there was supposed to be five or six
of us, but three couldn't show up, and it so happened that the
Elder was there, a young man, and myself.

It's still a circle. I saw one [of] your comments, the part on intuition. I know this happens to me a lot in terms of being guided by
the Creator. I think I made some mention of it, that it [this circle]
was needed for the young man, just for the three of us to be there.
The Elder did the opening, listened while this person spoke, and
[then] did the closing. The things that the person spoke about were
really fascinating, so it was almost like it was needed for that to
happen. I did the usual thing in terms of tobacco, and everybody
was okay with recording because I told them ahead of time. I said
that I could either take notes or try to remember after, but I said, to
really get the essence of your voice, I think recording would be the
next best thing. That is what we did. The other thing I did was,
let's say that one educator might not feel comfortable being in a
circle with another. I would make sure they were not in the same
circle. Or say, well, there is safety in there, it's your voice and the
person knows it's your voice. They know me, I have a good reputation and they know that I would be trustworthy.

The relationship is very important, and I did a lot of follow-up,
too. What I did in terms of making space, creating the space to
reflect on our traditions, our culture, our ways, and our knowledge, was before the circle. I would have a mini-feast. I prepared
the food myself, whether it was bannock and stew or bannock and
chili. I would prepare food, also keeping it open; if they needed to
bring their kids they could. That happened in a couple of
instances. In one instance, the child was old enough that she could
play off on her own while we were in circle. And in the other
instance, the kid was in the circle, running around, [*laughter*]
driving us crazy. That was kind of neat. I didn't want to say, 'Well,
this is my work, don't interrupt me,' because that is not our way.
Your kids are part of it, so how can I then say, 'Oh no, don't bring
them.'

You find a way to work it in, [even if] it takes longer. I mean,
that took a long time, about four hours, but that was okay. I was
talking about the opening and the closing. I think that there was

one circle where one of the participants was known to do Elder or traditional work, so I offered her the tobacco and asked her to open the circle for us, and that was okay.

MAGGIE: How did you handle things like consent forms?

LAARA: Well, these were all educators. I didn't go into a community, which I think might have been a different sense. I mean, they are used to stuff being written and signed and everything. They were okay with this, they were signing it ahead of time ... Again, it's the trust, the relationships, they know who I am. In the one-on-one interview, I did the same thing, I prepared food. In one case, I went to somebody's office and interviewed her and went through the same tobacco offering. This is where [consent forms] with methodologies or research ethics that you want to protect people's anonymity for various reason, for good reason, because people know each other. Although people will know that I interviewed one of eighty-eight people that are listed, they will not know who I interviewed.

In terms of a methodology, I didn't really name a methodology. What I did was talk about the inquiry, listening to the stories and providing meaning to the stories, what the teachers [were giving as] meaning to the stories through description and an analysis of their stories. I wanted to compare these to what Indigenous scholars were saying. The difficulty I was having with methodologies was getting them to fit what I was doing. I noticed you talk about allied methodologies. In one sense, that is kind of what I did. Then I looked at the Indigenous scholars. This is where the permission came for me to do the storying in lieu of research questions.

In the write-up, I think things start to unfold as you are doing it, things you hadn't thought of ahead of time. For example, what do I do with the Elders' words because you also transcribe them. That's why, for me, it was good to transcribe as opposed to somebody else because they might have excluded it because that's not part of the [research] participants. They might exclude the Elders' words. As I was going through, I would transcribe their [Elders'] words, too, and I thought, 'Wow, it's so right-on,' and then I thought, 'What do I do with the Elders' words in the stories?' You talk about, how do you work with intuition. There were many times when I would feel stuck. I would smudge, I would pray, and then I would get an energy flow. I even smudged my computer. So,

I was wondering what to do with the Elders' words. You know, how do I work this in?

I thought it would just be a major omission if I didn't acknowledge the Elders and say thank you. How do I write it up? When he [the Elder] was present, each time he opened he didn't say exactly the same words, but similar words. What I did was take the bulk of what he said for the bigger circle, because he is acknowledging everybody. When I was writing it up, I put his opening before the stories and his closing after the stories. Anyway, that meant that I had to backtrack and phone him because I can't do it without his permission.

MAGGIE: Overall, I think you have responded to this, but do you believe there is an Indigenous methodology and distinctive way we approach research?

LAARA: I think it's a lot more mindful, respectful of the bigger picture and the individuals within the bigger picture. It's not just the institution that matters or what publications can come out of it. It is about how it [research] can benefit the community.

After leaving my conversation with Laara, I felt extremely grateful, not just for the knowledge that she readily shared about Indigenous research, but for the opportunity to participate in what felt like a Cree research seminar. I was responding with questioning along the lines of: What did you do next? How did you handle that? What approach did you use there? What kept you going? I found this conversation to be very instructive on the nuts and bolts of gathering and interpreting data. From a pragmatic perspective, Laara said at various times that the Western approach to research and Cree ways did not reconcile with each other (e.g., exclusivity of sampling, rationalizing, and utilizing a circle as a method as opposed to using a focus group method). Identifying these places of divergence and sharing how she managed to uphold a Nêhiýaw epistemology was important to hear because it showed that it could be done and that there was room for Indigenous methodologies. It just took some extra elbow grease in developing a methodology that explained research-sharing circles as an Indigenous method, as well as having supportive allies in the institution to hear it.

From having Elders open the circle gatherings to offering tobacco, smudging, and receiving help, Laara was working with a broader range of knowledges. This asked me to reflect upon that which method and procedure can never really encapsulate, but which are a part of Indigenous inquiry. A Cree epistemic research framework honours the Cree values of respect, kindness, and giving back to the community. The offering of tobacco or pipe ceremonies may not be written as a formal part of research methodology, but these protocols are fundamental to Indigenous research frameworks. The sacredness of Indigenous research is bound in ceremony, spirit, land, place, nature, relationships, language, dreams, humour, purpose, and stories in an inexplicable, holistic, non-fragmented way, and it is this sacredness that defies the conventional. The sacred would never reveal itself in isolation of the life that swelled amid, among, and around it. Laara said that she did not write much about intuitions, dreams, or energy, and it occurred to me that much of the sacredness of our research would never appear in my written research document – family gatherings, kind words, friends, smiles, teasing, tears, teachers, a deer sprinting across the open prairie, or manitow giving energy when I could go no further. These experiences constitute meaning that cannot be written, only felt, remembered, and at best spoken.

After our conversation, it occurred to me that meaning-making with Indigenous inquiry involved observation, sensory experience, contextual knowledge, and recognition of patterns. It drew upon external and internal sources and was highly interpretative, combined with a form of inductive analysis. Indigenous researchers are grappling with how to present meaning in a way that honours tribal knowledges, and are stating as much. As with most researchers, those operating under an Indigenous paradigm recognize patterns that transcend the local and particular. However, the difference is that those ascribing to tribal methodology will likely return to the particular and local to validate claims because our truths are found in our places. Presenting findings congruent with Indigenous inquiry holds much promise in bringing Indigenous epistemologies into Western sites of research. The extent to which Indigenous-specific forms of knowledge production are welcomed will be a litmus test as to the ability of Western research sites to engage Indigenous knowledges on their own terms.

8 Doing Indigenous Research in a Good Way – Ethics and Reciprocity

'Expert continued to use native blood without consent. Blood taken from a Vancouver Island native group and used for unauthorized genetic studies in the U.S. and England has been returned to B.C' (Munro, 2005: A18). This quote was taken from a newspaper article that appeared in *The [Vancouver] Province* in January 2005. The article reported on a 1986 research project that studied the genetic incidence of arthritis. The research was carried out through the University of British Columbia and funded by Health Canada. Eight hundred and eighty-two Nuu-chah-nulth individuals donated blood for the project. The project reported inconclusive findings, and when the researcher left the University of British Columbia he took the blood samples with him without informing the Nuu-chah-nulth. I was living on Vancouver Island at the time that this story broke, and was jolted by the extractive and exploitive incidence of Western research into Indigenous life. I was, however, not surprised. In reading this article and subsequent newspaper items on this story, it became evident that there was an urgent need to clarify overall ethical regulations of genetic and biological material gathered for research purposes. However, as much as the overarching ethics were a concern, I was deeply affected by the Nuu-chah-nulth experience because it represented another betrayal of Indigenous people.

Other recent incidences were not hard to find. Brazilian ethnopharmacologist Elaine Elisabetsy (1991) reports on the extraction of Indigenous plant knowledge to develop pharmaceutical products. Non-Indigenous stakeholders appropriated the knowledge for financial gain but gave nothing back to the Indigenous community. Lynne Davis (2004) writes of Haida texts published without Haida permission in Robert Bringhurst's

1999 work, *A Story as Sharp as a Knife: The Classical Haida Myth Tellers and Their World*. In tandem with taking tribal stories without collective permission, it also raises an ethical question about interpreting Haida myths from a non-Haida perspective. With its publication in a scholarly work, there is a potential for a general readership to assume that it is a tribally authorized interpretation. Clearly, such practices reinforce, benefit, and serve outside interests, and do little to assist the community, leaving ethical queries about the research practice (Davis, 2004).

Infringement on Indigenous communities by Western research is not localized to one specific research methodology or its procedures, and analysis as to why it happens varies. A neo-liberal standpoint suggests ethical misconduct is a predicament of researchers having a lack of cultural knowledge but good intentions, while a critical analysis points to a power dynamic sustained by societal and institutional structures that allow the privileged to take, take, and take. Seen from a decolonizing lens, ethical infringement through research is an extension of the Indigenous-settler colonial project. Much has to do with divergent beliefs around ownership of knowledge stemming from collectivist and individualist orientations that hold deep philosophical assumptions about how a society should work. The homogeneity of large research centres makes them suited for maintaining monoculture traditions. Decolonizing voices questioning the rightness of unilaterally imposed Western research methods are intellectually marginalized. There has been plenty written on the why and the how of ethical misconduct in Indigenous communities, with most learned academic individuals acknowledging the abhorrent Western research history. Although the research landscape is shifting, it cannot be situated as a purely historical phenomenon.

This chapter focuses on the application of Indigenous research ethics, ranging from governance to methods of giving back to community. Indigenous ethical guidelines, statements of principles, and protocols of research with Indigenous communities are highlighted as powerful tools for ensuring ethical conduct. Yet engaging in cultural codes of ethics, as often happens in research, brings with it challenges. In concluding this chapter, Kathy Absolon reflects upon the ethical quagmire of this intersection from the viewpoint of an Indigenous researcher. As much as it has been localized as a specific issue, an Indigenous perspective finds it impossible to separate ethics from the totality of research. Thoughts here will have appeared elsewhere in this work, but then repetition in matters such as ethics can never hurt.

Principles, Guidelines, and Protocols

In the past decade, Indigenous research protocols have been developed to protect against ethical misconduct. A portion of this task has been educative, with Indigenous peoples identifying why a research action may have an ethical implication on a tribal culture where it might not in a Western setting, such as collective permission to use community knowledge. Still, a substantive function of protocols has been to decolonize the research relationship. The Nuu-chah-nulth example cites scientific empiricist research, but regardless of the methodology any disrespectful research relationship with Indigenous people is colonial and raises ethical quandaries. Because of such occurrences, Indigenous research protocols have arisen from a community dialogue and substantive scholarship on ethically responsible research (Brandt-Castellano, 2004; Battiste and Henderson, 2000).

Indigenous research protocols, be they in protocol form or as a statement of principles, outline specific guidelines that counter objectionable research practices around governance, consent, ownership, and use. Furthermore, protocols stress the responsibility on the part of the researcher who seeks to work with Indigenous peoples who hold their cultural knowledges as sacred. Such protocols work to strengthen the overall ethical foundation of a research project, for in elevating tribal epistemologies Western ontology reveals itself in contrast, providing a more conceptually transparent/starting place. Any researcher wishing to carry out research with Indigenous communities possesses an awareness of such protocols, and the broader the breadth the better. (This also applies to those who evaluate Indigenous research, such as academic faculty.) While most protocols cannot provide a specific direction on a particular research project, they will offer guidance as to how to assess the ethical implications. Protocols are most useful when followed in conjunction with local community protocols (which may be research specific or not).

Within Canada, examples of specific protocols include the Royal Commission on Aboriginal People's *Ethical Guidelines for Research* (1996); the Mi'kmaq Ethics Watch (1999); local, collaborative protocols such as the *Standard of Conduct for Research in Clayoquot and Northern Barkely Sound Communities* (Clayoquot Alliance for Research, Education and Training, 2003); *Section 6: Research Involving Aboriginal Peoples* of the Tri-Council Policy Statement (1998); and the Canadian Institute of Health Research's *Guidelines for Health Research Involving Aboriginal*

People (2007). Schnarch's 2004 article on ownership, control, access, and possession (OCAP) details a well-known statement of principle that, if followed, can offset extractive research practices. The protocols and principles mentioned have been either developed by Indigenous communities or in dialogue with them.

Released in 1996, the report of the Royal Commission on Aboriginal Peoples (RCAP) is the most substantive study to date of conditions in Aboriginal communities. Researchers from across Canada were invited to submit proposals to the commission. To ensure ethical conduct, RCAP published guidelines to which all research conducted under RCAP was subject. The guidelines were applicable to both individual and community-based research. In community research projects, researchers were required to spell out how the Indigenous communities would participate, how they would provide consent, and how they would benefit from the research. The guidelines associated with Aboriginal knowledge asked researchers to clarify that their research and subsequent findings were, indeed, coming from an Aboriginal perspective. Furthermore, researchers had to show how their research design incorporated local protocols on knowledge-sharing, and how findings involving Aboriginal knowledges would be validated. The commission monitored work to ensure that these guidelines were followed (RCAP, 1996). This was the first government-funded research project to develop ethical research guidelines specifically with the Indigenous community in mind. While it did not generate a broad awareness among the larger research community, it showed leadership on protocol development. The RCAP principles became a practical tool for concerned researchers and have since been used broadly to guide research in Aboriginal communities (Brandt-Castellano, 2004).

The phrase *ownership, control, access, and possession* (OCAP) was first coined by the First Nations Regional Longitudinal Health Survey Working Committee, and was brought into further awareness through the article by Brian Schnarch for the First Nations Centre, National Health Organization (Schnarch 2004). While the article was written with on-reserve communities in mind, it has applicability for the larger Indigenous population. Schnarch summarizes a non-exhaustive, but significant list of thirty points that itemize the ways in which Western research has aggrieved the Indigenous community and from which the OCAP document has emerged. The list includes researchers pre-empting community involvement by presenting research designs constructed without community participation yet requesting a community stamp of approval, and the use of biological samples (e.g., blood) for further research without community consent. Schnarch's article goes on to say that though the thirty points mentioned can occur in non-Indigenous research sites, the potential for ethical infringement within Indigenous communities is increased by their relatively small size and inability to wield power within dominant society.

To counter such exploitive research practices, four key principles are proposed, beginning with ownership. *Ownership* assumes that a community owns cultural knowledge or data collectively, in the same manner that an individual owns personal information, and so the community's consent is required to use its knowledge. The principle of *control* asserts that First Nations people have a right to control various aspects of the research on them, including the formulation of research frameworks, data management, and dissemination. *Access* is the ability for Indigenous people to retrieve and examine data that concern them and their communities. The principle of *possession* refers to the actual possession of data. 'Although not a condition of ownership per se, possession (of data) is a mechanism by which ownership can be asserted and protected' (Schnarch, 2004: 81). While Schnarch's OCAP article is a position paper, the principles of OCAP have gained moral force within the Indigenous community. OCAP outlines clearly the governance that Indigenous people are asserting over their knowledges. It is a set of principles that work to decolonize the Indigenous–Western research relationship, and provides researchers with explicit guidelines for assessing whether said research is exploitive or beneficial to Indigenous interests. Certainly, such a research approach takes effort, but it is required to defend against the 'smash and grab' (Martin and Frost, 1996: 606) approach.

There are additional resources available to further assist in the ethical practice of research within Indigenous communities. The *Guidelines for Health Research Involving Aboriginal Peoples* (CIHR 2007) is a protocol document that has taken several years to develop and is now finalized. These *Guidelines* represent a collaborative effort by Indigenous and non-Indigenous people to develop a protocol for the Canadian Institute of Health Research (CIHR), a national academic research-funding body. Of the three major academic funding bodies in Canada, the Natural Sciences and Engineering Research Council (NSERC), the Social Sciences and Humanities Research Council (SSHRC), and the CIHR, the latter is the first to develop a substantive guideline document in consultation with the Indigenous community. (It should be noted that Section 6 of Tri-Council Policy Statement (1998) on research acknowledges Indigenous research ethics.)

The CIHR *Guidelines* discuss the protection of Indigenous knowledges, community control, benefit-sharing, recognition of cultural protocols, and involvement in interpretation of findings, to name a few of the issues (CIHR, 2007). The document is to be read within the context of an Aboriginal worldview that honours qualities such as relationship, reciprocity, collectivism, and sacred knowledges. There is an expectation that researchers who hold alternative worldviews will respect these values. When used in conjunction with local protocols, this document provides researchers with clear standards. However, they are merely guidelines, not policy, and their effectiveness depends upon how well they are monitored and followed. That they have been developed specifically for a national academic research-funding organization is promising in that it shows a desire for change. Granted, such ethical guidelines will make for a more intensive research experience with increased checks and balances in place, and, as Schnarch concedes, there will be a tendency to fall back on 'tried and true' methods (2004: 84). However, there is an expectation that institutional research centres will support their researchers to make certain that inquiry into Indigenous life is carried out in a good way.

Decolonizing the research relationship begins with strategies devised in conjunction with Indigenous advisory committees for specific research projects and tribal ethics review boards, and the integration of university ethics reviews that specifically consider research in Indigenous communities. I believe that praxis is a combination of both attitudinal adjustments and practical steps. Protocols and guidelines that outline ethical research conducted within Indigenous communities are methodical. If one chooses, they can be learned and practised. For many, they must be learned, as adapting to the ethical protocol of another's culture does not come easily. Adhering to such protocols offers deeper appreciation for the holistic quality of Indigenous knowledges. As Indigenous scholar Marlene Brandt-Castellano suggests, Indigenous ethics can never be limited to a defined set of rules; they are about knowing who you are, the values you hold, and your understanding of how you fit within a spiritual world (2004). Being on the front line of knowledge creation, individual researchers who learn and commit to ethical protocols for research within Indigenous communities are in a privileged position to not only create change from the bottom up, but also to further broaden their understandings on a deeply personal level.

Ethics as Methodology

Specific ethical considerations and their complexities occur within Indigenous research frameworks themselves. In the practice of research, certain ethical standards cross cultures, such as informed consent and member checks. Within institutional contexts, these are often associated with liability concerns, and are acknowledged by the larger community of researchers. However, Indigenous epistemic research conducted under Western funding or academic parameters holds a unique ethical complexity that is less about liability and is more relational. First, Indigenous frameworks inevitably have to accommodate parties with philosophically distinctive worldviews. Right from the start, one can assume an external source of ethical tension. Second, Western research has a bad reputation in Indigenous communities for good reason. Simply because a researcher is Indigenous (or following an Indigenous framework) does not automatically translate into community trust. Trust needs to be earned internally. Trusting relationships are engendered in a variety of ways: following protocol, showing guardianship over sacred knowledges, standing by cultural validity of knowledge, and giving back. In Cree, the word *miýo* means 'good, well, beautiful, valuable.' The word 'ethics' is not differentiated (Wolvengrey, 2001a: 109). Values and ethics are interconnected and are about *miýo*, about goodness. In thinking about Indigenous research ethics, the overarching theme is to conduct oneself in a way that reflects *miýo*. Within this broad interpretation of ethical responsibility, several reccurring themes associated with Indigenous research ethics arise.

Among Indigenous researchers there is a deep concern about the risk to cultural knowledges in research. Indigenous knowledges are holistic and encompass knowledge sources that Western science may not acknowledge as legitimate. The difficulty of bringing such knowledges into the academy is the risk of them being appropriated or diminished. Once in the public realm, guardianship is difficult. Michael Hart urges care in sharing sacred ways of knowing, like dreams, when their validity is questioned. For her research, the Niitsitapi Elders helped Betty Bastien (1999) determine which cultural knowledges could be shared. Betty was ethically bound to use any shared information in a helpful way. If a researcher is conducting research within a community, Elders, tribal ethics boards, and local protocols can be particularly helpful in determining what knowledge to share. I did not want to exploit community or familial knowledge, and so I referenced only minimal knowledge from my own experience when writing specifically about Nêhiyáw sacred knowledge. I relied upon sources by Elders and others already in the public realm. When I spoke with the Indigenous researchers for my study, I was confident that they were aware of risks associated with bringing cultural knowledges into Western research projects. They could and would monitor their contributions. This participant group's vulnerability level was lower than for those who lack the same familiarity with Western research. As mentioned above, if a researcher is unclear, local protocols, community relationship, and advisory groups can be helpful.

Integral to sharing knowledge is the matter of confidentiality. Clearly an ethical consideration, confidentiality can be interpreted differently in Western and Indigenous contexts. In some instances, university ethics boards allow research participants to have the choice as to whether they wish to remain anonymous. The choice, however, does not exist for everyone. A research participant in my study indicated that her institutional ethics regulatory board did not provide this option. Why does this matter? It matters because our stories are our truth and knowledge. It is about standing behind one's words and recognizing collective protocol, that one is accountable for one's words. It is difficult to honour this cultural tradition if it is disallowed. Of course, some research projects (Indigenous or not) demand confidentiality for good reason. However, in instances where risk is minimal, there should be an option.

From an Indigenous perspective, ethical implications arise within the evaluative context of research. Such concerns about validity are identified in the RCAP guidelines (1996). Validation of knowledge differs across cultures. Attempting to validate Indigenous knowledges according to Western terms and assumptions creates an ethical problem. From a Cree perspective, Winona Stevenson (2000) states that truth (validity) or *tapwê* is bound with the integrity of the person sharing knowledge. Stevenson makes the following suggestion to the Indigenous historian: 'The tasks of tribal historians are to recover the past and to present it to the public in a form that meets the approval of the people whose histories and lives it represents' (2000: 298). Betty Bastien (1999) states that a peril of subjecting Indigenous epistemologies like Niitsitapi to Western validity is that tribal knowledge is meant to be understood in the (oral) language of that particular culture. Validity, then, is determined by methodology and community. Given the misinterpretations of Indigenous culture within research; this is a vital ethical concern.

Given the small number of Indigenous academics, non-Indigenous scholars are currently evaluating Indigenous academic research. These individuals may not have the background to appreciate validity from an Indigenous perspective, where truth is found in the subjective, and validity is in the nature of the relationship with culture. As found in Niitsitapi ways, 'Grandfather is saying, the validity and ethics of the epistemologies and pedagogy of Niitsitapi knowing lives through the manner in which I live my life' (Bastien, 1999: 97). No wonder validity is bound with giving back to community, which is integral to ethical research.

A relational research approach is built upon the collective value of giving back to the community. It is the *miýo* ethic. In my study, collective responsibility was a consistent theme among Indigenous researchers. Jeannine Carriere made the point that completing a doctoral degree was only part of a larger commitment to give back what was learned to the community: 'The bigger challenge and the more important work is to publish this information to get it out to people.' Kathy Absolon spoke about giving back in relation to purpose: 'So, the Ph.D. has to be meaningful, it has to help, that there is a purpose in terms of the bigger picture of who we are as Anishnabe.' There are a host of ways to give back, and for Indigenous academic researchers sharing knowledge is the most obvious means.

Relevancy is integral to giving back. Did the research assist the community, and could the community make sense of the research? Dissemination of the research is a central issue, and it is important to ensure that the research is available to the community in a manner that is accessible and useful. This means ensuring that the research is grounded in community needs, as opposed to the needs of the academy. Graham Smith emphasizes this point: 'At the end of the day it belongs to the community, the Maori, and that's why I keep talking about praxis.' Giving back is not a difficult concept, yet one of the most egregious actions of Western research into the lives of Indigenous peoples is the negligence of this ethic. Giving back does not only mean dissemination of findings; it means creating a relationship throughout the entirety of the research.

A Conversation with Kathy Absolon

Kathy Absolon's conversation with me concludes this chapter by reflecting on what it means to be in a holistic and ethical research relationship with Indigenous communities and the challenges in being true to the inherent responsibilities.

Kathy Abosolon is Anishnabe, from the Flying Post First Nation, and is first degree Midewiwin of the Three Fires Society. She completed her doctorate through the Department of Adult Education, Community Development and Counselling Psychology, at the Ontario Institute for Studies in Education (OISE), University of Toronto. I have known Kathy for many years as a colleague, friend, and Anishnabe sister. It was so nice to have this conversation with Kathy about Indigenous research methodologies because it was also the focus of her doctoral studies. When I talked with Kathy, I was feeling alone with a lot of uncertainties. I wanted to learn how she integrated her cultural knowing into her research amid such tensions. Having this talk with a friend, about a subject that is near to our hearts, was the boost that I needed.

MAGGIE: What prompted you to enter into Ph.D. studies? What was it that made you decide that it was time to go back?

KATHY: For me, I don't think I can say that it was one thing. It was a number of things. I am still not even sure if this is a useful thing to do as an Aboriginal person, as an Anishnabe. I am not sure if it's contributing to the community or our overall healing, recovery, and self-determination. But I guess it's simply that I've been an educator. My community said it was okay, and it was timely in that I was feeling I needed to change my job. It was all winding up to say this is the doorway. I don't completely understand why we go through those doorways or why the universe or the spirits present those doorways, but I think not all of us are medicine people, not all of us conduct sweats, Rain Dances, or Sun Dances. Some of us are educators, some of us healers, some of us are a little bit of this and a little bit of that. I think I can accept that I am an educator. At a structural level, one of the roles of the educator is to bring validation and help widen the path for other Aboriginal people to be okay with who they are. To know that if you choose the path of education you can still come in and be who you are. This one student, her methodology is water walks across the [Great] Lakes, her reflection on her water walk and the understanding and insights that come out of that. If doing this Ph.D. gives me the power to say to somebody, 'It's okay for you to do your research that way,' then that's an important reason to do it.

A big part of it is a lifelong journey, and I know that when I am talking about my research it has to feel like it's meaningful. It means something to me that I know how to sing the songs in my language. When I go to ceremony and my Elders are saying the ceremonies in Anishnabe, that I know what they are talking about. So, the Ph.D. has to be meaningful, it has to help, that there is a purpose in terms of the bigger picture of who we are as Anishnabe. When my daughter does the ceremonies, I tell her that she is bringing those lines back into the world. That's more important to me than my Ph.D. So, yeah, it's important, but there are other things that are more important, but it's [the Ph.D.] also the catalyst, the doorway. I believe that if I wasn't meant to do my Ph.D., that doorway wouldn't have been there, that path wouldn't have been created. That's what I believe.

[In doing this Ph.D.,] my challenges have been around how does this learning, a Ph.D. in the academy, support me to become more who I am. The answer is that it doesn't. Where I have been supported – to be who I am, know what I know, and have that grow – is in our lodge. In our lodge, in our communities, I can talk the way I talk and people get me and they understand where I am at. The other thing is that I get them. They teach me. Working at the community level has helped me know myself and to feel the strength, pride, and identity as an Anishnabe person. The struggle, if that's what you need, is not in academia. You have to get that from your family, your community, your own teachings, and your culture. You have to go there ...

What I feel frustrated or constrained by [in] doing research in the academy is that you are forced to begin from a colonized place, and we are forced to begin from that place for two reasons. One is that we are colonized – Indigenous people are colonized. The second reason is that the academy reinforces that and we are in that place. Yet, within me there is an Anishnabe thinker, person, and my European side. It's not just Anishnabe, it's not just European. It's about what *I* am. It's also what a lot of other Aboriginal people are, too. We haven't·had an education system that has helped us to reconcile those different parts within ourselves, so I begin with that kind of frustration ...

My topic is around how do we search for knowledge as Indigenous people. I believe that if we look at some of the methodologies along the continuum that are less oppressive, they might be supportive of Indigenous methodologies or they might even be in alliance with Indigenous methodologies, but they are still not Indigenous methodologies. They happen to come from their paradigm and their reference point, and while they might fit, they are not based in Indigenous thinking. They are not based in spirit and where spirit comes from. A couple of people said that to me, and so that's been imprinted in my notions. More recently, a colleague who has finished his Ph.D. said, 'Indigenous research is in the language. All you have to do is learn language.' If we learn our language, the methodology is in learning your language because then you'll understand what the Elders are talking about. The knowledge is in the language.

When I was writing up my methodology and thinking about it, the first thing is that it has to be Indigenous, but that's a contradiction and kind of a state of anguish right off the bat. All of the things I've learned about in academia don't come from an Indigenous paradigm. Even the idea of doing interviews, I was writing about that and thought, 'Well, we don't do interviews in Aboriginal culture. We have discussions and talks.' I talked to my committee advisor and said, 'I think I am going to reword it to say this is what we are doing.' She said the committee might not get that, but I reworded it anyway. We don't have focus groups, we have circles. I am trying to rethink the methodology, but that's a real hard thing because none of us can say we know what is authentically Indigenous.

We are all colonized. The people who do know are not in the academy … [T]he people who understand are the Aboriginal people who are poor, who are living in rez housing. If you want to know your culture, they will do the ceremony for you or they will help you understand the roles. If you need help, they will help you. They will teach you about friendship and community and about what it means. What those teachings really mean versus just rhetoric. I don't know if I am articulating that clearly but our teachers are not really in the academy. Our teachers are in community.

I think of our methodologies. We have to be able to start from a slate that is not influenced by the other, so that it is okay to have your dreams be your methodology. If you go on a water walk or quest, that is your methodology. I was reflecting when you were talking about yours [methodology]. If I said I am doing my Ph.D. and my methodology is my dreams, and I am going to go on a fast every year, and after that fast I had somebody come and visit me and talk to me about my fast and take [teachings] with them. I wouldn't propose that because I wouldn't want that to [be] measured. I know that is Indigenous methodologies, but I wouldn't propose it as a methodology within a mainstream setting because I don't want them to have the power to say that that's not research. But it is. What my friend was saying to me five years ago was true, that your research is through your dreams, that is where we go for our answers, and that is where we go for our knowledge.

What I have done with my methodology – I know it's a long-winded answer – is that my methodology has become a combination of looking at what other Indigenous researchers have used in their process, knowing that they are only speaking about a small piece. It's like an iceberg. Secondly, doing what you are doing, talking to other Indigenous researchers about their methodologies and then trying to create. The third is creating a learning circle, and facilitating Indigenous scholars to come together, to talk about what we are talking about right now, and what they consider to be Indigenous methodologies. The big dilemma and struggles is doing that in a Western methodological research context, trying to grow something Indigenous there. Out of a box, you're morphing a circle and there is something kind of wacky about that, but there is something kind of challenging about that, too [*laughter*].

I think our methodology is process. I don't know what kind of boundaries I am going to be pushing at the university, but you know that you will be pushing boundaries. My ultimate goal is that I want to privilege an Anishnabe worldview and Anishnabe methodology. I am here to uphold and uplift Indigenous methodologies, not for the world to see, but for my children and their children and other Anishnabe children. To say to them that they exist and they are beautiful and that they are amazing ways of growing and learning and being.

I often question, Should we be doing these methodologies? Even this conversation is making me think, 'Maybe I should scrap my methodology.' Maybe I should just be saying, 'I'm doing my methodology, using my dreams and I am going to do what I already believe is Indigenous.' Why do I need to go and talk to people about it when I already believe it? If you experience a fast, I know what that is like and so I know what comes for you. It's different for everyone. I know that experience is sacred. What do you call it, like in sci-fi movies, a portal? I know that there are portals and when you go into a sweat lodge there are portals. When you go into different ceremonies, there are portals for knowledge to come through. You take that knowledge and you go into a ceremony and tell people what you saw and what you experienced. That is research. That is bringing in knowledge ...

It's what we will hear people saying over and over again, in my research [and] in your research, we will hear people say that our methodologies exist in our dreams, in our fast. They will say that we traditionally knew about the portal, the doorway, how to get knowledge and that it was brought to the people by sharing, by community forums, by sitting in circles, by engaging in ceremony, by honouring your relationship to the spirit. When we do that, the spirit will reciprocate and we will be given what we are needed. The universe will provide for us if we honour the great circle and cycle of being, and that can only happen if we know how to do that. So why am I not doing the methodology based on what I already know? ...

If I was at home in my own community, I would be bantering back and forth with people in my community and saying, 'Well, Indigenous methodologies, what do you think I should be doing?' I would be doing more discussions. That is something that we talked about in terms of our own methodology and we haven't done very well to date. We do it when we are doing a conference, but on our own we should be doing more sitting and talking about our research. Like here, we are together doing our research, we need to be bouncing our ideas off each other because we are both in the same boat. We need to be talking about these things and creating a space for us to write, read, and get feedback from each other. I think part of it is that you get so used to working in isolation, you just don't think to ask. We can talk about this and how we ought to do that, and I find I create things where the process seems like a lot of work. I know that with Indigenous methodologies or traditional practices, it is more work.

Kathy's perspective on Indigenous methodologies was *miýo*. As she spoke, she was nesting her research practice within an Indigenous ethical framework that was respectful of relationship, purpose, sacred knowledge, and giving back. The theme of reciprocity was evident throughout her assertions that her research must be meaningful to her daughter, to her community, to Anishnabe people. She saw her role as post-secondary educator as assisting Indigenous students find their way through research, to assure them that their cultural knowledges, be they received through dreamtime or water walks, were respected as legitimate sources of knowing. As an Indigenous educator-researcher, she was giving back to the larger Indigenous community. Kathy spent time reflecting upon cultural knowledge sources and their role in Indigenous research. Cultural knowledges are powerful, and their sacredness must be respected. Her desire to serve Anishnabe ways of knowing was strong, but she acknowledged the struggle of conducting Indigenous research within a non-Indigenous system. She articulated the ethical anguish of bringing cultural knowledges into our research given they will inevitably be judged by those unfamiliar with them. At the same time, she acknowledged that it is tribal epistemologies that make Indigenous research distinctive.

She articulated the complexity of bringing cultural epistemologies into spaces not fully decolonized. After our conversation, I began to wonder about the ways that Indigenous researchers show guardianship of Indigenous knowledges. I wondered about a non-Indigenous researcher's role. It seems a challenge to confront the entire research community and break with polarities that divide to create a new kind of ethical space.

9 Situating Indigenous Research within the Academy

At the inaugural *Shawane Dagosiwin* Aboriginal research conference in Winnipeg in June 2005, Indigenous scholar Marlene Brandt-Castellano (2005) gave a keynote address. She said that the challenge of and responsibility for Indigenous research lie with all of us. In speaking specifically about research in the academy, she said that Indigenous people must suspend distrust and non-Indigenous people must suspend disbelief. Through the creation of a principled ideological space, a *miÿo* interval, there is a possibility to move forward with the exciting proposition of Indigenous and tribal research frameworks. But how do we create these environments? What are the philosophies, values, and practices that offer this freedom? The academy is grappling with an increasingly non-homogeneous environment. This is evoking new theoretical discourses of inclusiveness, engaging the once invisible and excluded. It is an exciting time for theorists and scholars, but it is also testing every aspect of the 'tried and true' customs of institutional knowledge centres. The new landscape asks that the academic institutions self-assess according to new terms – the hope of this critical examination is in the potential for re-invention.

As an Indigenous presence surfaces within Western universities, it brings with it all that is Indigenous: thought, custom, culture, practice, and self. This is causing the academy to pause for a number of reasons. For some, the hesitancy reflects an active resistance to change, while for others it is born of a passive non-awareness. Still others are uncertain as to how to include, without subsuming, Indigenous knowledges. They understand the risk to non-Western knowledges within the cultural terrain of a Western system that has strong established philosophies and practices. They know that 'add Indigenous and stir' is not a valid response, and that this new country requires new orientations. There is an understanding that inclusion of Indigenous knowledges requires multiple strategies for reconsidering the existing system. The strongest potential for fresh discourse rests with the ability of invested non-Indigenous academics to listen attentively to not only what diminishes Indigenous research scholarship, but also to what helps. Furthermore, a new non-homogeneous academic landscape asks that it not simply listen anew, but listen differently to what is being said. For Indigenous academics, there is a responsibility to not submerge identity under the weight of a worldview that is not our own. It is the courage to keep on swimming.

This chapter includes reflections from Indigenous researchers on the environmental challenges that they have confronted, and in doing so they identify circumstances where supportive relationships have assisted. They do not solely focus on research practice, but also on the holistic experience of being an Indigenous academic researcher, for the two are bound together. Some of the insights are ideological in nature, while others are practical. Still others are personal. While commentary in this chapter focuses on graduate research, the experience is applicable to other research sites. The chapter concludes with ways that non-Indigenous scholars can be supportive of Indigenous research in general. However, prior to delving into this discussion, there is a need for some contextual backdrop.

Imagining a new approach requires a specific analysis of the past that complicates the 'us–other/other–us' dynamic of Indigenous–settler relations that equates this relationship to one of simple dominance. Without tending to the particulars of this relationship, there is a tendency towards a single 'inclusivity strategy,' a perspective that is not particularly useful, even slothful. I argue that there can be no advance in Indigenous research approaches without acknowledging the historical influence of Indigenous–settler relations on educational policy, practice, and research. The urge to replicate historical responses, albeit in a nuanced manner, is so great that moving forward is impossible without first reckoning with them. Furthermore, if the academy is going to seriously consider Indigenous knowledges, there must be recognition of the distinct status of Indigenous people as unique from other minority groups. This is not to diminish other groups, but to point out that the relationship between post-secondary education and Indigenous people is distinctive and so must be the responses. Thus, this chapter provides a contextual backdrop for situating Indigenous researchers and research within the larger purpose of Indigenous cultural endurance amid Indigenous–settler colonial relationship. Because the focus of this chapter is academic research, this discussion cannot be isolated from the site of this research, which is the educational system.

Context

Indigenous scholars' desire to transform the exclusive domain of knowledge creation immersed in Western thought and held in the dominion of Western universities has its basis in at least three reasons: (a) to carry on a struggle borne by historical momentum; (b) to make visible the connection between cultural longevity, Aboriginal rights, and post-secondary education (with research being inherent to academic higher learning); and (c) to bring not only Indigenous bodies but Indigenous knowledges into the academy. While these factors relate to a broader discussion of Indigenous post-secondary education, they are necessary for understanding the historical backdrop from which Indigenous research methodologies have surfaced. The possibility of a research environment capable of engaging Indigenous thought cannot be abstracted from its history, nor can its full purpose be understood.

Below, a brief snapshot is offered of the historical progression, politics, and tensions that power Indigenous research frameworks. Creating room for Indigenous methodologies is not solely about setting forth another research option on the buffet table. It is about acknowledging an Indigenous cultural worldview and identity, which has long been a site of contention in this land. It is about recognizing the unique situation of Indigenous people that differentiates this group from other minorities. To this end, historical relations must be acknowledged or else transformative efforts will be blocked. This snapshot captures the intersection between educational policy generally, and post-secondary education and research specifically, in the lives of Indigenous people. It references the Indigenous–settler relations as formalized through legislation such as the Indian Act and subsequent policy.

Although this is a commentary on the Canadian experience, Indigenous people globally understand the connection to the land, which has long sustained Indigenous peoples, and the cultural identity bound to it. In the Canadian context, the historical relations between the original peoples of this territory and settler society illustrate the turbulent waters in which Indigenous knowledge-seeking systems have been immersed. The Royal Proclamation of 1763 set out the terms of engagement for settlement, decreeing that prior to settlement the Crown must enter into treaty agreements with the Indigenous habitants of this territory. The Proclamation signified the special relationship between the Crown and Indigenous nations, resulting in a series of treaty agreements. Prior to the British North American Act of 1867, Indigenous people and the British Empire entered into a number of peace and friendship treaties. However, it was not until 1870 that the historic numbered treaties were negotiated. Within these treaty agreements, educational consideration was paramount to Indian people and the frequency with which schooling is mentioned is evidence of this foresight (Barman, Hébert, and McCaskill, 1986). Further education was not viewed within the parameters of a specific time frame. Sheila Carr-Stewart identifies the links between treaty rights and education within Treaties One to Seven, clarifying that the headsmen negotiated the educational provisions because they believed that education was 'a holistic, life-long process' (2001: 130).

The British North American Act of 1867 assigned jurisdictional responsibilities to the federal and provincial governments, and identified educational matters as a federal responsibility. The Indian Act of 1876 became the instrument for regulating the relationship between the federal government and status Indian people, and it remains in force today. Educational policy and programming for status Indians flow from the Indian Act.

The policy of assimilation through educative means shifted back and forth, from the strategy of utilizing residential schools for full-scale cultural eradication to the educational policy of the early 1900s, which had as its goal preparing the Indian student for returning to the reserve (Barman et al., 1986). Preparing Indian students for returning to their community meant curricula that emphasized vocational studies and de-emphasized academic training, a transparent policy of maintaining the socioeconomic marginalization of Indigenous peoples. In the 1940s, a shift in philosophy emerged, and in 1946 a House Committee of the Senate and House of Commons was appointed to revise the Indian Act. The 1951 revised Indian Act permitted the federal government to provide financial compensation to the provinces for Indian children registering in provincial schools with non-Indian students. The Hawthorne Report of 1967, which was a survey of the social, economic, political, and educational needs of status Indian people in Canada, encouraged a policy of integration (ibid., 1986). While this shifted from a policy of educational segregation, registering Indian students into provincial schools was a form of cultural assimilation in a more nuanced guise. Consistent throughout the shifts in strategy, the philosophy governing educational policy for Indian peoples promoted cultural oppression in the form of assimilation, marginalization, or negligence.

Since the time of colonial settlement in Canada, Indian leadership has had a sophisticated understanding of the Western educative process and the foresight to appreciate its power to further nullify or nurture culture. Amid a growing desire to shake off paternalistic federal control through an assertion of self-governance, Indigenous contemporary political action began as early as the 1940s. However, it was not until 1970 that the National Indian Brotherhood formed. This organization was formed partly in response to the 1969 White Paper of the federal government, which called for a full-scale assimilation policy. The Brotherhood prepared a policy paper, accepted by the government in 1973, entitled *Indian Control of Indian Education*, which spoke to education issues broadly. This policy paper addressed the participation of Indian peoples in post-secondary universities by identifying the importance of adult education for Indian people (Richardson and Blanchet-Cohen, 2000). A clear message of the policy proposal was that educative policy and practice must affirm cultural identity (Barman et al., 1986), a principle applicable to all aspects of education involving Indian people, whether it was band-controlled education or within an integrated setting, whether it was compulsory education or higher learning.

The Canadian Constitution Act of 1982 built further momentum around Aboriginal issues. Section 35 of the Canadian Constitution recognizes existing Aboriginal rights, though the nature of these rights remains undefined. In conjunction with the Canadian Constitution, Section 25 of the Charter of Rights and Freedoms protects Aboriginal or treaty rights. Furthermore, as Battiste (1986) argues, Section 25 must be interpreted in a manner that is consistent with Section 27 of the Charter, which deals with the preservation and enhancement of the multicultural heritage of Canadians. Given the potential role of education in upholding cultural ways of knowing, and given the consistent attention to educational provision by the Indigenous community (first outlined in the written treaties), education has always been more than a matter of policy.

While compulsory elementary and secondary education for status Indians had been clearly delineated as a federal responsibility, post-secondary education has not been as clearly spelled out. In fact, where it was referred to within the Indian Act, was in the context of enfranchisement, which, in this context, means the relinquishment all rights and responsibilities associated with being a status Indian (such as the right to live on one's home reserve). Until 'the Indian Acts of the 1920s, Indians who attended university could face automatic enfranchisement.' The 'automatic enfranchisement' wording was changed in a 1927 revision (Stonechild, 2006: 5). However, 'until the 1940s, First Nations people enrolling in post-secondary education were required to surrender their status as "Indians"' (Standing Committee on Aboriginal Affairs and Northern Development [SCAAND], 2006: 2). The revised 1951 Indian Act allowed a board to decide whether an Indian was fit to be enfranchised upon completion of a post-secondary degree, as opposed to an 'automatic' determination. As with the general education policy, the underlying assumption was that a post-secondary education could deliver the Indian person to an acceptable level of whiteness, deliver him from his Indian identity.

It was not until 1968 that post-secondary programming for status Indian students was initiated, picking up momentum with the Post-Secondary Educational Assistance Program of the Department of Indian and Northern Affairs, which was put into place in 1977 (SCAANC, 2006). From a government perspective, post-secondary education was largely a policy mechanism, with subsequent educational programming seen as an initiative to bridge the equity gap between status Indians and mainstream (non-Indigenous) society. This differed substantially from the Indigenous community's perspective of education as a foundational right that should simultaneously serve culture and minimize socio-economic disparity. In his book, *The New Buffalo: The Struggle for Aboriginal Post-secondary Education in Canada* (2006), Cree scholar Blair Stonechild gives particular insight into the current dilemma of post-secondary education policy as it impacts status Indians. He states: 'The federal government's current policy is to limit First Nations aspirations by delivering such education [post-secondary] as a social program only in order to bring First Nations participation rates to a level comparable to the rest of society.' He goes on to argue that the difficulty with this approach is that it does not deal with Aboriginal rights (2006: 138). He ties the dilemma specifically to federal policy on First Nations, but the spirit of his analysis envelopes all people Indigenous to Canada. While the approach of post-secondary education as a socio-economic equalizer is laudable, it misses the larger point about Aboriginal rights, cultural longevity, and the responsibility of educational institutions within that larger discussion.

Not until 1996, and the release of the report by the Royal Commission on Aboriginal Peoples (RCAP), an inquiry into conditions impacting Canadian Indigenous people, did the spotlight again shine on the intersection between cultural longevity and education. The report acknowledged that, though much work had been done to reclaim education, Indigenous people were still dealing with assimilation through education, including the assimilative process of post-secondary education, and recommended that Indigenous knowledges be integrated into Western university settings (RCAP, 1996). Indigenous access to post-secondary education is critical, yet such education must not infringe on Indigenous peoples' ability to preserve their culture. Infusing Indigenous knowledges into the academy occurs only because of transformative efforts by Indigenous peoples committed to ensuring Indigenous access to a relevant post-secondary education. Those who have struggled for the right of relevancy in education include Indigenous community members, Elders, Indigenous political leaders, Indigenous post-secondary policy advocates, scholars, researchers, and writers. In this effort, they have implemented multiple strategies to ensure that higher learning (involving both pedagogy and methodology) is not a mechanism of assimilation but a tool for cultural survival.

So, what does this have to do with Indigenous research frameworks? Surely this history is known and it is more concerned with education than research per se. Why is it relevant? I argue that it is relevant because this historical accounting reveals a distinctive pattern of how Indigenous people have been regarded and treated by the dominant culture, whether the issue is education or anything else. It has been a pattern of exclusion and inclusion, but always according to their (non-Indigenous people's) terms. The example of status Indian people in Canada is used because it shows a consistent pattern of a majority culture attempting to push aside (through exclusion or assimilation) Indigenous culture and Indigenous people pushing back. The resulting change has been neither fully satisfying nor effective. Indigenous people have had to live with the changes, but the settler strategies so far have not fully challenged the settler–Indigenous power dynamic, acknowledged the uniqueness of this history of resistance, nor shown evidence of a new approach. To counteract the socioeconomic disparity experienced by the Indigenous community, one response has been to increase the enrolment of Indigenous people in post-secondary institutions, a strategy that certainly matters, but by itself it is insufficient. Welcoming Indigenous students but not allowing for learning, scholarship, and research that is congruent with Indigenous paradigms is simply a nuanced variation of a past strategy – same old, same old.

For Indigenous people, the push back has always been over the preservation of our culture. It goes beyond practising personal cultural identity, though by necessity that is part of it, and is about ensuring the existence of a tribal worldview for the next generation. Culture holds knowledge, knowledge holds culture; they are iterative, interdependent, and alive. The focus of this book has been on tribal knowledges with a purpose towards expanding the landscape where tribal knowledges can flourish. Academic research, concerned as it is with knowledge, is a highly relevant site. As a community of researchers, if we do not contest the formidable patterns of settler–Indigenous relations that continue to define us, if we do not take a field trip into our own mutual history, we are bound to replicate – subconsciously or not – the unsettling historical pattern. The history of research has been long and painful for Indigenous peoples, with only recent reconciliation gestures. The tension now for Indigenous researchers remains in the contemporary manifestations of a colonial response. No doubt this both angers and saddens, but as people seek a more sustainable way of living, perhaps there is hope for new possibilities.

Indigenous Graduate Research

Shape-shifting in the academy means opening windows for fresh air. Creating new conceptual tools is a powerful strategy, for these new tools demand new relationship dynamics. Indigenous research frameworks provide opportunities for tribal epistemologies to enter the tightly guarded academic research community and have great potential to serve Indigenous worldviews in the academy, as well as the academy itself. The development of Indigenous research frameworks (not research in Indigenous communities) is a new phenomenon, with limited investigation into the complexities confronted by Indigenous researchers conducting this form of inquiry. Supporting Indigenous research frameworks means supporting Indigenous researchers, and this cannot be achieved without hearing their perspective. Encompassed here are insights into the conflicts of traversing cultural paradigms. The conversations centre on the academic structures and relationships of graduate research. A focus on graduate programs is critical because it is here that Indigenous research frameworks are being honed and practised. The growing critical mass of Indigenous graduate students is best positioned to define and sustain Indigenous methodologies in the academy. To do so, these scholars require a supportive (or at least knowledgeable) mentoring environment. Because Indigenous research and scholarship do not only situate themselves within graduate research, this chapter offers concluding thoughts on how non-Indigenous academics seeking engagement with Indigenous scholarship can move forward generally.

A foundational challenge for Indigenous researchers is the inevitability of being accountable to culturally and epistemologically divergent communities. Jeannine Carriere describes this experience as a form of dual accountability: 'my intuitive self was saying you need to do things in a good way, you need to have the guidance of Elders ... and you need to satisfy this university.' Michael Hart articulates his experience: 'Part of the challenge for me is balancing that with ... how I would approach Elders if I wanted to learn from them. It doesn't reflect what the university expects.' There are myriad examples of tensions resulting from this dual responsibility, much of which is echoed in the pages of this book. The difficulty arises when research is told to look 'a certain way,' and follow the prescribed steps of a particular worldview that are incongruent with the steps (or order) that would occur in community. Furthermore, cultural sustainability is integral to Indigenous research frameworks, adding a dimension to Indigenous research that requires a particular type of attention. Serving community in this way becomes the individual Indigenous researcher's responsibility whereas sustaining Western culture through research is a highly institutionalized, supported project.

If one is feeling conflicted as an Indigenous graduate researcher, it is likely a good indicator that one has not lost her sense of self. While this may be affirming, serving divergent cultural authorities creates stress. Non-Indigenous faculty and administrators who show appreciation for this unique responsibility are a great support. Indigenous researchers understand that finding a respectful way of serving community through research happens in the research relationship. It is those non-Indigenous supports that are mindful of this accountability, that are non-directive but supportive of the Indigenous researcher–community relationships, that are open to Indigenous research frameworks, and that are able to assist Indigenous researchers with academic demands. The presence of such support (or lack of it) for Indigenous graduate researchers is felt most intensely through relationships established within the parameters of academic structures, such as committees.

Within the academic community, the committee structure has considerable power to support Indigenous graduate researchers and frameworks (or not). The power dynamic permeates regardless of cross-cultural membership. Within Indigenous graduate work, these committees represent intensely focused relationships between Indigenous and non-Indigenous members who are aware of the colonial history and its potential residue (some, arguably, are more acutely aware than others). What makes such committees work? While committee membership was not the focus of my research on Indigenous methodologies, it emerged as part of my conversation with Indigenous researchers, along with the significance of other academic support (i.e., peers) to balance a feeling of isolation. Such factors affirm the heightened relevance of relationship in and around Indigenous research. It harkens back to the notion of Indigenous research being process-oriented and relational in both its practice and supports.

Several Indigenous researchers in my study reflected upon the role of committee membership. Of these individuals, a majority had non-Indigenous supervisors. Most, however, had Indigenous people on the committee. A difficulty in finding an Indigenous supervisor reflected the small number of Indigenous faculty available to carry out this task. A recent article in the *Journal of Higher Education – Academic Matters* stated that less than 1 per cent of faculty in Canada are Aboriginal (Brelauer, 2007). This is a clear systemic barrier that influences knowledge creation itself. Why do Indigenous graduate supervisors matter for students who wish to uphold cultural knowledges? Cam Willett argued: 'When I think of the committee, I think of somebody, who is an Indigenous person, really should be my supervisor, who knows more about that part than anything because that's primarily what it is about.' Generally, Indigenous faculty members are better situated to recognize an Indigenous epistemic centring in a student's research design and validate the thinking behind such choices. In situations where students are having difficulty expressing an Indigenous research framework, Indigenous supervisors are well positioned to ask helpful questions and assist students in clarifying their methodology. Overall, it becomes a matter of good methodological supervision.

Even if the supervisor is Indigenous, it is important that there is the right match. Just being Indigenous is not enough. For example, Willett notes that he needed a supervisor 'who can stay out of my way just as much as give me guidance.' This is an equally important point, as there is a tendency to match Indigenous faculty with Indigenous students solely on the basis of shared cultural ancestry. Given that Indigenous people are not culturally or intellectually homogeneous, this can be problematic. That said, it is likely, given the numbers, that many Indigenous graduate researchers do not have much choice when it comes to Indigenous supervisors. At worst, Indigenous graduate researchers may struggle with a supervisor who is non-aligned with an Indigenous research approach.

In considering non-Indigenous supervisors, the favourable positioning mirrors Jeannine Carrier's experience. Her supervisor was non-Indigenous but was chosen because of her alliance to Indigenous peoples. 'My supervisor is not an Indigenous person, but she is very attuned to what needs to happen, she is a very strong ally.' On a similar note, Kathy Absolon shared this about her non-Indigenous advisor: '[She] is the one that is getting me through the hoops – she is the one that says you need to do this and don't worry about that – she is kind of the one that is helping me to be a good hoop dancer. So she is really great that way in giving me feedback.' Like Kathy, I was fortunate to have supportive non-Indigenous co-supervisors who were able to step up and step back at the right time. Where does this knowledge come from? Experience, instinct, having an attuned relationship with the student's context are all key factors. I sense that having an astute insight into holistic, relational learning (and, by extension, research) is immeasurable when working with Indigenous graduate researchers. It requires a degree of self-reflection in relation to the situation. My assessment is that successful committees involve both respect and good timing. It would be valuable to hear stories of non-Indigenous faculty and graduate student researchers exploring the dynamic of their shared journey. For those scholars who are interested in Indigenous higher education, this would be fertile ground for further exploration.

All the individuals with whom I conversed for this study had Indigenous people on their committee. From my own experience, it has been invaluable to have an Indigenous faculty committee member.

As well as being an esteemed Indigenous scholar, mine had an understanding of the Plains Indigenous culture. When I entered into the realm of this knowledge and did not know how to mediate this knowing with my academic research, he was the one who assisted me in navigating the environment.

In tandem with a supportive committee structure, the need for an Indigenous research community of peers was also identified as significant to Indigenous graduate researchers. This community allows for intriguing discussions around Indigenous research, and it makes graduate work feel less isolating. Prospective Indigenous graduate students look for programs that are amiable to an Indigenous perspective and have a cohort structure. Kathy Absolon identified the importance of Indigenous faculty and an Indigenous student cohort as part of her decision to enrol in OISE. She describes her experience of researching programs that could best accommodate this need: 'I was interested in primarily being in an Aboriginal cohort and going to a university that was developing something with Aboriginal Ph.D. students and I did not want to go through another degree program in isolation. Laara Fitznor spoke about being accepted into her doctoral program a number of years ago. Her experience reflects the absence of an Indigenous presence in universities at that time. She chose her program because it had the greatest likelihood of supporting her research curiosity. 'That was the only thing that was closest to what I thought could support Aboriginal perspectives because there was nothing when I went, so I took the courses and came back home and just kind of worked at what can I do with my research.' There are a growing number of programs that support Indigenous research, and those that are successful build into themselves a responsiveness to the relational dynamic of Indigenous scholarship, and offer openings for conceptual approaches that allow Indigenous perspectives to come through.

As more Indigenous students participate in graduate research, the need for Indigenous faculty to supervise and sit on academic graduate committees becomes more urgent. For Indigenous faculty who are currently in doctoral programs, supporting these individuals to successful completion becomes pressing, so that they, in turn, can supervise students. Faculties of graduate studies and senior administration at universities have a role in the recruitment, retention, and mentoring of Indigenous faculty, as well as in creating a principled space where Indigenous knowledges can flourish. One response to this need is the SAGE (Supporting Aboriginal Graduate Enhancement) project that operates through the University of British Columbia. Graham Smith spoke about this program, which has as its aim the growth of a critical mass of Aboriginal people with doctorates. In building a critical mass, race scholar Sherene Razack (2001) argues, numbers matter. However, Graham Smith points out that this is not simply about numbers, but about political reclamation. He cautions: 'The other important element about this is not just producing a large number of Ph.D. qualified Aboriginals, the program is designed to create a critical mass of Aboriginal leaders ... and working for Aboriginal change and transformation. So not just what I call privatized academics.' Programs such as SAGE, which build Indigenous capacity, reflect institutional support, and the individuals who deflect assimilative responses by focusing on cultural preservation in their scholarship will forge that change.

Supporting Indigenous Scholarship

Moving from the specific experience of Indigenous graduate researchers, there are myriad ways that non-Indigenous academics can support Indigenous research and scholarship. Within post-secondary settings, openness to Indigenous scholarship varies. Some disciplines (e.g., social work, law, education) have a history of nurturing Indigenous knowledge within their programs, and are better positioned to acknowledge that Indigenous methodologies matter. However, within these disciplines and across all disciplines more broadly, programs are at different levels of engagement, with some being further ahead than others. Effective engagement is multi-layered and holistic. It involves both process and content work. The following are some suggestions for non-Indigenous scholars who want to support Indigenous epistemology, and thus increase their ability to engage with Indigenous research in a respectful manner. These recommendations are non-exhaustive and arguably painted with broad strokes, but they offer an entry point. Increasingly, there are non-Indigenous academics who wish 'to jump on the Aboriginal bandwagon' because it is in vogue. Because their reasons are not grounded in actively challenging the colonial paradigm, they are quite easily identified. Fortunately, there are non-Indigenous academics that genuinely support Indigenous knowledges. They are already doing the following work – that is how we know them.

Decolonizing Self and Institution

The relationship begins with decolonizing one's mind and heart. Non-Indigenous academics who have successful relationships with Indigenous communities understand this. This means exploring one's own beliefs and values about knowledge and how it shapes practices. It is about examining whiteness. It is about examining power. It is ongoing. It is only after carrying out this personal and institutional examination that scholars and disciplines can be in a position to acknowledge Indigenous knowledge and what it means in changing an organizational culture.

Without this work, the alternative is, at best, tinkering with the colonial approach to Indigenous knowledges – which does not provide a foundation for Indigenous research frameworks or pedagogies. Once people, programs, and institutions commit to this work, they can intellectually consider Indigenous knowledges from a place of openness.

Knowing the History

Indigenous people do not have a long history with the academy. Non-Indigenous scholars who recognize this are best situated to be supportive. According to the Department of Indian Affairs statistics, in the 1930s, only one status Indian received a post-secondary degree; in the 1940s there were two; in the 1950s, there were thirty; and in the 1960s, a total of 107 status Indians acquired post-secondary degrees. In the period 1934 to 1976, there was only one status Indian Ph.D. recorded (Stonechild, 2006: 42). Many current Indigenous post-secondary students are the first in their families and/or communities to graduate from university. This creates transition complexities around navigating the academy. Furthermore, many have had a negative experience of Western schooling, which has compromised trust in the system. Non-Indigenous scholars must acknowledge that this is a time of trust-building. For many of us, entering universities means encountering a different cultural milieu on a number of levels. Non-Indigenous scholars who are interested in Indigenous scholarship, but feel discomfort in traversing cultures, ought to be able to empathize.

3

Moving beyond the Indigenous Exotic

For those seeking to support Indigenous scholarship, there is a responsibility to avoid the Edward S. Curtis lens. This means reconceptualizing the relationship with Indigenous communities from that of a studied, exotic 'other' to that of a partnering relationship. The spiritual, holistic nature of Indigenous knowledges can be problematic for the more traditional, empiricist approach to knowledge. Not all academic researchers will embrace Indigenous knowledges if doing so is too far from their level of comfort. However, this hesitancy, stemming from discomfort, should not translate into dismissing or objectifying Indigenous knowledges. Given the attention to this dynamic, it is shocking to see it continually replicated. This requires ongoing critical reflection.

4

Growing Indigenous Scholarship

Non-Indigenous scholars have a role in mentoring Indigenous researchers on the intellectual aspects of academia related to its operational requirements (e.g., research and knowledge). Mentorship that offers non-prescribed space for cultural epistemologies within academic production would be invaluable. Developing research proposals, particularly proposals for large funding bodies, can be a mystifying process for the novice researcher. While there is a great deal of generic mentorship for the development of these proposals, there are few individuals who can provide assistance for Indigenous researchers in preparing these proposals that meet funding criteria and cultural epistemologies that follow the community/tribal ethics of the Indigenous communities. Co-partnered workshops on Aboriginal proposal development would be a helpful support. Mentorship concerning publications, either through journal or book publication, is also valuable. A co-partnered workshop on the publication process, with a focus on publishing Indigenous writing, would be immensely helpful to Indigenous academics new to this process. The recommendation is not for a standard workshop delivered to Indigenous folk, but a workshop developed in specific consideration of Indigenous scholarly responsibilities and recognition of cultural epistemologies.

5

Evaluation of Indigenous Research and Scholarship

At this point, non-Indigenous scholars are evaluating Indigenous academic products. Supporting Indigenous scholarship means guarding against the tendency to adjudicate such scholarship based on the degree to which it conforms to Western academic custom. This requires non-Indigenous scholars to become intellectually open to and familiar with Indigenous knowledges (as a way of knowing distinct from Western thought). They must be able to evaluate, at least on a preliminary level, Indigenous scholarship as to whether it is congruent with an Indigenous paradigm when that is what it seeks to accomplish. Not all Indigenous researchers will use Indigenous conceptual models. This is fine as Indigenous researchers need choice to implement conceptual frameworks that align with their research question or inquiry. When Western frameworks are used, non-Indigenous assistance will be less complex. My point is about evaluating scholarship from a tribal perspective.

Any critique of Indigenous scholarship must follow the rules of collective relationship-building rather than the more competitive approach found in many university settings. Many non-Indigenous scholars are hesitant to critique Indigenous research. This is, in part, a result of not having enough familiarity with the subject area. Other factors include a fear that they will be considered colonial or that they will say something hurtful or be misinterpreted. Others are not hesitant at all. They critique Indigenous scholarship on narrowly prescribed Western terms, often harshly, without recognizing that their evaluations carry a cultural bias. It would be helpful if these individuals clarified and were upfront in stating that their evaluation was made in accordance with a specific cultural viewpoint.

In the adjudication of proposals comprising Indigenous research frameworks and publications incorporating Indigenous knowledges, there need to be more individuals with this background on both research and editorial review boards. Given the increasing demand, non-Indigenous mentors and editors play a significant role in encouraging publications of Indigenous research and writing.

Redefining Roles

As an Indigenous presence in the academy grows, there are concerns (by both sides) about the place for non-Indigenous scholars within Indigenous scholarship. What is the role? While this new relationship is evolving, it is safe to say that the role of non-Indigenous scholars within Indigenous research is not the same as it was ten, even five, years ago. Because it is relational, it is iterative and its nature cannot be prescribed, yet it must uphold, rather than weaken, the work of Indigenous scholars. The emergence of non-Indigenous 'Indigenous knowledge brokers' is a contemporary phenomenon. This group is comprised of non-Indigenous scholars who are reputable within Indigenous communities and can be called upon by other non-Indigenous scholars who wish to enter the area. It is likely more efficient and comfortable for the latter group of individuals, but it is counterproductive because it sidesteps the relationship-building aspect that gives credibility to the involvement of non-Indigenous scholars in Indigenous research. No doubt it puts the former group in an uncomfortable position. Non-Indigenous scholars must play a role in sorting through this concern.

Related specifically to research, there needs to be increased discussion on issues such as the Principal Investigator (PI) and Co-Investigator (CI). Generally, seasoned scholars (usually non-Indigenous) who have had held previous research grants tend to be PIs, while Indigenous academics work as CIs. Recently, the term Co-Principal Investigator (CPI) has emerged within Indigenous research contexts, where the Indigenous researcher is given the title of CPI. However, in actual fact it is unclear what this actually means. Non-Indigenous researchers need to be involved in this discussion. How does the structure of research funding bodies conflict with the collective value of Indigenous methodologies? How does the funding body structure work to maintain the status quo?

Do the Relational Work

In the new millennium, engagement with Indigenous knowledges means engagement with Indigenous peoples, communities, and cultures. In many instances it may demand taking direction from Indigenous communities (tribal ethics boards). Non-Indigenous scholars who wish to engage with Indigenous knowledges need to connect with Indigenous scholars, people, and communities. Without this work, they will never have a full sense of the knowledges and culture, and they will perpetually be confused as to how to engage with Indigenous knowledges. Those who try to sidestep the relational work will be forever frustrated by Indigenous knowledges, research, and methodologies.

This chapter is not about developing theory. It is about clearing a path of prickly brush so that theoretical progress can occur. It is included in a book on Indigenous research frameworks because such conceptual proposals will fall flat without redefining the relational context. The possibility of Indigenous forms of inquiry can exist only within a decolonizing academy. Otherwise, there is little utility for it here. Rather than summarize what has already been said, I close this chapter with a personal reflection from my research experience and concerning the hope I see around me, from my research journal:

> While I sit here, on a self-imposed writing retreat (a great strategy that I heard about from Graham Smith), I receive word from a Gitksan friend that she has just been accepted into a Ph.D. program in Toronto within the last two weeks. I have also heard that two more of my Indigenous colleagues have been accepted in Doctoral Programs in Education. This is praxis. Finally, the face of an Anishnabe sister comes to mind, a Master's level graduate student who attended one of my workshops in February of 2006 where I presented on this research. She has since been accepted into Ph.D. studies in Law. She said, 'Hurry up Maggie and get your research finished, I want to read it.' This is what this whole journey has been about. Through our minds, hearts, bodies and spirits we are pushing the edges here in these Western schools, we are taking a little bit of friggin' space ...
>
> And we hold our hands up to those who helped create it.

Conclusion

Why a book on Indigenous methodologies? Work such as this serves knowledge. It is participation in an invigorating conversation of the possibilities of tribal-based research. Re-emergent to Indigenous community and emergent to the academy, Indigenous inquiry is a relational methodology; its methods are dependent upon deep respect for those (or that) which it will involve, and those (or that) which will feel its consequence. In re-examining relationships that serve knowledge, Indigenous inquiry calls forth the inherent stewardship responsibilities. In both its procedure and consequences, Indigenous inquiry asks researchers to demonstrate how research gives back to individual and collective good. Research in service of social and ecological justice is inseparable from this value. Global warming, oil wars, religious dogma, poverty, isolation, unhealthy coping – there is evidence everywhere of a struggling world, angry and fragmented. The research community is becoming mindful of its complicity in this disorder. A desire to take responsibility is growing incrementally, albeit slowly, and in its wake is an appetite to learn of knowledge-seeking systems that are premised on stewardship.

More locally, this book seeks to serve culture, to honour Indigenous ways of being and doing in research. It does not propose theory development from a Western analytical lens – be it postcolonial, critical, postmodern, or otherwise – rather, it seeks to uphold Indigenous thought through a personal interpreted tribal lens. That said, its sole focus is not a tribal philosophy, though it goes into those places. It is an analysis that seeks to expose the problem of applying cultural methods to another culture's epistemology, theory, and/or philosophy. In doing so, this book advocates for research frameworks that unify

Indigenous theory and practice, identifies distinctive qualities, and proposes Indigenous inquiry as a valid and practical methodological option within academic environments. In concluding this book, I would like to offer a synthesis, not necessarily a summary, of opportunities for an ongoing dialogue on my original question: Why a book on Indigenous methodologies?

In an earlier chapter, Graham Smith highlighted the need for Indigenous methodologies as an option, a 'tool' available for Indigenous researchers. This statement not only emphasizes the necessity of choice itself, but how a lack of this methodological choice is intrinsically connected to an academy that is still colonial. The absence of tribal epistemic inquiry reflects a colonial institution that reproduces itself. The consequences of not having choice are, at best, maintaining a methodological status quo or, at worst, methodological discrimination (Ryen, 2000). The absence of Indigenous research frameworks is consequential for the Indigenous community because it is one less venue for exploring tribal knowledge. It has ramifications for the larger community, as nullifying the potential of Indigenous knowledge systems through methodological gatekeeping voids the contribution that this knowledge system can make to larger society. Indigenous methodologies, as a choice, heighten possibilities.

Decolonizing the academy means choice on political and on personal levels. Not all Indigenous researchers will choose Indigenous research frameworks, nor should that be expected. The tendency to categorize Indigenous people as a homogeneous culture, wiping out personal identity, haunts us everywhere. No doubt it will follow us into research practice. Simply because a researcher is Indigenous, it does not follow that she ought to, or will, conduct research via an Indigenous form of inquiry. Non-Indigenous researchers, as graduate supervisors, must not assume that all Indigenous researchers will go this route, though they should not to be discouraged either, even though Indigenous inquiry is less academically established. Indigenous researchers have a responsibility to clarify their methodology or methodologies and the rationale for their choices. My next research project, for example, will use grounded theory. I will use this methodology because the question I wish to research is best suited for it.

Creating methodological choice for Indigenous researchers is but one element of decolonizing research, a process that requires depth, breadth, and attention to various aspects of research. Continued effort to ensure the ethical conduct of research within Indigenous communities must proceed. Careful reflection is necessary on the differing implications for research within the range of Indigenous communities (e.g., urban, reserve, Métis, Inuit). Decolonizing research adjudication remains a priority. There are multiple strategies available for decolonizing research.

One of the emphases in this book is the interrelationship between epistemology and method, theory and practice. It is my belief that Indigenous research frameworks are those that centre and privilege Indigenous knowledges. It goes deeper than mere Indigenous methodologies that share a relational and holistic foundation, but rather the knowledge must be localized within a specific tribal group. This is not a methodological impossibility. The commonality of a holistic epistemology unites Indigenous approaches and a specific tribal knowledge directs method. This theme permeates because it is critical. The absence of either in a research design that involves Indigenous qualities is fragmenting and will lead to a methodological disconnect. As a research instructor, this frustrates and I look forward to progress in this area.

The act of naming is upheld in many tribal traditions. Naming gives purpose and offers grounding. One utility of this book lies in its argument that Indigenous research frameworks will share specific qualities. Tribal knowledge systems are holistic. They move beyond the cognitive to the kinetic, affective, and spiritual. They are fluid. Tribal knowledge systems are born of self-in-relation, and within that social nesting silent self-knowledge is valued. Story is an Indigenous method for sharing experience, and interpretative, subjective understanding is accepted. That which contextualizes life – place, kinship, ceremony, language, purpose – matters greatly in how we come to know. All of this tells us who we are and will surface in Indigenous research frameworks. Reclaiming is naming, and identifying Indigenous inquiry is a political act.

Given the necessity of naming, fluidity and flexibility are equally valued. Within Indigenous research design, there is no prescribed 'look.' How Indigenous knowledges are presented, the way in which the researcher binds epistemology with methods, and the framework that is utilized to show this relationship are all researcher-dependent. The extent to which the researcher shares self-knowledge and how she integrates cultural relationship may be implicit or explicit. Indigenous research design allows flexibility in the manner and extent to which the personal and particular are integrated; there can be no 'check-box' approach. In presenting the qualities of an Indigenous research framework, the intent has been to guide not prescribe. Several framework designs have been referenced in this text, for as Indigenous methodologies flourish there will be multiple expressions: their beauty lies in their ability to centre their epistemic roots while not giving way to a dogmatic interpretation.

Focused discourse on Indigenous inquiry must include the context, the place where it lives. The Indigenous community has much invested in this topic. Finding opportunities for community dialogue on the range of Indigenous research, including methodologies, needs promotion. Taking research to the community is integral to the growth of contextualized, holistic methodologies. Indigenous methodologies were not born in the ivory tower, nor can they be confined there. The larger research community is part of the context. While this means all researchers in all fields, I wish, however, to focus on qualitative researchers. The qualitative research landscape is in a period transformation (Denzin and Lincoln, 2003). Methodologies from the margins are validating the voices and the stories of those once excluded. Honouring subjective knowledge is nudging objectivity from centre-stage, thus challenging conventional definitions of 'real' research. Indigenous methodologies have a unique relationship with qualitative research, for they are both of it and not of it.

I argue that there are epistemological reasons for distinguishing Indigenous methodologies from qualitative approaches (see Chapter 1). There are also political motivations. Given the assimilative tendency of Western culture, highlighting the tribal-knowledge basis of an Indigenous research framework rather than identifying it as a more generic relational, holistic epistemology, lessens the risk of a qualitative research community assimilating it.

Positioning Indigenous inquiry relative to qualitative research that holds a simultaneous insider/outsider status calls for a particular type of relationship. There have been many proclamations of a 'new' relationship between Indigenous and non-Indigenous in various sectors. It is a relationship that must recognize both the distinctive and the common destiny, not as a polarized or conversely assimilative conjecture, but as something different, something more. This relationship gives purpose to discourses on ethical space, contributing to the invigoration of theory development, and a possibility of new ways of relating. Given a mutual desire, the relationship between Indigenous methodologies and qualitative research can deepen and build trust and openness. Certainly, coyote will appear, his teachings will cause a stir. But then growth mostly depends on the ability to hang in through the stir. Qualitative research has great potential as a support of Indigenous methodologies, and supporting Indigenous methodologies would enrich research overall.

This brings me to a closing thought about places for continued conversation. Indigenous methodologies, by their nature, evoke collective responsibility. Integral to its research methodology, there is an ethical responsibility to not upset a relational balance. Within the larger research theory and practice, there is a responsibility to 'take back' research, to work towards eradicating egregious research practices. Of these larger responsibilities, all researchers have a role. Relational responsibilities exist between the Indigenous researcher and the Indigenous community; the Indigenous community and the researcher; the Indigenous researcher and the Indigenous academic community; non-Indigenous researchers and the Indigenous community; and between the academic community and Indigenous methodologies. Specific responsibilities will depend upon the particular relationship. They may include guidance, direction, and evaluation. They may include conversation, support, and collegiality. Responsibility implies knowledge and action. It seeks to genuinely serve others, and is inseparable from respect and reciprocity. Why a book on Indigenous methodologies? It is a way to give back.

Writing these words, I have a flash of memory of the young Aboriginal student wondering about Indigenous methodologies. I think of all those who uphold culture, who find ways home, literally or figuratively, and who persist through long days of one step forward, two back. I hold my hands up to them. I know that not all are researchers, but for those who are, I hope this book is a friend.

Epilogue

Miskâsowin is a Nêhiyáw term that means going to the centre of yourself to find your own belonging (Cardinal and Hildebrandt, 2000: 79). It is personal knowing, it is *Nêhiÿaw Kiskêÿihtamowin*. This word found me when I was trying to connect inward knowing, preparation, and purpose to my research. For me, it asks: Why are you doing this research and why are you doing it this way? Answering those questions could only be found in my personal story. Eber Hampton (1995) argues that knowing personal motives behind research matters. Conceptually, I first understood this as good research practice; I came to realize that it asks that we move beyond intellectual rationales to spirit and heart.

I began doctoral studies thinking that this would be a cognitively taxing, intellectual commitment, but that would be the extent. The first year went as planned. Entering the second year, my perfect plan started to dissipate. I am not sure why. By this time I had chosen my topic, Indigenous methodologies, but it was not gelling as I expected. I was taking a pan-Indigenous approach, and it just did not feel intuitively or conceptually right. For one thing, I was trying to squeeze Indigenous holism into a Western methodological mould. The reasons for this were numerous: personal, unexamined Western bias; acquiescence to the Western thought that oiled the academic machine; a reluctance to commit to a methodology; and, the major reason – I could not conceptually envision an Indigenous research framework. There were few resources to help me. I see the predicament clearly now, but at the time I was lost. In a state of paralysing ambivalence about the possibility of holistic knowledge in the academy, I was simultaneously manifesting experiences that aggravated that which had worked well for me in the past. People I met and works I read-underlined the necessity of experiential knowing as a rich source of knowledge. And this was unnerving to me. Although unnerving, there was a need to persevere.

At that point, I cannot say that I really knew what I was looking for, but I just kept going. I was feeling uncertain, grappling with influences that challenged the detached linearity that I coveted. In short, my world was feeling gelatinous. I was reading works by Indigenous scholars who wrote of sacred knowledges, and the more that I read, the more I became acutely aware that knowledge is culturally defined and that Western notions of 'truth' or 'fact' are bound in their own paradigms or constructs of belief. So many Indigenous writers were saying that Indigenous knowledge dwells beyond what the Western knowledge paradigm can or will accommodate. This was not new to me from an analytical perspective. It was just that I was starting to integrate this possibility into my academic life on an intuitive, emotional, and experiential level. It was a visceral, raw, and bewildering time.

I opened myself to sacred offerings of knowledge coming from unexpected places. I paid attention to my dream life. This was not the first time I embraced holistic knowledges, but it was the first time in my academic world. I do not know how or why we are shown paths, how the Great Manitow, the universe, a sacred force, guides us along at the most confusing times. I still cannot explain exactly what happened except that I became confused, uncomfortable, alone, sad, and angry. I think I was confused and mad because I could not understand what was happening or why I was feeling so alone in this search. Because I was feeling so alone, I had a deep ache to go home, but it was more than that. I was also experiencing a strong gut feeling that I could not ignore and that would not go away. I could not explain this to others who may have helped. It was silent work.

I spiralled into a visceral journey back through memories of my Plains childhood. Sharon Butala (2004), a Saskatchewan writer, writes about her sacred connection to the landscape of the Cyprus Hills in southwestern Saskatchewan. She recounts how her spiritual relationship with the land emerged during a deep crisis in her life. As I read her experience, I realized that I could relate. I began to keep a journal of what I was remembering and the feelings that evoked. I wrote about my first memory as a young child at a Cree powwow, and how I stood there shaking. It was my first conscious awareness of a belonging that

would take me years to understand. I had flashbacks of myself searching for arrowheads on the prairie. These memories came back to me as
if no time had passed. I had not lived in Saskatchewan since 1987 and
only returned for yearly holidays, and though I had missed family, I
was comfortable with this arrangement. Yet, as I engaged with my
research, I was drawn into memories associated with this place on
both a conscious and subconscious level. I was having vibrant dreams
with unfamiliar symbols that were speaking to me of sacred knowing
and identity, and exploring the deep abyss of my personal story that
was intricately bound with place. I was having a journey into my own
private *miskâsowin*.

During that silent time, I had two significant experiences. These
experiences led me to consider cultural knowledges coming from a
non-rational, non-time sort of place about which Little Bear, Deloria
Jr, and others were writing. The first experience came in the form of
a dream. Without going into the specifics, I dreamed of the Pueblo
poet, Leslie Marmon Silko. Her message to me was that home was
important for Indigenous people and that I needed to think about
that. At the time of the dream, I had not been consciously planning
to go back to Saskatchewan for my research. I felt assured that I could
finish this work from the place where I was living, Sidney, British
Columbia. I sensed that this dream was alerting me, but I was not
quite sure what to do about it, and let things lie. In the back of my
mind, though, I knew enough about my culture to pay attention.
Later in the fall, the occurrence of a second extraordinary happening
resolved my ambiguity.

The second happening revolved around my own Indigenous identity. I was contemplating my upbringing and how this would impact
my research, and I questioned whether, given my experience, I could
authentically approach Indigenous knowledges. I knew that I had to
square with being raised outside the culture, particularly if my
research touched on cultural matters. One week in October, I was
obsessing on this. I was reflecting on European culture, and the
metaphor of white pearls kept reappearing in my mind. There were a
number of reasons for this association, but mostly because pearls for
me have strong associations with my childhood in rural
Saskatchewan. The Friday before that weekend, I wrote these thoughts
in my journal. On the following Sunday, I was feeling overwhelmed by
all the introspection and wanted to go for a drive. I headed out the
door, and when I got to the car there was a strange gift waiting for me

– hanging from the handle of the car door was a strand of pearls, costume, but unmarred. I was dumbfounded. It was the strangest synchronicity that I had ever experienced, and I did not know what to make of it. Yet, it sat with me, and I knew instinctively that it was about facing things, about *miskâsowin*.

I will not say that these two events were definitely causally connected, but by the winter of that year I made the exhausting, emotional decision to go home in the spring to conduct my research after completing my comprehensive exams and proposal.

After reaching my decision to go home, life had, to a certain extent, gotten back on track. I was busy teaching and preparing for my comprehensive exams. I put the strand of pearls out of my mind and packed it away out of sight. I had one vivid dream about it, and would fleetingly think about the necklace whenever I saw pearls, but otherwise I put it out of my mind. I wrote a proposal for my research outlining a project that involved going home to interview Cree researchers and scholars, and writing the dissertation while in my ancestral territory. In May, my partner and I left Vancouver Island for Regina.

In the spring, I arrived home in Saskatchewan and had the pleasure of meeting the five-year-old daughter of my cousin for the first time, a beautiful little girl of mixed blood heritage (Cree and Hungarian). She was with my Auntie, who was visiting my mother, and she was playing dress-up with my young niece when I stopped by. As I walked into the house, she ran into the kitchen to see who came in and my Auntie (her *kôkom*) introduced her to me. She had been into the make-up and costume jewelry and was having a fine time. When I saw her, I stopped short: she was wearing a child's toy necklace made of pearls. While this was not synchronicity or an extraordinary happening of any kind – it was simply a little girl wearing a child's toy necklace – it had meaning for me, bound in the memories of my own history. I chose to take this experience to be the universe giving me a nod that coming home was important. I still do not understand these experiences fully. I have tried to analyse, theorize, and rationalize, but there are some things that you cannot deconstruct. As an Elder said, some knowledges we cannot know. What I am left with is an acceptance that these knowings matter to me inwardly, and because I allowed them they impacted my research path in a good way.

By being in Saskatchewan, I was able to consider not just Indigenous ways of knowing but my own Nêhiýaw and Saulteaux heritage, and I spent time with each of my two families. I began learning Plains Cree. I crossed over from being a younger Auntie to a *kôkom* (because, as my sister says, that is what I am now). I made bannock and pickles. I attended traditional ceremonies and community fundraisers for school trips. I made road trips from Regina to Winnipeg, Vancouver, and Victoria where I had conversations with Indigenous scholars and researchers, simultaneously rekindling old friendships and making new ones. I developed a research framework based on a tribal epistemology or *Nêhiýaw Kiskêýihtamowin*. The list goes on. When I left Victoria, I was focusing so intently on how the sacred comes into research that I almost missed how the sacred is our research.

In the winter, just before heading back to Victoria, the dream, the pearls, and the conversations that they elicited became clearer. In December, just before Christmas, I arranged, at their request, for my two mothers to meet. Although it had its awkward moments, it was a mostly nice time. During the visit, I had an opportunity to hear the story of my birthfather. It took me forty years, but the story was waiting for me. After the visit, I had some difficulty returning to my research because I felt a sense of completion to this project. The hard work was done, and through it something changed. As my partner Monty said, 'You're different from when you started this research.' Of course, I wanted to know how, but he could not say; just that it was a 'good different.' About a week or so later, I was back on track with my research, began working with my data, flew back to Victoria, and started teaching again. I graduated and shortly afterward accepted a faculty position at the University of Saskatchewan, making the decision to return home permanently. The research in which I engaged and the approach that I took was deeply motivated by *miskâsowin*.

Everyone's experience is different, but the gift of Indigenous research frameworks is that it allows our story to be a part of our research. Research stories teach us much, they give us much. They tell us who we are as researchers, as people.

As I write this, I look over to the small bookshelf that is next to my desk. On top of the shelf sit several objects that have been companions to me. At the base is a miniature easel, upon which rests a small four-by-six painting by my Auntie. It is a painting of a wooded space with wild flowers growing among the trees. She painted this in the early 1970s, when I was around seven or eight years old. To me, this is a place of both magic and possibility. Sitting on the easel against the picture is a handcrafted dream catcher that my brother's son made in school. When I look at it, I feel hope. Hanging over the easel, on top of the picture, is the strand of pearls. It propelled me home. At my defence and convocation, I wore it with a beaded choker. Finally, in a protective circle around all these items lies a piece of sweet grass, signifying the sacredness of this work. I know that these symbols represent stories of my life. What I also finally get from this whole experience is that stories will wait for us until we are ready. Then they will reveal themselves in purposeful, powerful ways, and when this happens we are in the midst of the sacred.

References

Absolon, K., and Willet, C. (2004). Aboriginal research: Berry picking and hunting in the 21st century. *First Peoples Child and Family Review – A Journal on Innovation and Best Practices in Aboriginal Child Welfare* 1(1): 5–17.

Absolon, K., and Willett, C. (2005). Putting ourselves forward: Location in Aboriginal research. In L. Brown and S. Strega (Eds.), *Research as Resistance,* 97–126. Toronto: Canadian Scholars' Press.

Ahenakew, E. (1995). *Voices of the Plains Cree.* Regina: Canadian Plains Research Center.

Ahenakew, F. (1987). *Cree Language Structures.* Winnipeg: Pemmican.

Ahenakew, F., and Wolfart, H.C. (Eds.). (1998). *Kôkhominawak Otâcimowini-wâwa – Our Grandmothers' Lives as Told in Their Words.* Regina: Canadian Plains Research Center.

Alfred, T. (2005). *Wasáse – Indigenous Pathways of Action and Freedom.* Peterborough: Broadview.

Alford, R.R. (1998). *The Craft of Inquiry: Theories, Methods, Evidence.* New York: Oxford University Press.

American Indian Movement of Colorado (13 Nov., 2005). In Honor of Vine Deloria, Jr. (1933–2005). Retrieved January 2006 from http://www.coloradoaim.org/blog/2005/11/in-honor-of-vine-deloria-jr-1933-2005.html.

Archibald, J. (2001). Editorial: Sharing Aboriginal knowledge and Aboriginal ways of knowing. *Canadian Journal of Native Education* 25(1): 1–5.

Atleo, E.R. (2004). *Tsawalk: A Nuu-chah-nulth Worldview.* Vancouver: UBC Press.

Barman, J., Hébert, Y., and McCaskill, D. (Eds.). (1986). *Indian Education in Canada, vol. 1, The Legacy.* Vancouver: UBC Press.

Basso, K.H. (1996). *Wisdom Sits in Places: Landscape and Language among the Western Apache.* (1st ed.) Albuquerque: University of New Mexico Press.

Bastien, B. (1999). *Blackfoot Ways of Knowing – Indigenous Science.* Unpublished doctoral dissertation, California Institute of Integral Studies, San Francisco.

Battiste, M. (1986). MicMac literacy and cognitive assimilation. In J. Barman, Y. Hébert, and D. McCaskill (Eds.), *Indian Education in Canada, vol.* 1, 23–44. Vancouver: UBC Press.

Battiste, M. (2007). Research ethics for protecting Indigenous knowledge and heritage: Institutional and researcher responsibilities. In N. Denzin and M. Giardina (Eds.), *Ethical Futures of Qualitative Research: Decolonizing the Politics of Knowledge,* 111-27. Walnut Creek, CA: Left Coast Press.

Battiste, M., and Henderson, J.Y. (2000). *Protecting Indigenous Knowledge and Heritage: A Global Challenge.* Saskatoon: Purich.

Bishop, R. (1997). Maori people's concerns about research into their lives. *History of Education Review* 26(1): 25–41.

Boyd, S. (2005). *What knowledge do you privilege*? Paper presented at Graduate Student Conference for the University of Victoria, Studies in Policy and Practice, Victoria, 18 Nov.

Brandt-Castellano, M. (1993). Aboriginal organizations in Canada: Integrating participatory research. In P. Park, M. Brydon-Miller, B. Hall, and T. Jackson (Eds.), *Voices of Change: Participatory Research in the United States,* 145-55. Toronto: Ontario Institute for Studies in Education.

Brandt-Castellano, M. (2004). Ethics of Aboriginal research. *Journal of Aboriginal Health* 1(1): 98-114.

Brandt-Castellano, M. (2005). Keynote address given at the *Shawane Dagosiwin* Aboriginal research conference, Winnipeg, Manitoba, 1–3 June.

Brelauer, H. (2007). Academic restructuring and equality. *Journal of Higher Education – Academic Matters,* April, 20–2.

Bringhurst, R. (1999). *A Story as Sharp as a Knife: The Classical Haida Myth Tellers and Their World.* Vancouver: Douglas and McIntyre.

Brown, L., and Strega, S. (Eds.). (2005). *Research as Resistance: Critical, Indigenous and Anti-oppressive Approaches.* Toronto: Canadian Scholars' Press.

Brown, R. (1996). *A Description and Analysis of Sacrificial Stall Dancing: As Practised by the Plains Cree and Saulteaux of the Pasqua Reserve, Saskatchewan, in Their Contemporary Rain Dance Ceremonies.* Unpublished Master's Thesis, University of Manitoba, Winnipeg.

Bruyere, G. (1999). *'Empowerment,' in Aboriginal Social Work Training Project – Curriculum.* Victoria: Caring for First Nations Children Society.

Buendía, E. (2003). Fashioning research stories: The metaphoric and narrative structure of writing research about race. In G. López and L. Parker (Eds.), *Interrogating Racism in Qualitative Research Methodology,* 49–69. New York: Peter Lang.

Butala, S. (2004). *The Perfection of the Morning*. Toronto: HarperCollins.

Cajete, G. (1999). *Native Science: Natural Laws of Interdependence*. Santa Fe, NM: Clear Light Publishers.

Cajete, G. (2004). Philosophy of native science. In A. Waters (Ed.), *American Indian Thought: Philosophical Essays*, 45–57. Malden, MA: Blackwell.

Canadian Institute of Health Research (CIHR). (2007). *Guidelines for Health Research Involving Aboriginal Peoples*. Ottawa: Author.

Cardinal, H., and Hildebrandt, L. (2000). *Treaty Elders of Saskatchewan: Our Dream Is that Our Peoples Will One Day Be Clearly Recognized as Nations*. Calgary: University of Calgary Press.

Cardinal, L. (2001). What is an Indigenous perspective? *Canadian Journal of Native Education* 25(2): 180–2.

Carr-Stewart, S. (2001). A treaty right to education. *Canadian Journal of Native Education* 26(2): 125–43.

Chrystos. (1988). *Not Vanishing*. Vancouver: Press Gang Publishers.

Clayoquot Alliance for Research, Education and Training. (2003, June). *Standard of Conduct for Research in Clayoquot and Northern Barkley Sound Communities*. Prepared by the Protocols Project of the Clayoquot Alliance for Research, Education and Training. Victoria, BC: Author.

Coffey, A., and Atkinson, P. (1996). *Making Sense of Qualitative Data: Complementary Research Strategies*. Thousand Oaks, CA: Sage.

Cole, P. (2002). Aboriginalizing methodology: Considering the canoe. *Qualitative Studies in Education* 15(4): 447–59.

Colorado, P. (1988). Bridging native and western science. *Convergence* 20(2/3): 49–68.

Creswell, J.W. (2003). *Research Design: Qualitative,Qquantitative, and Mixed Methods Approaches* (2nd ed.). Thousand Oaks, CA: Sage.

Cruikshank, J. (1998). *The Social Life of Stories: Narrative and Knowledge in the Yukon Territory*. Vancouver: UBC Press

Davis, L. (2004). Risky stories: Speaking and writing in colonial spaces. *Native Studies Review* 15(1): 1–20.

Deloria, V., Jr. (1969). *Custer Died for Your Sins: An Indian Manifesto*. New York: Avon.

Deloria, V., Jr. (1991). Commentary: Research, redskins, and reality. *American Indian Quarterly* 15(4): 457–68

Deloria, V., Jr. (2002). *Evolution, Creationism, and Other Modern Myths: A Critical Inquiry*. Golden, CO: Fulcrum.

Deloria, V., Jr. (Ed.). (1999). *Spirit and Reason: The Vine Deloria Reader*. Golden, CO: Fulcrum.

Deloria, V., Jr., and Wildcat, D.R. (2001). *Power and Place*. Golden, CO: Fulcrum.

Denzin, N., and Lincoln, S. (Eds.). (2003). *The Landscape of Qualitative Research: Theories and Issues*. Thousand Oaks, CA: Sage.

Dibajiimo Masinahikan 'Newspaper.'(2007). Chief Paskwa Pictograph Returns Home. (Summer), 3.

Dyck, N (1986). Negotiating the Indian 'problem.' In D.R. Miller, C. Beal, J. Dempsey, and R. Wesley Heber (Eds.), *The First Ones: Reading in Indian/Native Studies*, 132–9. Piapot: Saskatchewan Indian Federated Press.

Elisabetsy, E. (1991). Sociopolitical, economical and ethical issues in medicinal plant research. *Journal of Ethnopharmacology* 32(1–3): 235–9.

Ely, M., Vinz, R., Downing, M., and Anzul, M. (2001). *On Writing Qualitative Research: Living by Words*. London: Routledge Falmer.

Ermine, W. (1999). Aboriginal epistemology. In M. Battiste (Ed.), *First Nations Education in Canada: The Circle Unfolds*, 101–12. Vancouver: UBC Press.

Estrada, Jimenez V.M. (2005). The tree of life as a research methodology. *Australian Journal of Indigenous Education* 34: 44–52.

Fanon, F. (1963). *The Wretched of the Earth*. London: Penguin.

Friesen, J.W. (1998). *Sayings of the Elders*. Calgary: Detselig.

Gergen, M., and Gergen, K. (2003). Qualitative inquiry: Tensions and transformations. In N. Denzin and S. Lincoln (Eds.), *The Landscape of Qualitative Research*, 575–610. Thousand Oaks, CA: Sage.

Gitlin, A., Peck, M., Aposhian, N., Hadley, S., and Porter, A. (2002). Looking again at insider knowledge: A relational approach to knowledge production and assessment. *Journal of Teacher Education* 53: 303–15.

Graveline, F.J. (1998). *Circleworks: Transforming Eurocentric Consciousness*. Halifax: Fernwood.

Graveline, F.J. (2000). Circle as methodology: Enacting an Aboriginal paradigm. *Qualitative Studies in Education* 13(4): 361–70.

Hall, B. (1998). Knowledge, democracy and higher education: Contributions from adult and lifelong learning. In B. Hall (Ed.), *Lifelong Learning and Institutes for Higher Education in the 21st Century*, 17–29. Mumbai: Department of Adult Education and Continuing Education and Extension, University of Mumbai.

Hampton, E. (1995). Memory comes before knowledge: Research may improve if researchers remember their motives. Paper presented at the First Biannual Indigenous Scholars' Conference, University of Alberta, Edmonton, 15–18.

Hart, M. (2002). *Seeking Mino-pimatisiwin. An Aboriginal Approach to Helping*. Halifax: Fernwood.

Henderson, J.Y. (Sakej). (2000). Postcolonial ghost dancing: Diagnosing European colonialism. In M.A. Battiste (Ed.), *Reclaiming Indigenous Voice and Vision*, 57–76. Vancouver: UBC Press.

Herising, F. (2005). Interrupting positions: Critical thresholds and queer pro/positions. In L. Brown and S. Strega (Eds.), *Research as Resistance*, 127–52. Toronto: Canadian Scholars' Press.

Kandinsky, W. (1977). *Concerning the Spiritual in Art*. Don Mills, ON: Dover.

Kimpson, S. (2005). Stepping off the road: A narrative (of) inquiry. In L. Brown and S. Strega (Eds.), *Research as Resistance*, 73–96. Toronto: Canadian Scholars' Press.

Kirby, S., Greaves, L., and Reid, C. (2006). *Experience, Research, Social Change – Methods beyond the Mainstream*. Peterborough, ON: Broadview.

Kovach, M. (2005). Emerging from the margins: Indigenous methodologies. In L. Brown and S. Strega (Eds.), *Research as Resistance*,19–36. Toronto: Canadian Scholars' Press.

Kovach, M. (2006) *Searching for Arrowheads: An Inquiry into Approaches to Indigenous Research Using a Tribal Methodology with a Nêhiýaw Kiskêýihtamowin Worldview*. Unpublished doctoral dissertation, University of Victoria, Victoria, British Columbia.

Kuhn, T.S. (1996 [1962]). *The Structure of Scientific Revolutions* (3rd ed.). Chicago: University of Chicago Press.

Ladson-Billings, G. (2003). Racialized discourse and ethnic epistemologies. In N. Denzin and S. Lincoln (Eds.), *The Landscape of Qualitative Research*, 398–433. Thousand Oaks, CA: Sage.

Lerat, H., and Ungar, L. (2005). *Treaty Promises, Indian Reality – Life on a Reserve*. Saskatoon: Purich.

Liamputtong, P. (2007). *Researching the Vulnerable*. London: Sage.

Little Bear, L. (2000). Jagged worldviews colliding. In M. Battiste (Ed.), *Reclaiming Indigenous Voice and Vision*, 77–85. Vancouver: UBC Press.

Little Bear, L. (2004). Land: The Blackfoot source of identity. Paper presented at the conference Beyond Race and Citzenship: Indigeneity in the 21st Century, University of California, Berkeley.

Mandelbaum, D.G. (1979). *The Plains Cree*. Regina: Canadian Plains Research Center.

Martin, J., and Frost, P. (1996). The organizational culture war games: A struggle for intellectual dominance. In S. Clegg, C. Hardy, and W. Nord (Eds.), *Handbook of Organizational Studies*, 599–619. Thousand Oaks, CA: Sage.

McLeod, N. (2005). *Songs to Kill a Wîhtikow*. Regina: Hagios.

McLeod, N. (2007). *Cree Narrative Memory – From Treaties to Contemporary Times*. Saskatoon: Purich.

McTaggart, R. (Ed.). (1997). *Participatory Action Research: International Contexts and Consequences*. Albany: State University of New York Press.

Memmi, A. (1965). *The Colonizer and the Colonized*. New York: Orion.

Mertens, D. (2005). *Research and Evaluation in Education and Psychology: Integrating Diversity with Quantitative, Qualitative, and Mixed Methods*. Thousands Oaks, CA: Sage.

Meyer, Aluli M. (2001). Acultural assumptions of empiricism: A Native Hawaiian critique. *Canadian Journal of Nature Education* 25(2): 188–98.

Meyer, Aluli M. (2004). *Ho'oulu Our Time of Becoming: Hawaiian Epistemology and Early Writings*. Honolulu: Ai Pohaku Press.

Mi'kmaq Ethics Watch. (1999). *Principles and Guidelines for Researchers Conducting Research with and/or among Mi'kmaq People*. (Author's copy.)

Moustakas, C. (1990). *Heuristic Research: Design, Methodology and Applications*. Newbury Park: Sage.

Munro, M. (2005). Controversial blood samples return to B.C: Expert continued to use native blood without consent. *The Province*, 19 Jan.: A18.

Neuman, W.L. (1997). *Social Research Methods: Qualitative and Quantitative Approaches*. (3rd ed.). Needham Heights, MA: Allyn and Bacon.

Pillow, W. (2003). Race-based methodologies: Multicultural methods or epistemological shifts? In G. López and L. Parker (Eds.), *Interrogating Racism in Qualitative Research Methodology*, 181–97. New York: Peter Lang.

Potts, K., and Brown, L. (2005). Becoming an anti-oppressive researcher. In L. Brown and S. Strega (Eds.), *Research as Resistance*, 255–86. Toronto: Canadian Scholars' Press.

Razack, S. (2001). Racialized immigrant women as native informants in the academy. In *Seen but Not Heard: Aboriginal Women and Women of Color in the Academy*. Ottawa: Canadian Institute for the Advancement of Women.

Richardson, C., and Blanchet-Cohen, N. (2000). *Survey of Post-secondary Education Programs in Canada for Aboriginal Peoples*. Unpublished report for UNESCO, Institute for Child Rights and Development and First Nations Partnership Programs, University of Victoria.

Rossman, G., and Rallis, S. (2003). *Learning in the Field: An Introduction to Qualitative Research* (2nd ed.). Thousand Oaks, CA: Sage.

Royal Commission on Aboriginal Peoples (RCAP). (1996). *Gathering Strength*, vol. 3. Ottawa: Canada Communications Group.

Royal Commission on Aboriginal Peoples (RCAP). (1996). Renewal: A Twenty-Year Commitment, Appendix E: Ethical Guidelines for Research, vol. 5. Ottawa: Canada Communications Group.

Ryen, A. (2000). Colonial methodology? Methodological challenges to cross-cultural projects collecting data by structured interviews. In C. Truman, D.

Mertens, and B. Humphrey (Eds.), *Race and Inequality,* 220–33. London: UCL Press.

Schnarch, B. (2004). Ownership, control, access, and possession (OCAP) or self-determination applied to research: A critical analysis of contemporary First Nations research and some options for First Nations communities. *Journal of Aboriginal Health* 1(1): 80–94.

Schwandt, T. (2007). *The Sage Dictionary of Qualitative Inquiry* (3rd ed.). Los Angeles: Sage.

Silko, Leslie Marmon. (1977). *Ceremonies.* New York: Viking, Penguin.

Smith, G.H. (1997). *The Development of Kaupapa Maori: Theory and Praxis.* Unpublished doctoral dissertation, University of Auckland.

Smith, G.H. (2005). The problematic of 'Indigenous theorizing': A critical reflection. Paper present at the AERA Annual Conference, Montreal, 11– 15 April.

Somekh, B., and Lewin, C. (2005). *Research Methods in the Social Sciences.* London: Sage.

Standing Committee on Aboriginal Affairs and Northern Development (SCAAND). (2006). *No Higher Priority: Aboriginal Post-secondary Education in Canada.* Ottawa: Author

Steinhauer, E. (2002). Thoughts on an Indigenous research methodology. *Canadian Journal of Native Education* 26(2): 69–81.

Steinhauer, P. (2001). Situating myself in research. *Canadian Journal of Native Education* 25(2): 183–7.

Stevenson, W.L. (2000). *Decolonizing Tribal Histories.* Unpublished doctoral dissertation, University of California, Berkeley.

Stonechild, B. (2006). *The New Buffalo: The Struggle for Aboriginal Post-secondary Education in Canada.* Winnipeg: University of Manitoba.

Strauss, A., and Corbin, J. (1998). *Basics of Qualitative Research: Techniques and Procedures for Developing Grounded Theory.* (2nd ed.). Thousand Oaks, CA: Sage.

Strega, S. (2005). The view from the poststructual margins: Epistemology and methodology reconsidered. In L. Brown and S. Strega (Eds.), *Research as Resistance,* 199–236. Toronto: Canadian Scholars' Press.

Stringer, E. (1999). *Action Research.* (2nd ed.). Thousand Oaks, CA: Sage.

Struthers, R. (2001). Conducting sacred research: An Indigenous experience. *Wicazo Sa Review* 16(1): 125–33.

Thomas, R. (2005). Honoring the oral traditions of my ancestors through story-telling. In S. Strega and L. Brown (Eds.), *Research as Resistance,* 237–54. Toronto: Canadian Scholars' Press.

Tri-Council Policy Statement. (1998). Section 6 – Research involving Aboriginal peoples. Reterived 2 April 2009 from http: pre.ethics.gc.ca/eng/policy-politique/teps-eptic.

Tuhiwai Smith, L. (1999). *Decolonizing Methodologies – Research and Indigenous Peoples*. London: Zed.

Van Manen, M. (2001). *Researching Lived Experience*. London, ON: Althouse Press, University of Western Ontario.

Waters, A. (Ed.). (2004). *Language Matters: Nondiscrete Nonbinary Dualism*. Malden, MA: Blackwell.

Weaver, H. (2001). Indigenous identity – What is it, and who really has it? *American Indian Quarterly* 25(2): 240–54.

Weber-Pillwax, C. (1999). Indigenous research methodology: Exploratory discussion of an elusive subject. *Journal of Educational Thought/Revue de la Pensee Educative* 33(1): 31–45.

Wilson, S. (2001). What is Indigenous research methodology? *Canadian Journal of Native Education* 25(2): 175–9.

Wolvengrey, A. (2001a). *Nêhiyawêwin: Itwêwina,*vol. 1, *Cree–English*. Regina: Canadian Plains Research Centre.

Wolvengrey, A. (2001b). *Nêhiyawêwin: Itwêwina,*vol. 2, *English–Cree*. Regina: Canadian Plains Research Centre.

Yon, D. (2003). Highlights and overview of the history of educational ethnography. *Annual Review of Anthropology* 32: 411–29.

Index

Aboriginal rights 20, 158, 161–2
Absolon, Kathy 58, 115, 149, 167; on
    the academy 85–6, 112, 126–7, 142,
    150–5
academia, homogeneity of 12, 25, 28,
    79, 83–4, 142, 156–7; restrictions in
    for Indigenous research 12–13, 14,
    25, 28, 128
access 59, 72, 87, 123, 144–5
accountability to community 14,
    48–9, 52, 60, 85, 92, 120, 148–9,
    164–5
advisory boards/committees 49,
    114, 127, 146, 148
Ahenakew, Edward 95
analysis vs. interpretation 53, 130–2
ancestral knowledge 37, 48, 94, 130
ancient knowledges 9, 40, 66–7, 105,
    120
animistic philosophy 34, 56, 62, 66
anti-oppressive methodology 18, 33,
    41, 110, 152
appreciative inquiry 32
Archibald, Jo-ann 94
assimilationist policies 36, 75, 77, 89,
    159–60, 161–2, 168, 177
autobiographical narrative 110–11

autoethnography 33, 35, 96, 110, 130

Basso, Keith 6–7, 23–4
Bastien, Betty 53, 116, 129, 147–8,
    148–9
Battiste, Marie 35–6, 56, 160
benefits of research 29, 48, 81–2, 93,
    130, 142, 145; to the community
    11, 48, 50, 81, 86–7, 115, 139, 141–2,
    144, 146, 149, 174. *See also* giving
    back
bias 26, 33, 41, 81, 90, 103, 171, 179
binaries 12, 21, 59, 60–1; dualist 24
biological/genetic material 141, 145
Blood, Narcisse 61
Brandt-Castellano, Marlene 57, 146,
    156
British North America Act 1867
    (BNA Act) 159
Brown, Leslie 41–2, 130
Brown, R. (Randall) 66–7
Buendía, Edward 41, 43
buffalo 64–5, 68, 73
Butala, Sharon 180

Cajete, Gregory 34, 131
Canadian Charter of Rights and

Freedoms, sec. 25 (Aboriginal
rights) 160
Canadian Institute of Health
Research (CIHR) 143–4, 145–6
capacity building 86, 168
capitalism 78, 79
Carriere, Jeannine 28, 68, 99, 103–8,
125, 138, 149; on self 85, 127, 164
ceremony 50, 56, 64–5, 66–8, 116–17,
119; as cultural protocol 36, 69,
140; and research 47, 50, 73, 120,
140, 176
circles 104–5, 126–7, 128, 139, 152, 153.
See also research/sharing circles
co-constructing/co-creating knowledge 100, 111
coding 35, 52–3, 55, 122, 130, 131–2
collectivism 19, 44, 48, 62, 142, 146,
148
colonial history 12, 24–5, 28–9, 47,
75–9, 80; and interruption of
Indigenous culture 12, 24, 59,
76–7, 86, 158–9; necessity of
acknowledging 18, 21, 24–5, 30,
38, 44, 48, 59, 76–9, 80, 84;
present/ongoing effects of 20, 28,
37, 75–93, 103, 129, 142, 143,
151–2, 163, 169, 171, 185
Colorado, Pam 77
community-based research 13, 25,
36, 144; and RCAP guidelines 144
conceptual frameworks 25, 27, 40–3,
39–54, 62, 64, 65, 130, 171; need
for 16, 39, 40–4
confidentiality 148
consent/permission 14, 138, 141–3,
144–5, 147
consent forms, use of 138
Constitution of Canada, 1982, sec. 35
(Aboriginal rights) 160

constructivism 26, 29, 30, 111
consumerism 76
control 81, 82, 87, 90, 124, 125, 144–5,
146
conversation as method 14, 15, 17,
19, 51–3, 99, 100, 123–5, 127–8
creation stories 57, 95
credibility 36, 52, 132–3, 172
Creswell, John W. 33
critical reflexivity (self-reflection) 33,
42, 85, 112, 170. See also reflexivity
critical theory 6, 28, 39, 47–8, 50, 53,
75, 78, 80, 86, 92–3, 174
cultural capital 28, 36
cultural catalyst activities 50, 57, 66,
71, 72, 126–7, 150–1, 152–5, 180
cultural exoticism 27, 67, 78–9, 170
cultural grounding/location 18, 54,
62, 85, 109, 115–17, 121, 158, 176
cultural longevity/sustainability 12,
158, 162, 164

Darwinian theory 77
data 19, 26, 68, 145; analysis 35, 41,
53, 121, 129, 130–4, 139; collection
23, 28, 42, 51, 86, 98, 101, 121–9,
136, 139
Davis, Lynne 141–2
decolonizing: aim of research 28, 35,
45, 47–9, 53, 115, 132, 143, 145;
efforts 28, 79, 92, 98, 103, 143, 146,
173, 175–6; perspective 18, 30, 33,
43, 75–9, 80–2, 83–7, 121, 125, 142,
169; theory 54, 80–2
Delgamuukw decision 95
Deloria, Vine Jr 23, 34, 53, 77, 93,
131, 181
Denzin, Norman 26, 27
Descartes 78
dreams 50, 57–8, 66–7, 70–2, 120,

140, 180–1; as knowledge source 57–8, 70, 117, 126–7, 140, 147, 153–4, 155, 180–1; as method 34, 70–1, 126–7; as methodology 70–1, 120, 152–3

education 13, 14, 27–8, 48, 76, 86, 87–8, 89, 151, 157, 158–60; graduate research 163–73; post-secondary 155, 157, 158, 161–3
Elisabetsy, Elaine 141
empiricism 57, 72, 82, 101, 129, 132, 143, 170
Ermine, Willie 21, 57
essentialism 28
Estrada, Jiménez 40
ethical responsibility in research 19, 34–5, 73, 99–100, 141–6, 147, 149, 178
ethics 43, 44, 49, 127, 141–54, 170, 174–5; as methodology 19, 54, 86, 147–9
ethnography 7, 27–8, 33, 36, 83
experiential knowledge 34, 43, 44, 49, 61, 67, 110–11, 115, 153, 180
exploitation 77, 79, 81, 87, 125, 141, 145, 148; Indigenous complicity in 91; prevention of 36, 92, 103, 145
extractive research 12–13, 27–8, 29, 57, 59, 79, 86–7, 92, 98, 99, 101, 112, 125, 127, 141, 144, 149; 'smash and grab' 28, 36, 99, 145

fasts 66, 71, 153–5; as methodology 126–7
Federated Saskatchewan Indian College 127–8
feminist methodology 25, 32, 33, 96, 110; as relational 35
field notes 33, 50, 113

Fitznor, Laara 116–17, 124, 127, 128, 131, 134–9, 137; on circles 135–8; on relationships 98–9, 126, 137
focus groups 19, 152; as knowledge-gathering structure 123, 124, 136, 139

genetic material 141, 145
giving back 44, 45, 48, 63, 109, 115, 147, 151–5, 164, 176, 178; to community 4, 27, 81–2, 100, 140, 142, 149, 155. See also benefits of research; reciprocity
globalization 76, 78
governance 19, 142, 143, 145
Graveline, Fyre Jean 14
grounded theory 25–6, 35, 36, 83, 130, 133, 175
guidelines 42, 124, 127, 133, 143–6, 148. See also protocol

Habermas, Jürgen 6, 80
Hall, Budd 79
Hampton, Eber 29, 50, 114, 119, 122, 179
Hart, Michael 58, 68–73, 115, 126–7; on the academy 86, 147, 164; on language 62, 69–70
Hawthorne report 159–60
healing 86, 125, 150
Heidegger, 30
Henderson, James Youngblood 56
holistic knowledge in academia 17, 34–5, 59, 73, 157, 146, 147, 166, 170, 179–80; resistance to 59, 67–8, 80, 84
human-subject research 39, 132; decision to avoid 122

inclusivity 27, 56, 93, 156, 157

Indian Act 158, 159–60, 161
Indian Affairs 161, 169
Indigenous Control of Indigenous Education 160
Indigenous culture: at risk 24, 27–9, 36, 77, 85, 86–7, 92, 147, 177; in academia 12–13, 84, 92, 147, 148–9, 156–7; colonial interruption of 12, 24, 59, 76–7, 86, 158–9; and education 158–63; as holistic 40–1, 47, 49–50, 58, 61, 73, 96, 102–1, 109, 140, 147
Indigenous epistemology, as holistic 34–5, 44, 49–50, 55, 56–9, 60, 61, 62–3, 68, 72, 84, 96, 111, 130, 176–7
Indigenous inquiry. *See* Indigenous methodology
Indigenous knowledge: as holistic 17, 58, 67–8, 96, 140, 146, 147, 170, 176; sharing of 48, 67, 75, 92, 158, 172
Indigenous knowledge systems 11, 12, 17, 19, 25, 36, 42, 46, 63, 77, 55–6, 95–7, 108, 110, 131, 147, 153, 155, 159, 171, 175–6
Indigenous language 17, 47, 57, 63–4, 65–6, 90–1, 119, 140, 176; and thought 24, 30, 41, 59–61, 62, 69–70, 73, 110, 140, 152
Indigenous methodology / inquiry / frameworks 15, 17, 18, 21, 24–5, 30, 32, 34, 36–7, 40, 56, 60, 80–2, 96, 98, 109–12, 121–3, 125–9, 132–3, 139–40, 159, 165–6, 174–8; as holistic 32, 40–1, 56–9, 73, 81, 94, 96, 108, 111, 140, 142, 147, 176; as inclusive 27, 44, 48, 56, 70, 73, 112, 156; meaning making 129–34, 140; need for 13, 16–17, 24–5, 28, 30, 38, 39, 41, 83–4, 88–9, 92–3,

153, 167; as political 18, 29, 123, 176–7; as pragmatic 56–7, 87, 125, 134; as relational 32, 51, 57–8, 111, 123, 147, 149, 165, 172, 174; research ethics as 54, 96, 98, 147–9; room for in academia 25, 30–2, 35, 43, 44, 58–9, 69, 82–5, 140, 153, 158, 165–7; as sacred 67, 92, 140, 146, 147, 155, 180–1; as unique 36–7
Indigenous people: as distinct from other minorities 157, 158–9; experience with and distrust of Western research 12–13, 24, 27–8, 36, 86–7, 126, 141–4, 147, 149, 156, 169; oppression of 28, 96, 91, 160
Indigenous research ethics 19, 34–6, 42, 44, 48, 49, 65, 73, 127, 142–7, 154; in CHIR guidelines 146; as methodology 54, 96, 98, 147–9
Indigenous scholarship 15, 24, 57, 84, 932, 131–2, 143, 149, 153, 157, 158, 163–8, 168–73; evaluation of 170–1; non-Indigenous role in 171–2; supporting 29, 32, 79, 168–73
Indigenous theory 20, 48, 59, 64, 87, 88–9, 91, 174–5
Indigenous vs. Western research approaches 18, 20–1, 28–9, 31, 35, 38, 39–40, 43, 53–4, 58–9, 78, 82, 86–7, 96, 102, 107, 128–9, 132, 133, 139, 143
Indigenous vs. Western thought 21, 29, 53–4, 58–9, 77–8, 76, 78, 84, 129, 148–9, 171, 179–80. *See also* Indigenous language: and thought
Indigenous ways of knowing 67–8, 81, 94, 97, 130–1, 147, 148–9, 155,